D1738260

# The
# Reorganization of
# Soviet Foreign Trade

## LEGAL ASPECTS

M. M. Boguslavsky and P. S. Smirnov

# The Reorganization of Soviet Foreign Trade

## LEGAL ASPECTS

EDITED WITH A FOREWORD BY
## SERGE L. LEVITSKY

PUBLISHED BY ARRANGEMENT WITH THE
DOCUMENTATION OFFICE FOR EAST EUROPEAN
LAW OF THE UNIVERSITY OF LEYDEN

M. E. Sharpe, Inc.
Armonk, New York
London, England

Translated by Denis M. McCauley

**Library of Congress Cataloging-in-Publication Data**

Boguslavskiĭ, M. M. (Mark Moiseevich)
    [Novaia sistema organizatsii i upravleniia vneshneekonomicheskoĭ
deiatel'nost'iu v SSSR. English]
    The reorganization of Soviet foreign trade : legal aspects / M. M.
Boguslavsky and P. S. Smirnov; edited with a foreword by Serge L.
Levitsky.
        p.    cm.
    Translation of: Novaia sistema organizatsii i upravleniia
vneshneekonomicheskoĭ deiatel'nost'iu v SSSR.
    "Published by arrangement with the Documentation Office for East
European Law of the University of Leyden"—T.p.
    ISBN 0-87332-508-7
    1. Foreign trade regulation—Soviet Union. 2. Joint ventures—
Soviet Union. 3. Soviet Union—Foreign economic relations.
I. Smirnov, P. S. II. Levitsky, Serge L. III. Title.
LAW < USSR 7 Bogu 1989 >
343.47'087—dc19
[344.70387]                                                        88-26348
                                                                        CIP

Printed in the United States of America

# CONTENTS

## Appendices

# FOREWORD

## I

The changes now being introduced in Soviet foreign trade are an important element of *perestroika* initiated in the USSR under General Secretary Mikhail S. Gorbachev. They are part of the answer to what Mr. Gorbachev referred to as the need for "a profound structural reorganization of the economy" and of its management. Although the principle of *state monopoly* of foreign trade has been retained—i.e, the planning of future foreign economic relations will remain an integral part of the overall planning of the Soviet national economy and of economic policy towards the *socialist* countries (by promoting further cooperation and integration), the *developing* countries (by serving as the "principal instrument of Soviet economic policy" towards these countries (*Pravda*, 22 May 1987), and the developed *"capitalist"* countries (by promoting "cooperation on the basis of mutual advantage")—the rigid centralized structure of the administration of foreign trade is being dismantled, in the direction away from what Gorbachev called "an excessively centralized management system relying on orders and injunctions."

Where once the USSR Ministry of Foreign Trade was the principal state organ through which foreign trade operations were conducted by subordinate "foreign trade organizations" (FTOs), more than twenty ministries and government departments, and sixty-seven major Soviet enterprises have now been granted the right of direct access to foreign markets through foreign trade firms of their own, and many existing FTOs have been transferred out of the jurisdiction of the Ministry of Foreign Trade to become the foreign trade arms of other ministries and departments.

The foreign trade firms have themselves been fundamentally reorganized: they have received a greater degree of managerial autonomy and have been converted over to self-financing and full cost accounting. For the first time, the foreign trade firms will act mainly as intermediaries on behalf of foreign buyers/ sellers and the domestic Soviet producers-suppliers or consumers-importers, although they will conduct their commercial activities as legal entities in their own right.

A precondition for the Soviet producers-suppliers' and importers-consumers' ability to exercise their right of access to foreign markets was their competence to make business decisions on their own within the structure of the domestic economy. This is what the Law on the State Enterprise (Association), of 30 June 1987, was enacted to accomplish. Beginning 1 January 1988, a full year after the grant of foreign market rights went into effect, all Soviet enterprises, industrial and service organizations in all branches of the Soviet economy, including trade, whether endowed with foreign market rights or not, began to operate on the principles of self-financing, full cost accounting, and economic self-management. In Article 1 of ch. I, the Law on the State Enterprise (Association) characterized the new enterprise as the most fundamental link in the entire new structure of the Soviet economy. ''Plan making will begin within the enterprise''—Gorbachev had said, adding that it is against this Law that all reorganization of the central apparatus and its functions under *perestroika* ''will be strictly matched.''

To be sure, central supervision and coordination of the new-type state enterprises, including the new-style FTOs, will remain; but the nature of central control will change: gone will be the day-to-day direct interference of the central organs in the operations and the management of the decentralized enterprises and commercial firms. ''We will free the central management of operational functions in the running of the enterprises, and this will enable it to concentrate on key processes determining the strategy of economic growth''—wrote Gorbachev in his book *Perestroika: New Thinking for Our Country and the World*. Control of the enterprises by central organs is to be confined, in the future, to a limited number of areas: the fulfillment of contractual obligations and of orders placed by the state; profits; labor profitability; and general indicators of scientific and technological progress.

''The replacement of the predominatly administrative method of management by a predominatly economic method'' became the *leitmotiv* of *perestroika* in the field of national economy and foreign trade.

At the very top, the guidance and coordination of the central administrative and policy-making bodies of the Soviet government in the field of foreign trade was entrusted, by a Joint Decree of the CPSU Central Committee and the USSR Council of Ministers of 19 August 1986 (''Decree No. 991'') to the State Commission of the USSR Council of Ministers for Foreign Economic Relations. Subordinate to it were, according to Decree No. 991, not only the Ministry of Foreign Trade, the State Committee for Foreign Economic Relations, and the Bank for Foreign Trade, but also the State Committee for Foreign Tourism, the Main State Customs Administration of the USSR Council of Ministers, and all ministries and departments in the discharge of their functions relating to foreign economic relations, as well as the Soviet contingents in the intergovernmental commissions for economic and scientific-technical cooperation with foreign countries.

For the new enterprises endowed with foreign market rights and especially for the new FTOs, there will be a different type of control as well: *that exercised by the market mechanism itself.* This means, according to Soviet analysts of the *perestroika* legislation, that in the conduct of foreign trade operations, the FTOs must be at all times guided by commercial considerations and by economic principles customarily applicable in international markets. In the words of a noted Soviet economist writing in *Pravda* on 22 May 1987:

> The basic parameters of the regulations of foreign economic relations based on full economic cost accounting will be established by prices for export and import goods, the rates of foreign exchange . . ., customs tariffs, taxes, interest rates on loans, costs . . . [etc.].

Soviet enterprises which had received the right to enter foreign markets, as well as the foreign trade organizations themselves, have a brief to succeed in world markets on the strength of the quality of their goods, which must measure up to international standards, their overall competitiveness, and their drive to secure a larger share in world markets for Soviet exports, A tall order, indeed.

In reorganizing the apparatus of foreign trade, the Soviet leadership took account of its changing nature by increasing the importance of those components which go beyond the traditional functions of exports and imports. Particular attention was given to agreements and contracts on scientific-technological and industrial cooperation with other countries, particularly socialist, and to joint ventures with ''capitalist'' countries. Recognition of the more comprehensive concept of foreign trade is reflected, in part, also in the renaming of the central bodies dealing with international trade. Thus, for instance, the USSR Ministry of Foreign Trade was abolished on 15 January 1988 (as was the State Committee for Foreign Economic Relations). Their place was taken by the new USSR Ministry of Foreign Economic Relations, which, however, has not yet had its own Statute confirmed, six months after its creation. Another example is the USSR Bank for Foreign Trade, which has been renamed the USSR Bank for Foreign Economic Relations.

The changes in the names of the new institutions reflect, in reality, both the change in the concept of ''foreign trade'' *and* the prevailing uncertainty about the proper place of many central institutions within *perestroika*. As Gorbachev himself has readily conceded: ''We have yet to divide the functions of the center and localities, to change the essence of ministries' work, and their very purpose.'' In fact, the structure of many familiar Soviet institutions continues to change before our very eyes. This ''experimentation,'' too, is an integral aspect of *perestroika*. One of the latest institutions relating to foreign trade to change its name was the Foreign Trade Arbitration Commission of the USSR Chamber of

Commerce and Industry, which became the Arbitration Court of the USSR Chamber of Commerce and Industry. In approving the Statute of the new Arbitration Court, on 14 December 1987, the Presidium of the USSR Supreme Soviet eliminated more than the terms "Foreign Trade" from its name. It also deleted clause 2 of the old Statute of 1975 which stipulated that "Parties must orginate from different countries."

The co-authors of the present monograph, Professor M. M. Boguslavsky and P. S. Smirnov, offer the reader an exceptionally thorough analysis of the current Soviet legislation on the organization and the mechanism of foreign economic relations under *perestroika*. They comment on the relationship between the state monopoly of foreign trade and the nature of the current decentralization of foreign trade operations; discuss the nature and the meaning of the changes brought about by the new Law on the State Enterprise (Association), of 30 June 1987, particularly in relation to foreign economic operations; follow up with a detailed commentary on the functions of various state administrative agencies in the area of foreign trade following the reforms, and, conversely, on the legal status of foreign trade organizations at various levels of the present decentralized management of foreign trade in the USSR. Of particular interest is also their penetrating legal analysis of the legal forms of reciprocal relations between industry and foreign trade under the conditions of *perestroika*. Mature scholarship and practical involvement in the topics discussed are also combined in their presentation of the Soviet view on direct relations with enterprises of CMEA countries and on legal aspects of scientific-technical and industrial cooperation contracts and agreements.

## II

Of special interest to practitioners in the industrialized Western countries will be the authors' commentary on the Soviet *joint ventures* legislation—the most detailed thus far presented by Soviet jurists, and the most authoritative, given the respective positions of the authors, even though they present here their own views rather than those of their respective institutions.

Most Western practitioners will by now be familiar with the text of the decrees of 13 January 1987 issued by the USSR Council of Ministers on joint ventures with enterprises, international associations and organizations of the USSR and other member countries of the CMEA (Decree No. 48), and joint ventures on Soviet territory with participation of Soviet organizations and firms from capitalist and developing countries (Decree No. 49)—or at least with the latter.

Under the expert guidance of the authors, the joint venture decrees are analyzed, clause by clause. To the skeptics who saw but *lacunae*, inadequate legal regulation, and hastily drafted, unacceptable clauses, it will soon become clear how many of these "*lacunae*" are left for the parties themselves to define and agree on, in the charter of establishment, within, of course, the general provisions of Soviet law, which is the *lex corporationis*. Decree No. 49 merely lays down the mandatory provisions among the principal matter that the charter should contain (provisions relating to the object[s] of the joint venture, formation of its charter capital, valuation of the respective contributions, shares of the Soviet and the foreign partners, distribution and repatriation of profits, composition of management and hiring of personnel, duration and legislation of the joint venture, settlement of disputes, etc.). Decree No. 49 makes clear in clause 3 that approval of the joint venture (which must be moved by the Soviet partner) is tied to the joint venture's ability to attract the latest foreign technology, to stimulate exports, and to make possible the elimination of unnecessary imports.

The authors go into considerable detail in suggesting what questions the parties should strive to settle and stipulate in the "foundation documents" (i.e., the charter) of the joint venture. The authors then turn to the discussion of the actual operation of the joint venture and indicate (*a*) how the existing provisions of Decree No. 49 are to be interpreted; (*b*) what changes have been made in the text of the Decree since its publication, as a rule on the basis of practical experience in its application; (*c*) which questions are to be dealt with, *according to the language of Decree No. 49*, under separate implementing and substatutory legislation; and (*d*) how the legislation can improve the existing texts.

Among significant amendments of Decree No. 49 which have already been placed on the books are, *inter alia*, the extension of the right to decide independently on the creation of joint ventures (subject to the standard procedure of approval) to federal ministries and government departments as well as the councils of ministers *of the union republics* (Joint Decree of 17 September 1987); extension of the exemption from payment of taxes on profit, from "two years from the start of operations" (para. 2 of clause 36) to "two years from the date of showing profit" (Edict of 17 March 1988); and the permission presented to parties to a joint venture to agree on the valuation of their respective contributions to the charter capital in rubles as well as in foreign currency (Joint Decree of 17 September 1987). A decree issued by the State Committee for Material and Technical Supply (*Gossnab*) on 4 June 1987 added a special provision to the joint venture decree on the supply of local materials and services on the basis of contracts with agencies of *Gossnab*, and other local economic organizations, with payment in rubles at wholesale and negotiated prices.

Since the publication of Decree No. 49, the list of enacted implementing and substatutory normative materials has grown steadily, particularly in the areas of taxation, procedure for registration of joint ventures, rules on auditing and accounting procedures, keeping of statistical data, insurance, etc. The authors cite the most important of these acts published prior to 1 October 1987. P. S Smirnov, one of the co-authors of this monograph, continued the list in *Vneshniaia torgovlia* (Foreign trade) 1988, No. 1, where he also lists the first joint ventures with foreign firms approved by the competent

Soviet authorities under Decrees No. 48 and 49.

To be sure, the joint venture legislation as it now stands still contains many *lacunae* and areas in which improvements have been suggested, some by the present authors themsleves. (Smirnov has devoted a major article in *Pravovedenie* [Jurisprudence] 1987, No. 5 [Sept.–Oct. issue], to the need for improving the regulation of legal relationships arising from foreign economic activities by means of civil-law legislation). Foreign practitioners have added to the roster of needed improvements the clarification of the method of valuation of partners' respective contributions to the charter capital; of the scope of protection of industrial property rights; of the distribution of managerial positions; of the approval procedures for loans from Soviet banks; of the depreciation rules (at present there is only a reference to the rules applicable to state enterprises, without spelling out the details); of the powers of the trade unions; etc. (see, e.g., Hobér, in *International Financial Law Review*, November 1987). One might also question the present legal protection of investments in the Soviet Union and wonder about the legal force of clause 45 in Decree No.49, in the parent country of the foreign partner. Clause 45 prohibits the disclosure, by the joint venture, of any accounting or business data to the government or other authorities of a foreign country. Such provision invites direct violation of the law (including tax laws) of many foreign countries. The settlement of disputes under the new Statute of the Arbitration Court also deserves a fresh look.

The authors of the monograph anticipate that in time a more detailed, complex, and comprehensive *Law on Joint Ventures* will be drawn up which will incorporate answers to the many still outstanding questions. In the meantime they have successfully shown how the existing legislation on joint ventures, with its black/white as well as gray areas, can be utilized by prospective participants to their best advantage. As two Western practitioners have put it in an article in *The Law Society's Gazette* (9 September 1987), "Now is the time for companies to approach the Soviet market with a joint venture in mind."

# III

Professor M. M. Boguslavsky is one of the most respected Soviet scholars and an internationally recognized specialist in the fields of private international law, intellectual property, and legal-economic and cultural relations with other countries. P. S. Smirnov is a high-level Soviet foreign economic relations official known also for his practice-oriented legal contributions to the major Soviet scholarly and business journals. Both jurists are among the best informed sources in the Soviet Union on the progress of *perestroika* in the field of foreign trade and foreign economic relations in general. The present monograph which they have co-authored, was intended, in the first place, for the lawyer and the business executive, and, in the second place, for the academic jurist and the student of *perestroika* in a vital area of the Soviet economy and of Soviet economic relations with other countries. Both groups will appreciate the wealth of technical detail. Both will equally welcome the care which the authors took in presenting the material in the kind of style that General Secretary Gorbachev has himself introduced in his speeches and writings. The result is a pragmatic, matter-of-fact account of the changes now being introduced in the USSR in doing business abroad and in managing both, the foreign economic relations and the changes themselves.

In addition, this systematic and authoritative guide to the reforms in Soviet foreign economic relations will prove invaluable to prospective partners in joint ventures with the USSR and to international bodies (such as GATT, for instance) who follow attentively the direction of Soviet reforms in this field.

The editor wishes to thank both authors for their willingness to make this study available at a time when it is vitally needed. Denis M. McCauley has translated the Russian manuscript in a most professional manner which all readers will appreciate.

SERGE L. LEVITSKY

# The Reorganization of Soviet Foreign Trade

## LEGAL ASPECTS

# INTRODUCTION

The Twenty-seventh Congress of the Communist Party of the Soviet Union formulated the task of substantially improving all work in the sphere of foreign economic relations and of integrating this task more closely with the program for the economic and social development of the USSR and the acceleration of the entire economic mechanism. "In advancing the goal of the more active utilization of foreign economic operations in the acceleration of our development," noted at the Congress the General Secretary of the CPSU Central Committee M. S. Gorbachev, "we have in mind to reorganize step by step the structure of our foreign trade turnover and to make our exports and imports more effective."[1] One facet of the wholesale restructuring of the USSR's economic mechanism, which is proceeding in accordance with the decisions of the Twenty-seventh CPSU Congress, are measures provided for in the joint decrees of the CPSU Central Committee and the USSR Council of Ministers aimed at the radical improvement of the structure and management of foreign economic operations.[2]

There were a number of factors involved in the approval of these measures. As we know, the USSR's foreign trade turnover has grown to very substantial proportions in recent decades. At the same time, the CPSU Central Committee and the Soviet government have noted that the existing scale of trade, scientific-technological, and production ties with other countries have come into contradiction with the demands of the intensification of the national economy and the acceleration of scientific-technological progress. The USSR's share in international trade does not correspond to the level of economic development we have achieved or the nation's developmental needs. And we are only slowly making the conversion to broad scientific-technological and production cooperation and to other new forms of international economic cooperation.

The CPSU Central Committee and the USSR Council of Ministers have pointed out that the existing situation is also a consequence of the maintenance of

---

The views expressed in this monograph are those of the authors and do not necessarily reflect the views of the organizations with which they are affiliated.

1. *Materialy XXVII s"ezda KPSS* [Materials of the Twenty-seventh Congress of the CPSU], Moscow 1986, p. 30.

2. See Decree No. 991 of the CPSU Central Committee and the USSR Council of Ministers of 19 August 1986, "On Measures for Improving the Management of Economic and Scientific-Technological Cooperation with the Socialist Countries," *Sobranie Postanovlenii Pravitel'stva SSSR* [Gazette of Decrees of the Government of the USSR; hereinafter *SP SSSR*] 1986, No. 3, item 172; *Vneshniaia torgovlia* [Foreign trade] 1987, No. 4.

outmoded methods in the organization and management of foreign economic operations in the USSR and industry's isolation from foreign trade. In the resulting system, production associations and enterprises have indeed found themselves cut off from direct participation in foreign economic operations.

The above-mentioned decrees of the CPSU Central Committee and the USSR Council of Ministers call for substantial, far-reaching, and long-term changes in the structure and management of the USSR's foreign economic operations. In particular, they envisage measures aimed at improving planning and strengthening economic cost accounting in this sphere. They recognize the need for broadening considerably the rights of branch ministries and agencies, production associations, enterprises, and organizations in the administering of foreign economic operations. And they have posed the task of introducing new and promising forms of economic cooperation with foreign countries; of establishing direct production ties between enterprises of CMEA member countries; and of expanding production specialization and scientific-technological and industrial cooperation and creating joint enterprises, including on the territory of the USSR. In essence, we are talking about radical reforms in the sphere of foreign economic operations and the creation of a new structure and organization for this sphere that would completely correspond to the conditions of economic activity in the USSR.

The current restructuring and radical improvement of the USSR's foreign economic operations have given rise to major changes in the system of legal norms regulating this sphere. Undoubtedly, the achievement of the stated goals and the success of reorganization will depend in no small measure not only on whether the approved measures are realized, but also on the directions that the further development of the legal regime of foreign economic operations will take.

Since the approval of the abovementioned decrees by the CPSU Central Committee and the USSR Council of Ministers, a number of important normative acts have been drafted and confirmed. And while work continues on some documents, the basic features of the legal regime of foreign economic operations in the USSR at the present stage have already been codified in a system of sufficiently detailed regulations. This allows us to present and comment on them and to provide a general assessment.

In this monograph, we hope to provide the reader with a general overview of a few of the most important issues in the modern legal regime of the structure and management of foreign economic operations in the USSR. In so doing, we will stress not only the theoretical side of these problems, but more so their practical aspects which may be of broad interest. In this connection, the authors consider it helpful to take a detailed look at the powers of state organs of management of foreign economic operations, the rights and responsibilities of industrial organizations that enjoy the right to carry on export-import operations, and the legal regime governing the creation and operations on the territory of the USSR of joint enterprises consisting of Soviet organizations and foreign firms.

In writing the present monograph, the authors made use of normative materials *in statu juris* as of 1 October 1987.

# 1

# RECENT NORMATIVE ACTS AFFECTING
# FOREIGN ECONOMIC OPERATIONS

We should first of all note that the basic normative acts establishing the legal norms for foreign economic operations remain in force. Foremost among them is the 1977 USSR Constitution, which establishes that at the basis of foreign trade and other forms of foreign economic operations in the USSR lies the state monopoly (Article 73).[1] Aside from the Constitution, other such fundamental acts are the Principles of Civil Legislation of the USSR and the Union Republics of 1961[2] and the civil codes of the union republics, as well a number of other sources.[3]

The decrees of the CPSU Central Committee and USSR Council of Ministers of 19 August 1986 laid down the goals and directions for the radical improvement of foreign economic operations in the USSR and the basic contours of its new structure and management. These contain both norms of a general and fundamental nature and instructions on the drafting of a series of normative acts on individual problems and issues. Moreover, new documents may flow directly from the abovementioned decrees of 19 August 1986, although this is not expressly called for. As well, the realization of the stipulated measures may require the further definition of approved norms and principals, which is usually provided for with the publication of supplements and revisions, rules and directives, especially at the level of ministries and departments.

As concerns those normative acts that are already on the books and that are to provide the foundation for the legal basis of the new structure and management of foreign economic operations, we should take particular note of the following:

—Decree No. 1513 of the USSR Council of Ministers of 22 December 1986,

---

1. *Svod zakonov SSSR* [Digest of Laws of the USSR], Vol. 1, pp. 14–42.
2. *Svod zakonov SSSR*, Vol. 2, pp. 6–42.
3. See M. M. Boguslavsky, *Mezhdunarodnoe chastnoe pravo* [International private law], Moscow 1982, pp. 56–60; V. S. Pozdniakov and O. N. Sadikov, *Pravovoe regulirovanie otnoshenii po vneshnei torgovle SSSR* [The legal regulation of the USSR's foreign-trade relations], part I, Moscow 1985, pp. 12–20.

"On the Confirmation of the Statute of the USSR Ministry of Foreign Trade"[4];
—the Statute of the USSR Ministry of Foreign Trade;
—the Statute of the USSR State Committee for Foreign Economic Relations, confirmed by Decree No. 1514 of the USSR Council of Ministers of 22 December 1986[5];
—the Statute of the All-Union Cost-Accounting Foreign Trade Organization (Association) of a Ministry or Department, and the Model Statute of the Cost-Accounting Foreign-Trade Firm of a Science-Production or Production Association, Enterprise, or Organization, confirmed by Decree No. 1526 of the USSR Council of Ministers of 22 December 1986[6];
—the Procedures for the Establishment of Direct Production and Scientific-Technological Ties between USSR Associations, Enterprises, and Organizations and Enterprises and Organizations of Other CMEA Member Countries[7];
—the Edict of the Presidium of the USSR Supreme Soviet of 13 January 1987, "On Questions Connected with the Creation and Operation on the Territory of the USSR of Joint Enterprises, International Associations, and Organizations Consisting of Soviet and Foreign Organizations, Firms, and Administrative Agencies"[8];
—Decree No. 48 of the USSR Council of Ministers of 13 January 1987, "On the Procedures for the Creation and Operation on the Territory of the USSR of Joint Enterprises, International Associations, and Organizations of the USSR and Other CMEA Member Countries"[9];
—Decree No. 49 of the USSR Council of Ministers of 13 January 1987, "On the Procedures for the Creation and Operation on the Territory of the USSR of Joint Enterprises Consisting of Soviet Organizations and Firms from Capitalist and Developing Countries."[10]

4. *SP SSSR* 1987, No. 7, item 30.
5. *SP SSSR* 1987, No. 5, item 20.
6. *SP SSSR* 1987, No. 6, p. 24.
7. *Ekonomicheskaia gazeta* [Economic Gazette] 1987, no. 9. p. 23.
8. *Vedomosti Verkhovnogo Soveta SSSR* [Gazette of the USSR Supreme Soviet] 1987, No. 2, item 35.
9. *SP SSSR* 1987, No. 8, item 38.
10. *SP SSSR* 1987, No. 8, item 40.

# 2

# THE STATE MONOPOLY ON
# FOREIGN ECONOMIC OPERATIONS IN THE USSR

As we know, at the basis of foreign economic operations in the USSR is the state monopoly. The wholesale restructuring of the structure and management of this sphere issuing from the aforementioned decrees of 19 August 1986 proceed from the fact that the state monopoly on foreign economic operations will be retained and developed further.

## The state monopoly and the structure and
## management of foreign economic operations

The idea of the state monopoly on foreign trade was integrally tied in with the theory of socialist revolution and with the economic platform of the CPSU drafted by the founder of the Soviet state, V. I. Lenin, in the period leading up to the Great October Socialist Revolution of 1917. Lenin proposed its actual establishment in the first months of the Soviet state's existence. On the economic policy agenda of the proletarian state, drawn up by Lenin for the meeting of the Council of People's Commissars on 27 November (10 December) 1917, establishment of a "state monopoly on foreign trade" occupied third place after the nationalization of banks and compulsory syndication.[1]

The state monopoly in this sphere flowed from the planned nature of the management of the national economy, which itself was a product of the establishment of social ownership of the basic means of production. As L. B. Krasin noted in his time, "this is nothing other than the application . . . of the general Soviet

---

1. V. I. Lenin, *Polnoe sobranie sochenenii* [Complete collected works], vol. 35, p. 123. This issue was again addressed in the draft of the program of economic measures as well as in other documents. See *V. I. Lenin o vneshnekonomicheskikh sviaziakh Sovetskogo gosudarstva* [V. I. Lenin on the foreign economic ties of the Soviet state], Moscow 1974, p. 11, etc.

principle of planned state regulation to the Soviet Union's foreign trade relations."[2]

The state monopoly on foreign trade came into being with the Decree of the Council of People's Commissars of 22 April 1918, "On the Nationalization of Foreign Trade."[3] This act was preceded by a number of others that were aimed at the establishment of Soviet state control over foreign trade.[4]

The introduction of the state monopoly on foreign trade was one of the most important of the acts promulgated in the first months of the existence of the Soviet state which were directed at the cementing and development of the new socioeconomic order. While the Decree of 22 April 1918 spoke of the "nationalization" of foreign trade, in an actual and juridical sense it pronounced this sphere a monopoly of the Soviet state. As a result, no foreign trade transaction could take place without the prior approval of the People's Commissariat of Foreign Trade, and this approval otherwise translated into its control. This came to be considered one of the juridical principles of the structure and management of foreign trade in the USSR. The very term "state monopoly" was first used in a decree of the All-Russian Central Executive Committee of 13 March 1922; it was reproduced in later normative acts and was codified in the USSR's constitutions. The establishment of "the state monopoly" did not require that foreign trade could be carried out only and exclusively by the Soviet state as such, or its agencies or organizations. In actuality, due to a number of reasons and factors, it happened that for a certain amount of time the Soviet state directly or through its organizations conducted all foreign trade, or at least the majority of it. In general, the Soviet state and state ownership have played a decisive role in the USSR's economy. However, it seems that the principal content of the 1918 Decree was to confirm the authorization-type system for the conduct of foreign trade transactions and for the import and export of goods, which is characteristic today of the regulation of foreign trade in many countries. The term selected then best reflected the nature of the established structure and management of foreign trade, and it is still used today in existing Soviet foreign economic legislation.[5]

---

2. L. B. Krasin, *Planovoe khoziaistvo i monopoliia vneshnei torgovli* [The planned economy and the foreign trade monopoly], Moscow 1925, p. 37.

3. See I. Kovan, "Pravovoe soderzhanie Dekreta o natsionalizatsii vneshnei torgovli" [The legal content of the Decree on the nationalization of foreign trade], *Vneshniaia torgovlia* 1967, No. 4, pp. 13–14.

4. See V. Timofeev, "Istoricheskii opyt gosudarstvennoi monopolii vneshnei torgovli SSSR" [The history of the USSR's state monopoly on foreign trade], *Vneshniaia torgovlia* 1967, No. 7, pp. 24–25.

5. A similar analysis of the content of this institution can be found in the Soviet juridical literature. See, in particular: G. P. Kaliuzhnaia, *Pravovye formy monopolii vneshnei torgovli SSSR v ikh istoricheskom razvitii* [Legal forms of the USSR's foreign trade monopoly in their historical development], Moscow 1951; V. S. Pozdniakov,

For a number of decades, it was that facet of foreign economic operations that is traditionally associated with foreign trade that was not only the subject of legal regulation by the Soviet state, but also a sphere of administrative management on the part of state agencies. After all, other forms of foreign economic activity were practically nonexistent at that time. Thus, the USSR's first two constitutions (1924 and 1936) still spoke of the state monopoly on foreign trade. The present Constitution provides a wider definition of the state monopoly to comprise all forms of foreign economic activity in the USSR. This was occasioned by the development of new forms of foreign economic relations, forms that went beyond normal trade.[6] The monopoly of the Soviet state on all forms of foreign economic activity was established before 1977, but it was the 1977 Constitution that codified it as a legal institution.[7]

An important question in the structure and management of foreign economic operations was and remains that of the jurisdiction of the USSR's federal government in this sphere.

Due to external and domestic conditions, unified and generally agreed-upon principles were established for the regulation of foreign trade operations even prior to the formation of the federated Soviet state, and a single state agency was created to manage the implementation of these principles (the People's Commissariat of Foreign Trade). This agency played the directing role in all the Soviet republics in the sphere of foreign economic policy.[8]

On 30 December 1922 the First Congress of Soviets convened, and it was at

*Gosudarstvennaia monopoliia vneshnei torgovli SSSR* [The state monopoly on foreign trade in the USSR], Moscow 1969; idem, *Sovetskoe gosudarstvo i vneshniaia torgovlia (pravovye voprosy)* [The Soviet state and foreign trade (legal aspects)], Moscow 1976; E. T. Usenko, "Sushchnost' i formy sotsialisticheskoi monopolii vneshnei torgovli" [The essence and forms of the socialist monopoly on foreign trade], *Vneshniaia torgovlia* 1967, No. 6, pp. 40–41; Iu. Shamrai, "Perestroika sistemy vneshneekonomicheskikh sviazei SSSR i gosudarstvennaia monopoliia vneshnei torgovli" [Restructuring of the USSR's foreign economic relations and the state monopoly on foreign trade], *Vneshniaia torgovlia* 1987, No. 4, pp. 2–7.

6. See V. S. Pozdniakov, "Konstitutsionnye osnovy gosudarstvennoi monopolii vneshnei torgovli v SSSR" [The constitutional foundations for the state monopoly on foreign trade in the USSR], *Vneshniaia torgovlia* 1978, No. 7, pp. 11–17; idem, "Konstitutsiia SSSR i vneshneekonomicheskaia deiatel'nost'" [The USSR Constitution and foreign economic operations], in *Iuridicheskie aspekty osushchestvleniia vneshneekonomicheskikh sviazei* [Legal aspects of the implementation of foreign economic relations], Moscow 1979, pp. 3–8.

7. During discussion of the draft of the 1977 USSR Constitution, proposals were advanced in the press for defining the sphere of state management and control of foreign economic relations by stating flatly that the state monopoly on foreign trade applies to all foreign economic activity.

8. See I. Kovan, "Obrazovanie SSSR i voprosy monopolii vneshnei torgovli" [The formation of the USSR and questions involving the monopoly on foreign trade], *Vneshniaia torgovlia* 1972, No. 7, p. 10.

this assembly that the Declaration and Agreement on the Formation of the USSR were approved. The Agreement authorized the supreme organs of federal power to establish "a system of foreign trade." The 1924 USSR Constitution, which was drafted on the basis of the Declaration and Agreement, placed under the jurisdiction of the USSR in the person of its supreme organs "the management of foreign trade." The present Constitution provides that foreign economic operations belong to the jurisdiction of the USSR in the person of its highest organs of state power and management.

## Foreign trade and industry

While the foundations of the structure and management of foreign economic operations and the state monopoly principle have remained unaltered, their legal and organizational forms have changed to meet the needs of the Soviet state at certain stages of the development of the economy. The examination of all these changes must be the subject of a separate study. Here it is important to direct the reader's attention to the conditions under which questions of industry's role in foreign trade were decided. Examining this question will allow us to better understand the nature of reforms taking place today in the sphere of foreign economic operations and their principal orientation.

As is known, the Tenth Congress of the RCP(b) [Russian Communist Party (Bolsheviks)], meeting in March 1921, approved the transition to the New Economic Policy (NEP). With a view to the changing external conditions of that time, the transition to the New Economic Policy created the preconditions for changes in the structure and management of foreign trade that would place it on the very same foundations as the nation's entire economy. On 13 March 1922 the All-Russian Central Executive Committee published a decree "On Foreign Trade," which set down the basic regulations for the import and export of goods. The People's Commissariat of Foreign Trade was empowered to grant individual Soviet organizations direct access to foreign markets. Such organizations were required to obtain prior authorization from the People's Commissariat of Foreign Trade or its representatives before foreign trade transactions could be consummated.

The All-Russian Central Executive Committee and the Council of People's Commissars issued a decree on 16 October 1922 which provided that the Council of Labor and Defense could confer the right to conduct foreign trade operations, in accordance with this decree, on specified state, central, and local organs included in a special list. A further decree issued by these same organs on 12 April 1923 as a supplement to the first decree provided that these rights could also be granted to state production enterprises and associations that had made the transition to commercial accounting.

The 12 April 1923 decree provided that industrial enterprises and associations that had been provided access to foreign markets could only export their own goods and import only those products that were required for in-house production. Thus, access to foreign markets was extended as a rule only to production enterprises and associations that were included in the special list, and then only for the import of necessary goods and the export of their own products.

In their conduct of export-import operations, Soviet industrial organizations that had won access to foreign markets came under the control of the People's Commissariat of Foreign Trade and of trade missions abroad. The 16 October 1922 decree stipulated that central and local economic organs and their representatives were obligated to provide prior notification to the People's Commissariat of Foreign Trade and the appropriate trade missions of each and every proposed trade transaction. These state administrative agencies had the right to prohibit any such transaction on reasonable and verified grounds.

The proper relationship between production enterprises and associations having access to foreign markets and trade missions abroad was defined in the directive of the Council of Labor and Defense of 18 April 1923, which was based on the 12 April 1923 decree. The directive obliged enterprises and associations to submit to the trade missions financial and other reports on their activities within the time period and in the procedure required by the trade missions. All books and correspondence were also subject to examination.

This directive gave trade missions the right to prohibit any trade transaction of a Soviet organization on the grounds of political or commerical undesirability, or on the grounds that the specific transaction did not correspond with the state plan.

To allow trade missions to properly execute their control functions over the export-import operations of Soviet organizations, the latter were required to provide prior notification to the trade missions regarding planned agreements with foreign firms. Likewise, all inquiries and proposals addressed to foreign companies had also to be submitted to the trade missions. And the terms for proposed deals were also to be recorded upon the conclusion of negotiations with foreign partners.

The directive established short periods (of two to five days) within which trade missions had to make their decisions; the absence of objections was taken as approval of the activities of Soviet organizations. In practice, the regulating activity of the trade missions in fact served to aid Soviet organizations in their conduct of export-import operations and to enable them to gain more favorable terms for their transactions.

The structure and management of foreign trade described above grew, as noted, out of the specific conditions of the first half of the 1920s. This system had its advantages and its shortcomings.[9] [Its shortcomings led] the October 1925 Plenum of the RCP(b) Central Committee to order the system's reorganization.[10]

---

9. For greater detail, see V. S. Pozdniakov, *Sovetskoe gosudarstvo i vneshniaia torgovlia*, pp. 114–125.

10. *KPSS v rezoliutsiiakh i resheniiakh s"ezdov, konferentsii i plenumov TsK* [The CPSU in resolutions and decisions of congresses, conferences, and Central Committee plenums], Moscow 1953, ch. 2, p. 58.

Under the new system, specialized state joint-stock companies were now empowered to conduct foreign trade operations. As a rule, these joint-stock companies were production, procurement, and consumers' organizations.

The establishment of specialized companies made it possible to expand exports and to terminate imports of goods that could be produced in the USSR, and also to reduce the number of Soviet organizations operating in foreign markets. The joint-stock companies operated through special import and export departments of the trade missions, which precluded the duplication of foreign market efforts for a specific type of product. Also operating in this period alongside the specialized state export-import joint-stock companies were branch syndicates, for example "Neftesindikat" [The petroleum syndicate], which, under the supervision of the People's Commissariat of Foreign Trade, sold its members' products in foreign markets. The syndicates operated on the basis of economic cost accounting and conducted foreign trade operations in their own name.

In 1930, all-union foreign trade associations were authorized to conduct export-import operations. Initially subordinate to the People's Commissariat, these organizations came under the supervision of the Ministry of Foreign Trade, and later, under that of another specialized agency—the USSR State Committee for Foreign Economic Relations. Under this system, production enterprises and associations came to be merely suppliers of goods for export, fulfilling the schedule-orders of foreign trade associations, while branch ministries and agencies of industry became customers for imported goods. Notwithstanding the definite and continous broadening, beginning in the 1960s, of the rights of industry in foreign economic decision making and numerous changes of individual elements of the entire system of work in this sphere, the basic model of the structure and management of foreign economic relations established in 1930 remained until the middle of 1986.

## Defininition of the concept of the state monopoly as the structure and management of foreign trade operations in the USSR

In the modern understanding of the state monopoly, the Soviet state controls the conduct of foreign economic operations. It ensures the conduct of a unified state policy in this sphere, plans foreign economic operations, establishes procedures for their implementation and ensures observance of those procedures, determines the organizations empowered to conduct foreign economic operations, including the conclusion of economic (civil-law) foreign economic contracts, and determines the scope of these operations.

This understanding of the structure and management of foreign economic operations in the USSR has nothing in common with the view that the state monopoly is supposedly the monopoly of one agency (the USSR Ministry of Foreign Trade) or of two agencies (the Ministry of Foreign Trade and the USSR State Committee for Foreign Economic Relations). This idea had no basis in reality in the past, and this is especially true today, when the functions of state management of foreign economic operations lie not with one or two but a whole series of administrative agencies.

Another misconception too, must be pointed out, namely, the view that the Soviet state or the Ministry of Foreign Trade themselves transact foreign economic deals and themselves become the subjects of civil-law relations in specific export-import operations. In fact, the Soviet state, in the person of the government and other organs, merely determines the organizations (juridical persons in civil law) that are legally empowered to conclude and in practice do conclude foreign economic transactions. Of course, in the Soviet economy—and thus, in foreign trade—state enterprises and associations enjoy primacy, but in a number of cases, cooperative and social organizations have acquired the right of access to foreign markets, and, under the new structure and management of foreign trade, this is the case also with the joint enterprises of Soviet and foreign organizations and firms.

## Description of the fundamental principals underlying the Soviet structure and management of foreign economic operations

Notwithstanding its almost seventy-year existence in the USSR and the by and large considerable development of the USSR's economic and scientific-technological ties with foreign countries, there has been, as we know, quite a diversity of views and assessments of the state monopoly over the organization and management of foreign economic operations. Opinions on the state monopoly, its content and functions, range from unconditional and simplistic arguments of support and approval to groundless and misplaced criticism. There exists a rich literature on this issue.

Thus, there is the view that differences between socioeconomic systems, and especially in the structural forms of foreign economic operations of capitalist and socialist states, supposedly obstruct the development of economic relations between East and West. In particular, central planning is considered to be an obstacle to trade with the USSR. As this argument goes, planning restrains the free flow of foreign trade circulation to the extent that foreign trade is limited to the role ascribed to it by the overall plan of economic development. The idea expressed here is that the planned direction of foreign trade activity does not accord well with the spontaneously developing competition of world markets and thus blocks the natural course of international trade. In this scenario, foreign trade plans are some sort of rigid instructions that preclude the consideration of competitive conditions, thus making impossible flexibility, mobility, and adaptability to changes in world markets.

In actuality, however, the principles underlying the functioning of the Soviet economy provide for the combination of centrally planned management with the operational and commercial independence of each production and trade enterprise. This principle is the cornerstone of the activity of foreign trade associations, which, operating within the general contours of the national economic plan and acting on the basis of commercial considerations, resolve questions on the volume and term of purchases and sales, on the selection of partners, etc. Foreign trade associations can make meaningful corrections in initial import and export plans. The proposals of foreign trade associations are also considered in the drafting of long-term plans of national economic development. All this allows foreign trade associations to utilize, as commercial enterprises, competition in world markets.

There is also the view that the foreign trade plan, carrying as it does the force of law, represents the discriminatory application of quotas and nontariff barriers. Here once again we encounter the unfortunate transposition of economic features of one group of countries to the foreign economic activity of the USSR. The foreign trade plan has nothing to do with nontariff barriers or discriminatory quotas; there are no discriminatory aspects to it. In choosing partner countries and firms, foreign trade associations are guided by the normal commercial considerations. If, for example, a foreign firm's proposals are unsatisfactory and negotiations with it do not lead the achievement of an effective commercial agreement, the foreign trade association may opt for one of the following alternatives and make the corresponding proposals: to make the purchase in another country; to postpone the purchase until the following year, or even to the next five-year plan; or to pull back altogether from the import of the product, leaving to industry the sole production of that equipment and utilizing the foreign currency funds saved for other needs. On the other hand, under favorable commercial conditions, [the foreign trade association] may be able to increase purchases above those provided for in the initial plan.

At the same time, the planning of the foreign economic operations of the USSR and its structural forms is sufficiently diverse and flexible to cover not only the most vital products, but also all resources that can be available for inclusion in international trade turnover. The development of border trade with neighboring countries and deals along cooperative trade lines, etc., contribute particularly to this.

In fact, planning and the progressive, planned development of the USSR's national economy makes for a solid base for stable, long-term foreign economic ties.

With the structure and organization of foreign economic operations adopted in the USSR, the latter have become an integral part of the planned national economy. This could not have been otherwise in a situation where the entire economy is concentrated in the state and cooperative sectors, is based on public (state) and kolkhoz-cooperative ownership, and develops according to a single national plan. This type of organization allows foreign economic relations, like other branches of the economy, to develop in consonance with public interests. This system had helped to transform the USSR from a backward country rapidly into a mighty industrial and agricultural power and to achieve genuine economic independence.

We should also point out that the Soviet structure and management of foreign economic relations ensures advantages not only for the USSR but also for its trade partners. Intergovernmental trade agreements and the long-term and large-scale operations of Soviet foreign trade associations are capable of exercising a positive influence on the economy and level of employment in other countries by guaranteeing the stable sale of goods over a previously determined and lengthy period.

Beyond the views cited above, moreover, there is one that holds that the state monopoly of foreign economic operations makes it difficult to determine the actual significance of the obligations involved in the grant of the most favored nation status to socialist countries and to assess the advantages deriving therefrom, since the criteria by which socialist states select their partners and suppliers are unclear. The principle of the most favored nation status, according to this view, not only is ineffective in trade and economic relations between states with different socioeconomic systems, but it also accords one-sided advantages to socialist countries.

A corollary to this is that the grant of the most favored nation status in trade and economic relations would allow Soviet organizations to undermine the markets of the Western countries, since the former, so the theory goes, are not always motivated by commercial considerations or do not take into account domestic and foreign market prices. In this connection, we should note that Soviet organizations have long conducted their operations on the basis of economic cost accounting, which presupposes the pursuit of commercial interests.

The essence of the USSR's foreign trade policy consists in the stable development of mutually advantageous and balanced trade.

The planned organization of Soviet foreign economic operations guarantees nondiscriminatory practices toward all foreign partners and the full observance of the principle of the most favored nation status.

The planning principle makes for stable trade and economic ties that are less susceptible to spontaneous influences and that contribute to the consistent broadening of trade turnover in accordance with forecasts. All states have an interest in this. Moreover, regardless of the plan, the conditions for importing goods remain equal for all partners with whom [the USSR] maintains trade and economic ties which are based on the reciprocal grant of most favored nation status.

Neither is access to the Soviet market obstructed by the methods of price formation and the price system existing in the USSR. As is known, Soviet foreign trade organizations buy and sell goods in foreign markets at world market prices. The methods of internal price formation, on the other hand, are applied uniformly, without any sort of discrimination, to all analogous imported products.

The fact that export-import operations are conducted in the main by state organizations also presents no obstacle to mutually advantageous commercial operations. While the socioeconomic nature of Soviet foreign trade organizations and of corporations of other countries are often inherently different, Soviet organizations nevertheless carry out each foreign trade transaction in the same manner as private trade companies, that is, based on normal commercial considerations.[11]

Thus, it seems that it is not the USSR's economic institutions and practices that create special inevitable difficulties in trade for governments and firms in market-economy countries. Neither is it the state planning of the volume and structure of foreign trade turnover, or the mechanism of internal price formation and taxation, or foreign-currency regulation, or the implementation of export-import operations by state organizations, which block foreign firms from gaining access to the Soviet market, as some hold. This is far from the case—the situation is actually quite different. Obviously, there exist some objective differences in the structure and management of foreign economic operations which derive from the divergent socioeconomic systems. However, these should not and do not prevent the establishment, implementation, and development of economic and scientific-technological ties between interested organizations and firms in the USSR and abroad. Difficulties of a subjective nature can be successfully overcome if there is a mutual desire and will to search for and find spheres and objects for effective economic cooperation.

The authors are, nevertheless, far from attempting to idealize the existing mechanism. There is nothing so harmful as a simplistic approach to the problems of development and a striving to confuse wishful thinking with the truth. Taking a businesslike approach and rejecting all rhetoric will allow for an objective assessment of the phenomenon under investigation without prejudice or bias. Having said this, the conclusion is inevitable that the long-applied mechanism of foreign economic operations is imperfect. If there were no problems, there would, of course, have been no need to reform the existing methods.

### Development of the structure and management of foreign economic operations

Any system, of course, while it may rest on objectively modern foundations, cannot by itself attain the desired results if the forms and methods of its work and its organizational structures are not adapted to changing conditions, both internal and external. In this context, the decrees of the CPSU Central Committee and the USSR Council of Ministers of 19 August 1986 can be seen as quite unavoidable measures aimed at the radical improvement of the USSR's foreign trade activity in the interests of the Soviet people and of international cooperation.

The documents enacted speak directly of maintaining and developing the principle of state monopoly management of foreign economic operations. The structure and management built on that base must make foreign economic rela-

---

11. See B. Vaganov and A. Frumkin, "Nelepye razmyshleniia i razumnye golosa" [Absurd ideas and sensible voices], *Vneshniaia torgovlia* 1981, No. 11, pp. 43–52; and V. Shumilov, "Effektivnaia vzaimnost': kontseptsiia protektsionizma i diskriminatsii" [Effective complements: the concept of protectionism and discrimination], *Vneshniaia torgovlia* 1986, No. 4, pp. 45–50.

tions a more open, easier to study, and effectively operating branch, one that is flexible and sensitive to the needs of the USSR's national economy and the specific conditions of foreign markets. The state monopoly is the point of departure in this sphere, the economic and legal foundation of the sovereignty of the Soviet state and of its right to establish priorities in the foreign economic operations, goals, and tasks of state organizations, as well as to plan and regulate export-import activity.

It seems to us that within the framework of the new system the emphasis must be removed from administrative methods and placed on economic methods. The rapid expansion of the number of subjects of foreign economic transactions will inevitably lead to the creation of new and the activation of existing instruments for carrying out the policies of the Soviet state in this sphere, and these must correspond to the established economic foundations and the organizational and managerial model of foreign economic relations. The result should be such that the Soviet structure and management of foreign economic relations, open as it is to mutually advantageous and equitable international cooperation and operating according to generally recognized principles, norms, rules, standards, and customs of international trade, will finally attain the qualities that are necessary for the fulfillment of the tasks advanced for it.

# 3

# THE ORGANIZATION AND LEGAL FORMS OF
# FOREIGN ECONOMIC OPERATIONS TODAY

In the Soviet juridical literature the opinion has justly been expressed that of all the issues involved with the state monopoly, the most complex from the theoretical point of view, and at the same time the most important from the practical point of view, are those attendant on the determination of the organizational forms of state guidance [*rukovodstvo*] and the conduct of foreign economic activity.[1] We have already noted above that the organizational and legal forms of foreign economic activity in the USSR have not remained static over the course of the almost seventy-year existence of the state monopoly. One must concede that necessary changes have not always been brought about in good time, and that they have not always kept pace with the changing internal and external situations. Experience has shown that the organization of foreign economic relations must always be in accord with the system of management of the national economy as a whole and be able to meet its principal demands while at the same time taking into account the specifics of foreign markets.

## The network of administrative agencies

At present, there exists in the USSR a broad and multi-tiered system of state administrative agencies dealing with foreign economic relations. These include the State Planning Committee, the State Committee for Material and Technical Supply, the State Committee for Science and Technology, the Ministry of Finance, the State Bank, the State Committee for Inventions and Discoveries, the

---

1. See V. S. Pozdniakov, *Sovetskoe gosudarstvo i vneshniaia torgovlia*, p. 8.

Ministry of Foreign Trade,* the State Committee for Foreign Economic Relations,* the Ministry of the Fish Industry, the State Committee for Foreign Tourism, the Main Administration of State Customs attached to the USSR Council of Ministers, the State Committee for Publishing Houses, Printing Plants, and the Book Trade, the State Committee for Cinematography, the State Committee for Television and Radio Broadcasting, transportation ministries, as well as other ministries and departments.

Decree No. 991 of the CPSU Central Committee and the USSR Council of Ministers of 19 August 1986 extended direct access to foreign markets to almost twenty branch ministries and departments. The clause "access to foreign markets" does not mean that these state administrative agencies have the right to carry out foreign economic transactions or even to conduct economic activity in general. In the USSR, these functions are in principle the purview of enterprises, associations, and other organizations, including state organizations that have juridical personality (legal entities) and that do not normally execute the functions of state management. Some of these are specialized foreign trade organizations, while others conduct foreign operations supplementary to their other, primary economic responsibilities. The aforementioned Decree of 19 August 1986 extended access to foreign markets to almost seventy enterprises, associations, and other industrial organizations, which expanded the group of Soviet legal entities empowered to carry out foreign transactions. As for the ministries, departments, and state committees that were "provided direct access to foreign markets," their juridical and actual authority in the state management of economic operations in their respective industrial spheres has been broadened, and their authority now extends to both internal and external economic activity.

In our view, "access to foreign markets" means: the responsibility of the ministries, departments, and state committees concerned for the state of foreign economic operations in their industrial spheres; the right and also the obligation to administer state management of foreign economic operations in their respective spheres, including its planning; and the right to establish among the enterprises, associations, and other organizations comprising the system of that state agency, a specialized foreign economic organization—in most cases a foreign trade association, whose main function is to coordinate the export of the products and services of the corresponding enterprises, associations, and other organizations.

Thus, the system of state management of foreign economic relations has been expanded to include almost two dozen additional agencies, and its present form is as follows:

---

*Editor's note*—The Presidium of the USSR Supreme Soviet abolished the Ministry of Foreign Trade and the USSR State Committee for Foreign Economic Relations by Edict No. 8350–XI of 15 January 1988. (*Vedomosti Verkhovnogo Soveta SSSR* 1988, No. 3, item 43.) By the same Edict, a USSR Ministry of Foreign Economic Relations was created. No statute had been published for the new Ministry as of the end of June 1988. The Edict is translated and reproduced below in Appendix X.

—the USSR Council of Ministers;

—supra-economic agencies responsible for interbranch state administration: the USSR State Planning Committee, etc. Subordinated to some of these agencies are specialized foreign economic organizations (the USSR State Committee for Science and Technology, etc.);

—specialized agencies responsible for the management of foreign economic operations: the USSR Ministry of Foreign Trade,* the USSR State Committee for Foreign Economic Relations,* the USSR State Committee for Foreign Tourism, the Main Administration of State Customs attached to the USSR Council of Ministers;

—state administrative agencies for which supervision of foreign economic operations is just one of the tasks and functions involved in the management of economic activity in their respective spheres: individual branch-industrial ministries and departments, transportation ministries, etc.;

—state administrative agencies for foreign economic operations that are situated abroad. These include USSR trade missions which are specialized administrative agencies in this sphere, and whose tasks and functions have become considerably more complex today. Embassies enjoy overall authority in all the USSR's economic relations. We should note that the Decree (No. 991) of 19 August 1986 recognized the need to raise both the role and responsibility of Soviet embassies in questions of foreign economic relations with the respective countries of accreditation.

A major feature of the new structure and management of foreign economic operations is the investing of union-republic councils of ministers with certain functions in this sphere and with the prerogative to extend some of these rights and obligations to republic ministries and departments. In particular, the union-republic councils of ministers have been accorded the right to create union-republic foreign trade associations.

## Coordination of activity

It is obvious that the expansion of the network of administrative agencies and its extension beyond the national level to that of the union republics has made somewhat more complex the system of state management of foreign economic operations in the USSR. But at the same time, this offers the opportunity to strengthen the coordination mechanism and to create the conditions in which any divergence from the unified state policy in this area would be precluded. The resolution of this legal problem is an important task in the operation of the state monopoly under current conditions.

---

*Editor's note—Here and hereinafter, the reader is referred to the footnotes relating to the abolition of the Ministry of Foreign Trade and the State Committee for Foreign Economic Relations, and the creation of the USSR Ministry of Foreign Economic Relations.

The first step in this direction has already been taken: a new body was created with the goal of improving the management of the foreign economic complex—the State Foreign Economic Commission of the USSR Council of Ministers, whose responsibilities and functions we will examine below. We will only mention here that this Commission has been charged with supervising the foreign operations of all Soviet ministries and departments and the maintenance of systematic control over these operations. At the same time, the level of coordination has been improved between the state administrative agencies that maintain trade, economic, foreign-currency, financial, and scientific-technological ties with foreign countries.

With the expansion of the network of state administrative agencies responsible for foreign economic operations and its further ramification, the responsibilities and functions of two specialized agencies—the Ministry of Foreign Trade and the State Committee for Foreign Economic Relations—have also been redefined. These bodies are called upon, in particular, to ensure the observance of the state interests of the USSR in foreign markets by all ministries, departments, state committees, enterprises, associations, and other organizations.

## Expansion of the network of subjects of foreign economic transactions

The question of which economic organizations have the right to initiate import-export operations has been resolved anew with a view towards overcoming the separation between industry and foreign trade, of effecting changes in the structure of Soviet exports, of raising the interest of enterprises, associations, and other organizations in foreign economic activity, and of securing a more rational and effective import strategy.

The point here is not only that the number of legal entities that are empowered to effect foreign economic transactions has substantially increased, although this fact, of course, should not be underestimated. The main thing lies in something else, namely, that the majority of these legal entities consists of science-production enterprises, associations, and other organizations of industry. In other words, this radical improvement of Soviet foreign economic operations has provided access to foreign markets—that is, the right primarily to import and export goods, services, and results of their creative activity—to a wide range of producers and customers.

## The network of subjects of foreign economic transactions

For the sake of convenience, we can divide all the state organizations enjoying the right to effect foreign economic transactions into three groups. The first consists of specialized foreign trade associations, especially those subordinated to the Ministry of Foreign Trade and the State Committee for Foreign Economic Relations, as well as a number of other ministries and departments. The second group consists of the foreign trade organizations of branch-industrial ministries and departments. The third—foreign trade companies of science-production and production enterprises, associations, and other organizations. As the necessary preconditions are created, it is also intended that the right to conduct export-import operations will be extended to other industrial organizations as well.

We must take note, too, that Soviet industrial organizations have also been accorded broad rights within the framework of establishing direct ties with organizations of other member countries of the CMEA. In particular, they must independently resolve all issues involved with cooperation, and conclude economic agreements and contracts providing for the delivery of products and of services connected with cooperation and the development of production. By the same token, they have all, for all intents and purposes, been accorded access to foreign markets, albeit only to those of the CMEA. At the beginning of 1987, Soviet industrial organizations involved directly with organizations of the other CMEA member countries numbered more than four hundred. It is expected that this number will soon reach seven hundred.

In addition to those mentioned above, other Soviet organizations will emerge as subjects of foreign economic legal relations, particularly those that become parties to agreements on the creation of joint enterprises and international associations and organizations, including those on Soviet territory.

As before, cooperative organizations will also engage in foreign economic operations in the USSR. These include the Central Union of Consumers' Cooperatives of the USSR in the person of its association "*Soiuzkoopvneshtorg*" and individual local consumer cooperatives within the framework of border and coastal trade, and also public organizations: the USSR Chamber of Commerce and Industry and the All-Union Copyright Agency. The USSR Academy of Sciences occupies a rather special position in this area.

The active role played by cooperative and public organizations in the USSR's foreign economic relations, the emerging potential for joint venture activity, the activity of the USSR Academy of Sciences and noneconomic public organizations, and a number of other factors suggest that the concept of the state monopoly on foreign economic activity in the USSR is broad and reflects the actual state of affairs, and that its management and structure is not the exclusive purview of the Soviet state. At its base lies the system of authorization for the conduct of foreign economic relations, established and implemented by the Soviet state. The state monopoly has been preserved as a juridical institution: as a system of legal norms, principles, and guidelines for this sphere of administration.

We must consider the following as well. While the number of Soviet legal entities enjoying the right to conduct export-import operations can always be concretely determined—this number is static at any given moment—the number of organizations involved in direct foreign economic ties in the form of joint enterprises, international associations and organizations, is constantly changing, and its trend is upward.

## A general assessment of the changes

These are the fundamental legal and organizational changes that have been effected in the management and conduct of foreign economic operations. Although the process of change has yet to run its full course, we can see the basic elements of the new model of management in this vital sphere of the national economy: industry's closer proximity to foreign markets; expansion of the foreign economic rights, as well as responsibilities, of branch-industrial ministries and departments, production enterprises, associations, and other organizations, including the investing of some of these with the right to conduct export-import operations; and a certain measure of decentralization of management at the departmental level, along with the simultaneous strengthening of preconditions for the more complete coordination of actions in this sphere and the strengthening of state management at the governmental level of the USSR. Another important aspect is the enhancement of centralization in the implementation of the USSR's foreign economic policy, primarily thanks to the creation of the State Foreign Economic Commission of the USSR Council of Ministers.

An important feature of the new conception of the organization of foreign economic relations is the greater role given to their planning. The stronger role of planning consists in the fact that plans will be reviewed by a new government body—the State Foreign Economic Commission—prior to their confirmation.

As to who may designate the subjects of export-import operations, in the new system of administration this function is concentrated in the abovementioned Commission. This will create the conditions necessary for avoiding unjustified parallelism in operations in foreign markets.

In addition to the improvement of planning, and also the effecting of necessary changes in foreign-currency regulation, a major legal problem in the improvement of foreign economic operations in the USSR and the maintenance of the state monopoly on them under contemporary conditions is the determining of the procedures for conducting export-import operations and the forms of control over them. The establishment and implementation of such procedures and control is considered one of the most important features of the state monopoly on foreign economic activity.

In this connection we should note the following. When the USSR's foreign trade turnover was carried out primarily by organizations subordinate to the USSR Ministry of Foreign Trade and the USSR State Committee for Foreign Economic Relations, the drafting and approving of detailed procedures and ensuring their observance was not vitally necessary, and this question was resolved on the basis of direct administrative-law relations of each given network.

With the conversion to new conditions, when a large part of the export and import of goods and services will be a function not of just one or two large administrative agencies but of dozens of such agencies, one should imagine that different solutions will be required.

The function of ensuring systematic control over the foreign economic operations of all ministries and departments now belongs to the State Foreign Economic Commission of the USSR Council of Ministers.

Moreover, as noted above, the USSR Ministry of Foreign Trade and USSR State Committee for Foreign Economic Relations are charged with ensuring the observance of the USSR's state interests in foreign markets by all ministries and departments, enterprises, associations, and other organizations. In principle, this control can be exercised via fulfillment of the responsibilities and functions that have been assigned to these two state agencies in their statutes, confirmed by the Soviet government. But it cannot be excluded that it will become necessary in the future to draft special normative acts or to supplement the already-existing acts in this area.

# 4

# RESPONSIBILITIES AND FUNCTIONS OF STATE ADMINISTRATIVE AGENCIES OVERSEEING FOREIGN ECONOMIC RELATIONS

The 5 July 1978 Law of the USSR "On the USSR Council of Ministers,"[1] provides that the government of the USSR exercises, in particular, overall supervision in the area of foreign trade and other forms of foreign economic activity, as well as in scientific-technological cooperation with other countries, and that it secures the implementation of measures aimed at the expansion of the USSR's sphere of international cooperation and at increasing the effectiveness of foreign economic and scientific-technological ties. The USSR Council of Ministers organizes and directs operations connected with the nation's participation in socialist economic integration and in the international socialist division of labor, and it exercises a number of other functions in the USSR's cooperation with CMEA member countries.

## The State Foreign Economic Commission of the USSR Council of Ministers

Pursuant to the Joint Decree No. 991 of the CPSU Central Committee and the USSR Council of Ministers of 19 August 1986, the State Foreign Economic Commission came into being as a standing agency of the government of the USSR. It was formed with the goal of enhancing the management of the foreign economic complex and of improving the level of coordination between ministries, departments, and organizations involved in trade and economic, foreign-currency, financial, and scientific-technological relations with foreign countries.

The State Foreign Economic Commission of the USSR Council of Ministers supervises the work of the Ministry of Foreign Trade, the State Committee for

---

1. *Svod zakonov SSSR*, Vol. 1, pp. 131–144.

Foreign Economic Relations, the State Committee for Foreign Tourism, the Foreign Trade Bank, the Main Administration of State Customs of the USSR Council of Ministers, all ministries and departments engaged in the conduct of foreign economic relations, and Soviet delegations to intergovernmental commissions on economic and scientific-technological cooperation with foreign countries.

The State Foreign Economic Commission is charged with the following:

—drafting proposals in the area of foreign economic policy as well as conceptual guidelines for the development of foreign economic relations, covering both individual regions and countries;

—implementing measures directed at the wholesale improvement of foreign economic operations, as well as at the further development and enhancement of trade and economic, foreign-currency, financial, and scientific-technological ties with foreign countries in the interests of accelerating the nation's socioeconomic progress;

—ensuring the dynamic and comprehensive deepening of economic integration with the countries of the socialist community, enhancing the nation's standing and influence with developing countries, and strengthening the USSR's position in the world economy;

—securing the active participation of ministries, departments, associations, and enterprises in foreign trade activity, in production and scientific-technological cooperation, and in international cooperation;

—ensuring fulfillment of the USSR's foreign economic obligations, including those provided for in international treaties.

The State Foreign Economic Commission is called upon to pay particular attention to the following:

—the development of new and advanced forms of foreign economic relations, the further improvement of planning, stimulation, and management of foreign economic ties, and the broad applications of economic methods of management, especially in the organization of new forms of foreign economic relations;

—the implementation, in conjunction with other standing agencies of the Soviet government, ministries, and departments, of projects designed to bring about wholesale change in the structure of exports and imports and to broaden the nation's export potential;

—the drafting and implementation of measures aimed at increasing foreign-currency revenues.

In the area of cooperation with CMEA member countries, this government agency is charged in particular with exercising coordination and control over the work of ministries and departments in carrying out the Comprehensive Program for Scientific-Technological Progress of the CMEA Member Countries to the Year 2000.

The State Foreign Economic Commission:

—reviews drafts of current and long-term plans for foreign economic relations and the consolidated foreign-currency plan (the USSR's balance of payments), presented by the State Planning Committee and the Ministry of Finance, and ensures their correspondence to the strategic policy for the development of foreign economic relations, [at all times] maintaining balance between foreign trade and payment relations and the creation of vital foreign-currency reserves;

—has at its disposal material and financial, including foreign-currency, reserves to be used for the resolution of individual problems arising in the course of foreign economic cooperation; and

—exercises systematic control over the foreign economic activities of all ministries and departments, and examines the latter's reports on their observance of the CPSU Central Committee and the USSR Council of Ministers' decrees and fulfillment of state plans for foreign economic operations.

The State Commission will also carry out one function of the state monopoly on foreign economic operations: it is empowered to decide on the grant of export-import rights to associations, enterprises, and organizations.

Another result of the restructuring are the broad changes that have come about in the responsibilities and functions of such specialized state administrative agencies for foreign economic operations as the USSR Ministry of Foreign Trade (hereinafter, the MFT) and the USSR State Committee for Foreign Economic Relations (hereinafter, the SCFR).

## The USSR Ministry of Foreign Trade*

In conformity with the Statute approved on 22 December 1986, the MFT is responsible, within the limits of its authority, for the development of foreign economic relations and ensuring their effectiveness, as well as for the most complete utilization of the potentialities offered by the international division of labor. It develops drafts of consolidated export and import plans, bears responsibility for many facets of socialist economic integration, participates in drafting strategies for the development of the nation's foreign economic ties and trade policies, and participates in the drafting and implementation of measures aimed at the development of the export base as well as new forms of economic cooperation with foreign countries. The MFT sees to the protection of the USSR's interests in bilateral and multilateral economic and trade ties with foreign countries, and promotes advances in Soviet exports and imports in efforts to enhance the competitiveness of Soviet goods.

As a state administrative agency, the MFT exercises supervisory functions in the area of trade in fuels, raw materials, food products, individual types of machinery, and other goods of statewide significance.

Operating within the MFT network is a large group of foreign trade associations that conduct their operations on the basis of cost accounting. The MFT

---

*Editor's note—See editor's note on p. 19, ch. 3.

does not bear financial liability for subordinate foreign trade associations, and these foreign trade associations are not responsible for the obligations of the Ministry.

The MFT also exercises the following functions:

—prepares and submits consolidated export and import plans to the State Planning Committee and the State Committee for Material and Technical Supply, and provides the State Planning Committee with the necessary summary data on payments and revenues in foreign currency; and it develops drafts for its own foreign-currency and financial plans as well as plans for the carriage of import, export, and transit goods. Its drafts of consolidated export and import plans and the corresponding summary data on revenues and payments in foreign currency are based on the plan drafts of ministries, departments, associations, enterprises, and organizations that enjoy the right to conduct export-import operations;

—takes part in the drafting of proposals and measures aimed at promoting socialist economic integration on the basis of the international division of labor, the strengthening of intergovernmental specialization and broad cooperation in the production of machinery and equipment, and the introduction of new and advanced cooperative forms;

—drafts proposals on the coordination of the USSR's state plans with the state plans of other CMEA member countries;

—conducts negotiations, along with the USSR State Planning Committee, the USSR State Committee for Material and Technical Supply, and the appropriate ministries, departments, and organizations that have the right to conduct export-import operations, on trade turnover and payments with socialist and capitalist countries with whom it maintains clearing accounts, and it signs the appropriate documents;

—studies the export possibilities and the import needs of the national economy, and the economies, foreign trade, trade policy, and trade legislation of foreign countries, as well as questions of the development of international trade; and it conducts studies on competition in international commodity markets;

—in conformity with existing legislation, makes proposals on the conclusion by the USSR of treaties on foreign trade and on the USSR's adherence to international treaties, and it conducts negotiations and enters into international treaties on behalf of the USSR;

—organizes and exercises state control over the quality of goods exported from the USSR produced in associations and enterprises where State Acceptance [gosudarstvennaia priemka] has not been introduced.

Of tremendous statewide importance is the MFT's exercise of its functions of control over the observance of the USSR's state interests in foreign markets by all ministries and departments, enterprises, associations, and other organizations. With these goals in mind, and also in the interests of conducting unified economic and trade, foreign-currency, and price policies, the MFT:

—audits (with the participation when necessary of the USSR Ministry of

Finance, the USSR Foreign Trade Bank,* and other interested agencies and organizations) the conduct of export-import operations by ministries and departments, associations, enterprises, and organizations;

—ensures the coordination and systematic supervision of the activity of ministries and departments, associations, enterprises, and organizations related to the conduct of export-import operations;

—receives from and provides to ministries and departments, associations, enterprises, and organizations involved in foreign economic relations, the requisite documents, proposals, and findings on foreign trade issues, including data on the developing competitive situations in world commodity markets and on exports and imports of individual goods, services, and results of productive activity by country or groups of countries and by types of foreign currency;

—submits to the State Foreign Economic Commission of the USSR Council of Ministers reports on the Ministry's exercise of its control function, which include proposals on the elimination of violations and shortcomings.

The MFT has the right:

—in the established procedure, to create, reorganize, and liquidate subordinate foreign trade associations;

—to authorize, in the established procedure, the creation by subordinate foreign trade associations, both within the USSR and abroad, of branch offices, departments, representative offices, and joint-stock companies, and likewise for the participation of these foreign trade associations in any form of organizations whose activity is appropriate to the tasks of the association;

—to grant, in the established procedure, to foreign organizations and companies the right to establish representative offices in the USSR, to make decisions regarding the cessation of their operations, and also to examine information provided by the chiefs of those representative offices on their activities.

As a consequence of the restructuring of foreign economic operations in the USSR, the MFT's role has been considerably enhanced in the systematic supervision of the foreign trade activities of associations and enterprises, in the strengthening of economic and organizational work in this area, in the improvement of [the obtaining and provision of] commercial information, and in personnel training.

The MFT administrative apparatus has undergone substantial changes. The chief roles within the apparatus belong to the subdivisions, the activities of which are tied up with economic work and with the drafting and implementation of trade policy, and to the regional and commodity offices. The Ministry's administrative apparatus has been simplified, now consisting of a smaller number of subdivisions.

The MFT continues to supervise the network of USSR trade missions abroad as well as its own network of plenipotentiaries in individual regions and sectors of

---

*Editors note—More recently renamed the USSR Bank for Foreign Economic Relations.

the nation that are of special importance for Soviet exports. Within the MFT network, the All-Union Scientific Market Research Institute continues to function, its goal now being to provide industry with a broader array of commercial information. So does the All-Union Academy of Foreign Trade, whose role in the training and retraining of specialists for all organizations involved in foreign economic relations has been expanded.

## The USSR State Committee
## for Foreign Economic Relations*

The USSR State Committee for Foreign Economic Relations is an administrative agency whose functions fall in the area of the USSR's economic and technological cooperation with foreign countries.

The restructuring of the administration of the Soviet foreign economic complex also occasioned a review of the SCFR's structure and functions.

It was established that in providing economic and technical assistance to foreign states, the SCFR must be guided by the goal of increasing the effectiveness of this cooperation, of improving the structure of exports and imports of complete equipment and services, and of promoting the development of the nation's export industries as well as the cost-accounting operations of organizations in its network.

The SCFR is called upon to participate actively in the deepening of socialist economic integration, to provide wider scope for economic and technical assistance to foreign states, and to ensure protection of the USSR's interests in these areas.

As it has previously, the SCFR will take part in the planning of foreign economic operations in the USSR and in the drafting and implementation of the country's trade policy, and it will continue to carry out operations involving the provision of Soviet technical assistance within the framework of the United Nations.

All-union associations within the SCFR network (part of their personnel and senior staff have been transferred to industry) will carry out their operations based on the principals of cost accounting, self-recoupment of costs, and self-financing and in conformity with economic agreements concluded with clients.

As a supplement to its existing functions in foreign markets, the SCFR will in the future exercise overall supervision over the organization and management of construction work on facilities being built on the territory of the USSR with the participation of foreign companies. It is also responsible for ensuring a high level of economic and systematic work as well as the effective operation of the newly constructed facilities.

---

*Editor's note—See editor's note on p. 19, ch. 3.

Among the most important of the SCFR's functions are reviewing the proposals of foreign governments and also organizations and companies of foreign countries for economic and technical cooperation in the construction and reconstruction of enterprises and other production facilities abroad. In important cases, the SCFR evaluates the proposals of Soviet ministries and departments on involving foreign organizations and companies in the construction of production facilities on the territory of the USSR. In special cases, it exercises the functions of supplier and contractor.

For enterprises and other production facilities under construction or in operation, both abroad and in the USSR, the SCFR, pursuant to the USSR's international treaties and to concluded contracts, provides for surveying and drafting work; for deliveries of complete equipment, materials, and spare parts; and for the dispatching of Soviet specialists abroad, as well as the acceptance of foreign specialists and workers in the USSR for production and technical training and consulting.

As part of the SCFR network there operates a group of all-union associations whose status, operating principles, and interrelations with the SCFR equate fully with the foreign trade associations of the MFT network. Like the MFT, the SCFR has its own plenipotentiaries in individual regions of the USSR, directs staffs of consultants on economic issues in Soviet embassies abroad, and maintains a subordinate scientific-technological institute which studies questions of economic and technical cooperation between the USSR and foreign countries.

On the whole, the responsibilities and functions of the SCFR and the MFT are much alike. Where they differ is largely in their respective spheres of operation, in the fact that their responsibilities lie in different areas of the USSR's foreign economic operations. An example of the simultaneous convergence and divergence of their functions are their responsibilities in the authorization of the import and export of goods.

The fundamental rules in this area are contained in Decree No. 1513 of the USSR Council of Ministers of 22 December 1986.

It is the USSR Ministry of Foreign Trade that authorizes the importing to and exporting from the USSR of cargo and other property by state, cooperative, and other associations, enterprises, and organizations. This includes partners involved in direct ties with organizations of member countries, in joint enterprises and international associations and organizations. This also applies to the transportation of foreign cargo across Soviet territory.

The USSR State Committee for Foreign Economic Relations authorizes the importing to and exporting from the USSR of cargo and other property by organizations subordinate to itself, to the USSR Ministry of the Fish Industry, the USSR Ministry of Geology, and the Main Administration of Geodesy and Cartography of the USSR Council of Ministers.

Associations, enterprises, and organizations involved in direct production and

scientific-technological ties with enterprises and organizations from other socialist countries receive general authorization for the import to and export from the
USSR of cargo and other property for one year or a more extended period within
the limits of the duration of the agreement or the protocol upon which the direct
ties are based.

Authorization for the re-export of cargo is issued by both the USSR Ministry
of Foreign Trade and the USSR State Committee for Foreign Economic Relations.

# 5

# LEGAL STATUS OF THE FOREIGN TRADE ORGANIZATIONS OF BRANCH-INDUSTRIAL MINISTRIES AND DEPARTMENTS

In extending to a number of ministries and departments "access to foreign markets," the Joint Decree No. 991 of the CPSU Central Committee and the USSR Council of Ministers, of 19 August 1986, in effect aimed at the creation of specialized foreign economic organizations to operate under the umbrellas of the relevant state administrative agencies. Among such agencies are, in particular, the Ministry of Power Machine Building, the Ministry of Heavy and Transport Machine Building, the Ministry of the Electrical Equipment Industry, the Ministry of the Automotive Industry, the Ministry of Tractor and Agricultural Machine Building, the Ministry of Instrument Making, Automation Equipment and Control Systems, the Ministry of the Machine Tool and Tool-Building Industry, the Ministry of the Chemical Industry, the Ministry of Chemical and Petroleum Machine Building, the Ministry of the Construction Materials Industry, the Ministry of the Medical and Microbiological Industry, and the Ministry of Geology. The foreign trade associations that were established within the networks of these state administrations originated from the foreign trade associations and their component specialized companies that had earlier come under the USSR Ministry of Foreign Trade and the USSR State Committee for Foreign Economic Relations. In the process, some foreign trade associations switched their organizational affiliation completely when they were transferred to the authority of branch-industrial ministries and departments.

In addition to the network of ministries and departments, foreign economic organizations are also being created in the union republics. They most likely will be subordinate to the councils of ministers of the union republics. Their responsibilities, functions, and status will exactly parallel those of the foreign trade organizations of branch-industrial ministries and departments.

The legal status of foreign trade associations belonging to this group of subjects of foreign economic transactions derives from the general provisions of Soviet civil law pertaining to legal entities (articles 11–13 of the Principles of Civil Legislation of the USSR and the Union Republics and the corresponding articles in the civil codes of the union republics, for example, articles 23–32 and 37 of the RSFSR Civil Code). It also derives from special norms, first and foremost, the regulations contained in the Statute of the All-Union Cost-Accounting Foreign Trade Organization (Association) of the Ministry or Department, confirmed by Decree No. 1526 of the USSR Council of Ministers of 22 December 1986.

The foreign trade associations of branch-industrial ministries and departments and those of the union-republic councils of ministers (hereinafter, foreign trade associations) have many common features notwithstanding all the objective differences that exist between them arising from the particular goods and services they provide, the results of their creative activity, and the exports and imports in which they deal. These common features are their operating principles, both legal and economic, their organizational structures, their interrelations with higher agencies, their liability, and other questions of a legal nature. Let's take a more detailed look.

**General description**

The foreign trade association is constituted on the basis of USSR legislation governing the conduct of export and import operations in an assigned list of goods and services. It also undertakes operations on the provision of technical assistance, on the basis of economic contracts with organizations belonging to the USSR State Committee for Foreign Economic Relations, including under contractor's agreements.

The administratively superior ministry or department (or the union-republic council of ministers) supervises the operations of the foreign trade association.

The foreign trade association possesses state property, which is assigned to its use or operative management. In utilizing these state assets, it conducts its operations on the basis of full cost accounting and in conformity with the ministry's or department's plan for economic and social development; discharges its assigned responsibilities and enjoys the rights connected with such activity; and it maintains its own account and is a legal entity.

The composition of the foreign trade association includes specialized companies. These latter organizations are not legal entities and are governed by a statute confirmed by the general director of the foreign trade association along the lines of the Model Statute of the Cost-Accounting Foreign Trade Company of a Science-Production or Production Association, Enterprise, or Organization, which we will discuss in more detail further below.

These specialized companies have the right, on behalf of the foreign trade association, to carry out foreign trade transactions and to conclude economic contracts with suppliers of goods for export as well as with customers of import goods and other organizations.

The foreign trade association's relations with Soviet enterprises and organizations are based on economic contracts and are governed by existing USSR legislation. Each foreign trade association has its own charter, which is drafted in conformity with the Model Statute of the Foreign Trade Organization (Association) and is confirmed by the administratively superior ministry or department with the agreement of the Ministry of Foreign Trade or the State Committee for Foreign Economic Relations.

Foreign trade associations coordinate their operations closely with USSR trade missions and with economic counsellors assigned to USSR embassies. The foreign trade association acquires the rights and responsibilities that come with its sphere of operations, and it is a legal entity from the day its charter is confirmed.

**Rights**

In the procedure provided for in Soviet legislation, the foreign trade association is granted the right:

—within the limits of its authority, both in the USSR and abroad, to effect transactions and other legal acts, including those of a credit and exchange nature, with institutions, enterprises, organizations, companies, partnerships and with individuals, and to appear in court and arbitration as either a plaintiff or a respondent;

—to build, acquire, alienate, or use or offer under lease, both in the USSR and abroad, subsidiary operations that are vital to its operations as well as all manner of movable and immovable property;

—if the need arises, to establish, both within the USSR and abroad, its own representative offices, departments, branches, offices, and agencies, as well as enterprises that are vital to its operations, upon agreement in the established procedure with the Ministry of Finance and also with either the Ministry of Foreign Trade or the State Committee for Foreign Economic Relations; to participate in organizations, including mixed companies, the operations of which correspond to the responsibilities of the foreign trade association;

—to maintain contact with foreign establishments, companies, and their representatives, as well as with foreign citizens, on issues that directly concern the association, while observing the existing procedure.

**Liability**

The foreign trade association is responsible for the property assigned to it which, according to Soviet legislation, may be subject to attachment.

The state and its agencies and organizations are not responsible for the obligations of the foreign trade association, and the foreign trade association is likewise not responsible for the obligations of the state or its agencies and organizations.

**Responsibilities and functions**

The foreign trade association:
—elaborates drafts of current, annual, and five-year plans for the development of foreign economic ties, secures confirmation of them in the established procedure, and ensures the fulfillment of the confirmed plans;
—carries out export and import operations based on its assigned list of goods and services while ensuring top-priority fulfillment of the obligations of the USSR's international treaties;
—conducts negotiations with foreign companies and organizations, concludes contracts on the export and import of goods and services and sees to their fulfillment;
—drafts and implements measures aimed at increasing exports of goods and services, at optimizing their structure and expanding their list, and also at increasing foreign-currency earnings and economizing on foreign-currency expenditures;
—concludes economic contracts with associations, enterprises, and organizations in the USSR for the supply of export and import products and services and the creation of a diverse manner of works that correspond to the specific charter governing the object of operations; meets requests for imported goods and services coming from ministries, departments, union-republic councils of ministers, science-production and production associations, enterprises, and organizations with its own foreign-currency funds regardless of whether such purchases are included in the plan for the import of goods;
—makes prompt transfers of foreign currency to science-production and production associations, enterprises, and organizations upon the sale of their products in foreign markets;
—coordinates the operations of, and renders assistance to, cost-accounting foreign trade companies established within science-production and production associations, enterprises, and organizations of the ministry or department to which the foreign trade association is subordinate;
—carries on active informational and advertising work with the goal of expanding the export of goods on its list, organizes special exhibitions and participates in international fairs and trade shows;
—takes part in the preparation and coordination of drafts of international treaties with CMEA member countries, and of economic agreements with these countries' organizations dealing with specialization and cooperation in the production of products included in the association's list;
—drafts and carries out measures aimed at improving the carriage of foreign trade cargo, and takes part in the drafting of measures designed to up-

grade its storage and safekeeping;

—conducts the dispatching, and supervises the activities, of economic specialists who are sent abroad in the established procedure in order to conduct commercial negotiations, to service machinery, equipment, instruments, and durable goods supplied by the USSR, to inspect and accept imported products after quality approval, and to undertake installation and other projects included in the association's list; and it hosts foreign specialists;

—promotes the optimally rapid assimilation of imported equipment;

—conducts comparative analyses of new domestic and analogous foreign machinery and other products that are assigned to the foreign trade association's list of goods, and its provides information to the relevant branch ministries and departments, associations, enterprises, and organizations regarding the quality demands for goods sold on the world market, regarding products enjoying especially high demand, and regarding the steps being undertaken by foreign companies to enhance the competitiveness of their goods.

The foreign trade association is called upon to promote with all the means at its disposal the expansion of mutually advantageous scientific-technological cooperation with foreign countries.

The foreign trade association drafts recommendations and proposals, pertaining to its assigned list of goods, that are aimed at enhancing the quality and competitiveness of export goods, and at ensuring that goods shipped abroad meet the highest technical and economic standards of domestic and foreign machinery. It also drafts recommendations and proposals designed to promote the import of the technologically most advanced machinery, equipment, industrial products and other goods, the application of which will produce a sizable economic effect.

Toward these ends, the foreign trade association systematically studies and analyzes achievements registered in domestic and foreign science and technology, the trends of scientific-technological progress abroad, patent and license documentation, prototypes of new technology, recommendations on standardization and standards, and the performance of products exported from the Soviet Union as well as of products purchased abroad.

The foreign trade association may contract with other enterprises and organizations to have carried out for it complex scientific-technological processes, as well as individual projects, and the provision of necessary services.

The foreign trade association plays a role in quality control and in the drafting of standards and technical conditions for export products that are assigned to its list of goods.

The foreign trade association draws up proposals on introducing the production of new goods designed for export and on improving the structure of imports, with the goal of promoting the most rapid possible acceleration of scientific-technological progress, the more complete satisfaction of demand for various goods, and an increase in the national economic effectiveness of production.

## Assets

The foreign trade association's assets consist of fixed and working capital, which make up its charter capital, and also of other types of capital and assets assigned to it.

The foreign trade association's profit arises when, in the course of its foreign economic operations, its earnings exceed its expenditures. The foreign trade association sets up in the established procedure a foreign operations fund and an economic incentive fund.

The foreign trade association may transfer the buildings, structures, and other fixed assets assigned to it to other enterprises and organizations in the procedure provided for in USSR legislation.

## Management

The management of the foreign trade association is based on the combination of one-man management and board management in the discussion and resolution of all questions involved in the operations of the foreign trade association. The council of the foreign trade association is constituted for this purpose. The administratively superior ministry or department appoints the members of the council and determines the council's authority.

The foreign trade association is headed up by the general director, who operates on the basis of one-man management and who is appointed to and relieved from his duties in the established procedure.

The general director, and his aides and other officials in their specific realms, enjoy the rights and discharge the obligations assigned to the foreign trade association, and where provided for by legislation, as a body, with the agreement or the participation of the work collective.

The general director supervises the work of the foreign trade association and bears full responsibility for its operations. Toward this end, the general director:

—supervises the operative sphere of the foreign trade association's activities, including making decisions on concluding sales or purchase contracts and on the provision of technical assistance and other services; acts on behalf of the foreign trade association without proxy and represents it in all institutions, enterprises, and organizations, both within the USSR and abroad; in conformity with existing legislation, disposes of the assets of the foreign trade association, enters into transactions and other legal acts, issues proxy authority, and opens current and other accounts for the foreign trade association in banks in conformity with the established procedure.

## Reorganization and liquidation

The reorganization (merger, annexation, division, separation) and liquidation of the foreign trade association is carried out in conformity with USSR legislation.
    The ministry or department sets the procedure and time period for the liquidation of the foreign trade association.
    The foreign trade association is liquidated either by a liquidation commission, which is appointed by the ministry or department, or by the association's general director on the authority of the ministry or department.
    The liquidation commission, or, in the appropriate cases, the general director of the association being liquidated, places a notice of liquidation of the foreign trade association and of the time period for the filing of claims by creditors in the journal *Vneshniaia torgovlia* [Foreign trade]. Independently of this, the liquidation commission or the general director of the association being liquidated must determine all outstanding claims of creditors on the foreign trade association and inform the creditors of the impending liquidation.
    Claims against the foreign trade association being liquidated are satisfied from its assets, against which by law claims may be brought.
    Claims that have been determined or filed after expiration of the time period established for the filing of claims by creditors, are satisfied from assets remaining after the satisfaction of claims that have been determined or filed within the established time period.
    Claims are considered invalid if they have been determined or filed after liquidation has been completed, and if they remain unsatisfied due to the absence of assets remaining from the liquidated foreign trade association. Likewise, claims that are not recognized by the liquidation commission or the general director of the association being liquidated are considered completely or partially discharged if the creditors do not file suit for the satisfaction of claims within three months of the date of notification of complete or partial rejection of the claims.

## Special features

On the whole, we can see that the legal status of foreign trade associations that constitute this new group of subjects of foreign economic transactions by and large parallel the legal status of the foreign trade associations belonging to the USSR Ministry of Foreign Trade. Their main distinguishing features from the legal point of view are the following:
    —the administratively superior ministries and departments draft their charters on the basis of a model charter, and these ministries and departments confirm the charters in conjunction with the Ministry of Foreign Trade or the State Committee for Foreign Economic Relations;

—they do not have the types of administrative agencies that play such a large role in the foreign trade associations of the USSR Ministry of Foreign Trade. At the same time, councils have been created for them to ensure observance of the board principle of management, and the councils' responsibilities, functions, and personnel are determined by the appropriate ministries and departments;

—their administratively superior ministries and departments supervise their operations. However, the aforementioned Statute reproduces among its regulations also the rule of the Decree No. 991 of 19 August 1986, which provides that the USSR Ministry of Foreign Trade and the USSR State Committee for Foreign Economic Relations ensure that foreign trade associations observe the USSR's state interests in foreign markets.

## Foreign trade associations—independent legal entities

In concluding the enumeration of the basic aspects of the status of foreign trade associations subordinate to branch-industrial ministries and departments, we should like to dwell briefly on a few of particular importance.[1]

Foreign trade associations are independent agents in property relations both within the country and in foreign markets. The rights and obligations realized by these organizations in conducting foreign economic transactions are for their own purposes alone, not for the Soviet state.

It is a mistake to confuse the liability of the Soviet state and its agencies as well as Soviet state organizations with liabilities of foreign trade associations.

The Soviet state and its agencies and organizations are not responsible for the obligations of foreign trade associations, and the latter are likewise not responsible for the obligations of the state or its agencies and organizations.

What independent property liability of each foreign trade association means is, in particular, that claims or suits may not be filed against them that derive from relations with other Soviet foreign trade associations or state organizations, or that are associated with the acts and actions of the Soviet state and its agencies.

Unlike the Soviet state and its agencies, foreign trade associations do not enjoy immunity from legal prosecution in foreign states.

The normative acts passed in recent years, including the statutes of the USSR Ministry of Foreign Trade and of the USSR State Committee for Foreign Economic Relations, frequently state that foreign trade associations are part of the "system" of the corresponding state administrative agency. We should note in this connection that the "system" as understood in these normative acts does not

---

1. For more detail on the subjects of foreign economic transactions, see V. S Pozdniakov and O. N. Sadikov, *Pravovoe regulirovanie otnoshenii po vneshnei torgovle SSSR*, part 1, pp. 23–54.

mean, in our opinion, that there exists a unitary whole within the meaning of civil law where those who issue administrative instructions, such as an act of state authority, and its addressees are one. On the contrary, this "system" presupposes, and cannot be anything other than, a delimitation of subjects that are independent in the civil-law meaning. The statutory definition of the group of independent subjects as a single "system" is more of economic significance, and is rooted in the constitutional designation of the Soviet economy as a unitary national economic complex which is managed based on the branch principle with the combination of centralized management and the economic independence of enterprises, associations, and other organizations.

# 6

# ENTERPRISES (ASSOCIATIONS) AND THEIR FOREIGN TRADE COMPANIES

As we have already noted, one of the key aspects in the radical restructuring of foreign economic operations in the USSR is providing science-production and production enterprises and associations, as well as other organizations, with direct access to foreign markets. This chiefly involves those industrial organizations that have substantial export capacity. On 19 August 1986 the CPSU Central Committee and the USSR Council of Ministers confirmed the list of large associations, enterprises, and other organizations that will have direct access to foreign markets and within which will be created foreign trade companies. They are situated in many cities across the Soviet Union (the majority are located outside of Moscow), and they operate under various branch-ministries and departments. And it is planned in the future to provide other industrial organizations with such access. Decisions on this question are made by the State Foreign Economic Commission of the Council of USSR Ministers.

The USSR Law ''On the State Enterprise (Association)'' gives considerable attention to questions of foreign economic operations. We will now take a more detailed look at this Law,* particularly in view of the important role that these organizations play in the USSR's national economy and their prominence in the plan for restructuring the entire economic mechanism.

## The Law on the State Enterprise

The Law was adopted on 30 June 1987. Its Draft was made public earlier that year, on 8 February. Following broad discussion and the close examination of all opinions and comments, it was completed and was submitted to the USSR

---

*Editor's note—When the present study was written, the *Law on the State Enterprise (Association)* was extant only as a Draft. The authors have subsequently brought it into conformity with the final text. The approved, final text of the Law is reproduced, in translation, in Appendix I, below.

Supreme Soviet for examination.

Naturally, the Draft, and subsequently the Law itself, met with great interest. Knowledge of what role state enterprises would now play in the USSR's foreign economic operations was especially important to those working in foreign trade and having scientific-technological and economic ties with Soviet organizations. Would they become full partners in foreign economic ventures, or would they remain as before, merely producers of goods and services for export and consumers of import goods? What kind of rights and obligations would they have in planning exports and imports? Would the preconditions be created for state enterprises to have an economic interest in participating in the international division of labor? Would they be provided with foreign-currency funds? These were just some of the questions impatiently awaiting answers following the June 1986 CPSU Central Committee Plenum's decision to complete work as quickly as possible on the Draft of the Law on the Enterprise.

Naturally, the Law that has been passed has been studied from all sides, and not only by business people. After all, the state enterprise, as we know, is the basic link in the USSR's national economy. Consequently, the organizational and operational configuration of the state enterprises and their legal status will in large measure determine the way in which will function the entire economic mechanism as well as many other areas of Soviet society.

We can today gauge at least partially how impatiently adoption of this Law was awaited in the USSR, what hopes accompany it, and what is expected from its promulgation. Even before it was passed into law it was acclaimed as a document of great political significance. Why has it generated so much interest? Mainly because it marks a huge step in the realization of the economic strategy, the concept and basic contours of which were formulated at the April 1985 CPSU Central Committee Plenum and developed, concretized, and approved at the Twenty-seventh CPSU Congress.

**The reasons for drafting the Law on the Enterprise**

As we know, the organizational and operational principles of the state enterprises and their legal status were governed up until recently by a series of normative acts. Among them we should single out the following decrees of the USSR Council of Ministers:

—No. 731 of 4 October 1965, which confirmed the Statute of the Socialist State Production Enterprise;

—No. 212 of 27 March 1974, which confirmed the Statute of the Production Enterprise (Combine), and No. 1062 of 30 December 1975, which confirmed the Statute of the Science-Production Association.

Obviously, the existing acts suffered from defects. Moreover, only a few of their provisions had legislative force. But eliminating these defects and upgrading the legal foundation of state enterprises was not why such monumental work was done in preparing the envisaged Law!

It is readily apparent that the need for a new normative act could only have arisen when the existing legal regime ceased to meet the requirements of the economy and came into contradiction with the nation's economic and social policy.

It is just such a situation that we had here. The statutes enumerated above were designed for an economic mechanism and a model of economic management that in contemporary conditions could no longer secure the necessary rate and quality of growth or ensure a forward thrust. So, this new economic policy envisages, and indeed stipulates, reform of the management of the USSR's national economy. Integral to it are:

—a decisive departure from the predominantly administrative methods of economic management that gave rise to petty tutelage over the state enterprises and intervention in their affairs;

—raising the effectiveness of centrally planned state management, which will make the strategic decisions and will create the conditions and stimuli for every enterprise to achieve the highest possible final results;

—the comprehensive diffusion of economic methods of management and the effective utilization of commodity-money relations in the operations of state enterprises;

—the decisive expansion of the state enterprise's independence, and the encouragement of an enterprising socialist attitude in management;

—the democratization of economic management and the deepening of socialist self-government in the economic sphere.

Managerial independence, property autonomy, and the initiative of state enterprises have always been important features in the organization of the Soviet economy. They reflect the position of the enterprises in the system of commodity production as well as objective economic laws. Cost accounting of state enterprises is the economic and organizational vehicle by which commodity principles are realized under the conditions of a planned socialist economy. But it must unfortunately be recognized that the principles of independence and initiative of state enterprises were for a long time implemented inconsistently and indecisively. The negative consequences of this, as well as a number of other phenomena, are well known. They are associated primarily with imperfections in the legal regime.

The sense of the new approach to economic management is effectively to subordinate all production to the requirements of society and the satisfaction of people's needs. It will orient management towards raising efficiency and quality, accelerating scientific-technological progress, fostering the interest of workers in the products of their labor, and promoting initiative and socialist enterprise in each link of the national economy, particularly in work collectives.

The restructuring of the economic mechanism and the reform of economic management are realities of our day, and we are both witnesses to and participants in the changes now underway. Thus, as of January 1987 all industrial enterprises have been converted to the experimentally tested new methods of management. A number of branches and enterprises, including some actively involved in foreign economic relations, have begun to operate on the basis of full cost accounting and self-financing. The agro-industrial complex, light industry, trade establishments, and the service sphere—branches of the economy that have a direct impact on the satisfaction of citizens' needs—have acquired broader independence and enhanced authority. The management of capital construction is also undergoing serious changes. Fifteen hundred leading enterprises have introduced the State Acceptance system with its quality control mechanism, with a view towards intensifying the struggle for higher product quality. And in order to complete the conversion to the comprehensive system of management of the national economy, the Council of Ministers has established permanently operating agencies that supervise whole groups of interrelated branches.

The enactment of the USSR Law "On the State Enterprise (Association)" is but one link in a long chain, one step on the path toward achieving the goals laid out before us.

**Goals of the Law on the Enterprise**

As we know, the idea behind the Law was to summarize recent experience, to give legal force to all the positive aspects that arose in the drive toward the broad expansion of economic independence and toward raising the role and authority of state enterprises. Its enactment should lay the basis for the optimal distribution of rights and obligations between ministries and enterprises, while for work collectives its should erect legislative barriers against petty tutelage and administrating and against unjustified interference in their affairs.

The Law is called upon to change radically the conditions and methods of business in the economy's basic link; it should reinforce the combination of the planning principle and full cost accounting, independence and liability in the operations of state enterprises, and it should codify new forms of self-management. Finally, it must translate into the language of law the new ideology of economic management.

The goals which this Law and a number of other normative acts are designed to achieve are of a radical nature. This requires the same of the legal regime being elaborated.

**A general description of the Law on the Enterprise**

The Law of the USSR on the State Enterprise (Association) has become a major source of norms for Soviet law: it consists of a preamble and three sections making for a total of twenty-five articles, each of which (except the last two) is subdivided into clauses (up to ten), the overall number of which is one hundred thirteen. In the volume of the lexical units it utilizes, the Law surpasses many other laws enacted by the Supreme Soviet. The extent of its regulations approaches those enactments which are traditionally termed codes in the USSR.

This is the first normative act of the USSR Supreme Soviet that resolves in a comprehensive manner manifold questions surrounding the organization, operations, and legal status of state enterprises. Its regulations will enjoy the highest measure of legal force after the USSR Constitution.

The question arises, does this Law in fact contain answers to the most important and as yet unresolved problems, does it offer solutions that meet the demands of the time? In order to find an answer, let us compare the text of the Law with the aforementioned Statute of 1965.

Six of the Law's twenty-five articles are devoted to subjects that are not even mentioned in the Statute, and the very concepts are absent there: the cost-accounting income of the collective and its distribution, the council of the enterprise's work collective, the social development of the work collective, the foreign economic activity of the enterprise, the utilization and preservation of the environment, and joint production and social activity. Of particular importance are such qualitatively new institutions as self-management, the electability of managers, and the creation and activity of the council of the work collective.

Thirteen articles address questions that are covered by the 1965 Statute, but they have been resolved [in the Law] quite differently. As an example we can take Article 1,* "The State Enterprise (Association) and Its Responsibilities." This article describes the enterprise as a socialist commodity producer (a description that not long ago was still a subject of debate); confirms the principles of full cost accounting, self-financing, and self-management; and affirms that [meeting] consumers' demands is obligatory and that this is the highest sense of the activity of the enterprise. In Article 2, however, "Principles of the Enterprise's Activity," only the fourth item contains much that is new; it introduces the concept of economic competition for customers, and stipulates the broad introduction of competitive design and production and the curtailment of the monopoly position of producers. Article 9, "The Enterprise's Relations with Administratively Superior Agencies and with Local Soviets of People's Deputies," should change at their very roots the relationships the enterprise maintains with central and local agencies of state power and management. Article 10, "Planning," forms one of the cornerstones of the whole reform: here it is stated that the enterprise itself drafts production plans and concludes delivery contracts on the basis of both state orders (these are mandatory) and direct customer orders.

The Law provides a concise and largely novel formulation of the principles of the operations of state enterprises. Their operations are based on the state plan—the most important vehicle in the implementation of economic policy. At the same

---

*Editor's note*—The quotations are taken from the Draft of the Law, the final version having been published only after this study had been completed. The final text appears in Appendix I, below.

time, however, enterprises are guided by the principles of full cost accounting and self-financing. Of course, only a few principles are set down in the Law, and these are of a general nature. For example, production and social activity and labor remuneration are to be financed from funds earned by the work collective. Profit is to be the overall indicator of enterprises' economic activity. Part of income will go to meeting obligations to the budget, banks, and superior agencies, while the other part will remain at the complete disposal of the enterprise and together with the wage fund will form the cost-accounting income of the collective of workers.

Thus, we have every reason to claim that this Law is more than just a re-fashioning of the old normative acts with a rewording and modified outline of its well-known regulations. This is a sociopolitical and economic document that is radical in its content, and if it is realized it will alter the entire landscape of the present economic mechanism. It was not only the ineffectiveness of previous attempts at change that paved the way for the concept of a new economic mechanism, but it was as well the effectiveness of the experiments that were carried out, the broad dissemination of the brigade contract, and universal demands for cost accounting.

But there exists still more proof of the innovative character of the Law on the Enterprise—it contains a series of important provisions on questions dealing with foreign economic relations.

### Foreign economic operations of enterprises (associations)

Quite naturally, the Law would have laid itself open to serious criticism had it repeated the mistake of the 1965 Statute and not addressed such a question vital to the state enterprises as their foreign economic ties. Article 19 of the Law, which consists of seven clauses, deals with this area.

The Law affirms that foreign economic operations are an integral part of the enterprise's work. Here, priority should belong to cooperation with socialist countries. The Law lays down the right of the enterprise to establish direct ties with enterprises and organizations of other member countries of the CMEA, including the conclusion of (civil-law) contracts with them.

Affirmation of the principle of foreign-currency self-recoupment and self-financing is a key element; as a rule, this must be the basis of the enterprise's foreign economic operations. The results of self-recoupment and self-financing must be a criterion of the overall success of the enterprise, and they must exercise direct influence of economic incentive funds.

The Law states that state enterprises may engage in export-import operations only with special authorization.

The Law assumes two categories of enterprises: those with direct and independent access to foreign markets and those without.

Enterprises not having direct access to foreign markets export their products through foreign trade organizations, but they do have a role in determining the optimal sales conditions for their products.

For those enterprises enjoying direct access to foreign markets, foreign trade companies have been created to facilitate their export-import operations, and their responsibilities, functions, and status are set out below.

In the interests of strengthening the cost accounting, increasing the economic interest and authority, and expanding the export-import independence of state enterprises, funds for foreign-currency payments [transfers] have been created. These funds are formed on the basis of stable long-term rates from monies earned from the export of products, as well as from all foreign-currency earnings from deliveries under cooperative agreements, and from the sale of licenses.

State enterprises must make good the damages resulting from the nonfulfillment of export assignments or contract obligations from their existing foreign-currency holdings.

The foreign-currency payments funds, as well as borrowed monies, will cover imports of equipment, technology, raw materials, and other goods and services vital to the enterprise. At the same time, [the Law] establishes the enterprise's right to receive bank credit in foreign currency for the creation and development of export production under the condition that the credit be repaid in foreign currency from export earnings.

Holdings of the foreign-currency payments funds are declared to be not subject to exaction. They may accumulate until their next utilization.

Of course, the Law sets down only a few of the legal provisions relating to the foreign economic ties of state enterprises. After all, it would be well-nigh impossible to include in the Law, for example, all those myriad (and recently carefully reexamined) regulations referring to direct ties with enterprises of CMEA member countries. This perhaps would do more harm than good. The nature of laws, as we know, demands that the stability of norms be observed. But direct ties are a relatively new area for state enterprises, and thus the legal regime governing them cannot be set in concrete. Consequently, it would be a mistake to include in the Law on the Enterprise all the regulations on questions involving direct ties and other issues. Therefore, the Law could only include the most important provisions of long-term relevance. Evidently, there is no other way.

### The potential impact of the Law on the State Enterprise (Association) on Soviet law

The Law on the Enterprise is the centerpiece of the legal framework for achieving the radical reform of the management and structure of the Soviet economy, approved by the Twenty-seventh CPSU Congress. This normative act can be considered a program for the construction of a new economic mechanism for the activity of state enterprises. Its enactment introduced a qualitatively new stage in the restructuring of the economy, and in large measure will determine the general orientation of the new system of management of the national economy.

A series of normative acts guaranteeing [the Law's] observation should follow on the heels of its confirmation. In the same measure that the rights and obligations of state enterprises have been changed, so should be changed the functions of the central economic and branch agencies. The efforts of the latter are to be redirected towards the elaboration and realization of the strategy of socioeconomic development and the optimal proportions and rates of economic growth, which includes drafting and implementing a strategy for foreign economic ties.

It is no secret that new statutes for a number of umbrella economic agencies are already in the works, as is the General Statute of USSR Ministries and a general statute of USSR state committees. It has been announced that work is underway on proposals for the creation of new forms of large-scale cost-accounting production structures building on enterprises and associations, as well as on a number of other important questions.

Obviously, reexamining the functions of branch ministries will raise the question of their number and structure. This is precisely where completion of work on the formation and optimization of the enterprise system is leading.

All this and much else is closely tied in with the Law on the Enterprise. One can also encounter in the literature, for example, calls for drafting normative acts on economic contracts, on wholesale trade in the means of production, on the credit system, and on the reorganization and liquidation of enterprises; and the need is recognized for the improvement of civil law, especially the system of norms of economic legislation.

The authors of the Law performed a special service in that their rendition of the proposed norms and regulations in many instances left no room for the need or even the possibility of publishing substatutory normative acts. We know all too well how some important initiatives and ideas came to naught under the guise of "explanation" and "concretization" of decisions reached at the highest level.

By itself, enactment of the Law of the USSR "On the State Enterprise (Association)" is naturally not likely to lead to positive changes. After all, major normative acts have been approved before that have held out great hopes. But have the expectations always proved out? The answer, of course, is no.

In our opinion, the Law represents an important step toward the achievement of the posited goals and the point of departure for further related measures. It is not a goal in itself but rather a means, an instrument for reform.

Let's assume, for example, that an enterprise does not have the capacity to produce goods for export, its fixed assets are obsolete, and it does not possess modern domestically produced equipment needed to modernize its plant. A dead-end situation, it would seem. However, the Law supports the enterprising: the enterprise can finance imported equipment with borrowed foreign currency, and it will repay the bank loan with earnings from the subsequent exports.

Clearly, if we limit ourselves to simply approving the new Law, the latter will just add to the list of palliatives and become but a patch with which to cover the aging economic mechanism. In order to justify its mission it must be reinforced by specific deeds. In the foreign economic sphere this means, first and foremost, developing exports, improving their structure via growth in the share of machinery and other final products, eliminating unnecessary imports, and increasing the overall efficiency of the whole of foreign economic operations.

While it accords priority to the development of cooperation with enterprises from CMEA member countries, the new Law orients Soviet state enterprises toward interaction with firms of all countries on the basis of mutual advantage and equality.

By consistently implementing the Law of the USSR ''On the State Enterprise (Association)'' in conjunction with the complex of measures that are already being undertaken in the economic sphere, including in the area of foreign economic ties, we can expect that an entirely new situation will crystallize in the USSR's national economy. And foreign economic operations will be given an entirely new face. In this connection, Soviet state enterprises are quite justified in assuming that in exporting their products and purchasing vital goods abroad, they will be accorded the same conditions enjoyed by firms of all other countries.

**Foreign trade companies**

The norms that determine the legal status of foreign trade companies are incorporated in their Model Statute, which was confirmed by the USSR Council of Ministers on 22 December 1986.

Foreign trade companies are constituted under the aegis of science-production associations, enterprises, and organizations that have the capacity to produce high-quality goods and to supply services.

A foreign trade company is constituted in an established procedure, and it conducts export-import operations in its assigned list of goods and services as well as other types of foreign economic activity in conformity with Soviet legislation. As a rule, the foreign trade company does not have juridical personality, but in some cases it may assume such. Decisions on this matter fall under the authority of its administratively superior ministry or department. The activity of such a company will be governed by the Statute of the All-Union Cost-Accounting Foreign Trade Organization (Association) of a Ministry or Department.

Its administratively superior enterprise exercises immediate supervision over the foreign trade company's activities. The foreign trade company conducts its operations on behalf and on the commission of the enterprise.

The enterprise may establish a separate budget for a foreign trade company established under its aegis.

The foreign trade company may be transferred over to a foreign trade association, ministry, or department.

The foreign trade company conducts its operations in conformity with the plan for the economic and social development of the enterprise on the basis of cost accounting, carries out its assigned obligations, and in connection therewith enjoys the rights granted to it by the enterprise; in so doing it is governed by its statute, which is approved by the enterprise manager on the basis of the Model Statute and of orders and other normative acts issued by the association.

The foreign trade company has its own title, which must also refer to the title of the enterprise to which it is subordinate.

**The principal responsibilities of foreign trade companies**

The following are the principal responsibilities of the foreign trade company:

—to conduct export operations, in conjunction with the enterprise's other production units, for the company's assigned list of products and services on the basis of concluded contracts in order to meet those requirements of the plan for the economic and social development of the enterprise relating to foreign-currency earnings; and to conduct import operations, coordinating trade, price, and foreign-currency questions with the appropriate foreign trade association, with a view toward ensuring the economical expenditure of foreign currency and toward satisfying demands on the qualitative and technical level of imported products and services;

—to promote exports of goods and services and improve their structure, to expand the product list, to enhance the quality and competitiveness of export goods, and to organize the technical servicing of exported machinery;

—to study and utilize competition in world markets, and to determine the optimal conditions for exports of goods and services that would ensure the maximum foreign-currency earnings;

—to study and analyze in a systematic manner the achievements of foreign science and technology, trends in scientific-technological progress, materials relating to patents and licenses, and the performance of domestically produced export products and analogous foreign products.

**The functions of foreign trade companies**

In order to fulfill its assigned responsibilities, the foreign trade company:

—takes part in the elaboration of drafts for long-term, five-year, and one-year plans of the enterprise, and secures fulfillment of the confirmed plans;

—finances export operations for the company's assigned list of products and services as well as imports of products and services from the enterprise's in-house foreign-currency holdings or with loans; in this it ensures for the enterprise the observance of principles of cost accounting and self-financing, and it assures conversion to foreign-currency self-recoupment for the technical retooling and reconstruction of plant and of scientific-technological, experimental-design and other projects;

—promotes for the enterprise the development of specialization and cooperation within the framework of the international division of labor, and of direct ties with enterprises and organizations of CMEA member countries; furthers the enterprise's participation in joint ventures and international associations and organizations; and it takes part in drafting proposals for the improvement of economic and scientific-technological cooperation;

—promotes the priority development of economic ties with the socialist countries and mutually advantageous relations with capitalist and developing countries; this is called forth by the need to take part in the international division of labor, to enhance the technical standards of the enterprise's products, and to increase production to meet the needs of the nation and of exports;

—studies the competitive situation in commodity markets for products on its assigned list and makes comparative analyses of exported machinery and analogous foreign machinery; provides information to enterprises and other interested organizations on the competitiveness of their exported products, on the demands being made on the quality of goods in foreign markets, on goods in high demand, and on steps being taken by foreign companies to enhance the competitiveness [of their products];

—drafts and carries out advertising and other [promotional] measures with the aim of expanding the export of goods, and participates in specialized exhibitions and international fairs and exhibitions;

—drafts and implements measures aimed at supplying technical services for exported products and at securing the same for machinery imported by the USSR;

—makes proposals on the dispatching abroad of the enterprise's specialists and supervises their activities in the servicing of exported machinery and the completion of installation and other projects, and it also sponsors foreign specialists;

—together with the relevant transportation organizations, drafts and implements measures designed to upgrade the carriage of foreign trade cargo, and takes part in drafting measures for improving its storage and ensuring its safekeeping;

—on the authority and on behalf of the enterprise, sees to the legal protection of the foreign economic interests of the enterprise.

**The rights of foreign trade companies**

The foreign trade company is vested with the following rights in accordance with the goals and responsibilities issuing from the statute of the foreign trade company, and in the procedure established by USSR legislation:

—to carry out, on the authority and on behalf of the enterprise, transactions and other juridical acts—including credit and exchange transactions—with institutions, enterprises, companies, associations, and individual persons, both in the USSR and abroad;

—to establish independent contact with Soviet and foreign institutions, companies, and their representatives, and also with Soviet and foreign citizens, involving issues within their competence;

—to represent the enterprise as both a plaintiff and a respondent in courts of law and in arbitration.

The foreign trade company enters into foreign trade transactions on the authority and on behalf of the enterprise. These are executed in the procedure established by USSR legislation.

On the authority and on behalf of the enterprise, the foreign trade company may enter into, and receive commissions for, economic contracts with other associations, enterprises, and organizations in the USSR for the implementation of export and import operations in supplying products and services; this takes place within the framework of the relevant [provision of the] statute of the foreign trade company covering the object of its activities.

**Assets of foreign trade companies, their liability, and management of their affairs**

The enterprise may directly assign to the foreign trade company part of its fixed and working assets that are necessary for foreign trade operations, and it may transfer to or create for the foreign trade company economic incentive funds as well as reserves.

The foreign trade company may transfer to other enterprises and organizations its allotted buildings, structures, and other fixed assets in the procedure provided for in USSR legislation. The enterprise is liable, and its assigned assets may be subject to claims in conformity with USSR legislation, for [unfulfilled] obligations undertaken by the enterprise in the person of its foreign trade company.

The state and its agencies and organizations are not responsible for the obligations undertaken by the enterprise in the person of its foreign trade company, and, likewise, the enterprise is not responsible for the obligations of the state or its agencies and organizations.

The special status of foreign trade companies as integral components of enterprises is also reflected in the resolution of issues bearing on their management.

The head of the foreign trade company is its director, who operates on the basis of one-man management and who is appointed and dismissed by the enterprise. The director of the company is aided by assistant directors.

The assistant director, chief accountant, and manager of the legal services office are appointed and dismissed by the enterprise.

The director of the foreign trade company has a seat on the enterprise council.

The director of the foreign trade company supervises its work and bears full responsibility for its operations.

The director exercises supervision over the operations of the foreign trade company, including decision making on the conclusion of contracts for the export or import of goods and services, and he represents the company in all institutions, enterprises, and organizations, both in the USSR and abroad, in conformity with the existing legislation and the foreign trade company's statute.

# 7

# DIRECT TIES WITH ENTERPRISES FROM CMEA MEMBER COUNTRIES

A major aspect of the reform of foreign economic operations in the USSR is the attention being paid to the development of direct ties between Soviet associations, enterprises, and other organizations and those of other CMEA member countries.

The deepening of socialist economic integration has been marked by a gradual relocation of the center of gravity in the economic cooperation of the countries of the socialist community directly to the sphere of material production. This has given rise to the further development of direct ties between industrial, scientific-technological, and design organizations.

The means of expanding direct (immediate) ties is the subject of section eight of the Comprehensive Program for the Deepening and Improvement of Cooperation and the Furthering of Socialist Economic Integration of the CMEA Member Countries. This section delineates the basic functions, methods, and organizational forms of direct contractual ties between economic organizations, as well as those extant in the creation of joint enterprises and other international economic organizations. These questions were discussed at the June 1984 Economic Summit Conference of the CMEA Member Countries. The Declaration on the Guidelines for the Further Development and Deepening of Economic and Scientific-Technological Cooperation between the CMEA Member Countries, adopted by the conference, stated that the broad development of industrial cooperation and the establishment of direct ties between associations, enterprises, and organizations represent an important trend in enhancing the mechanism for economic cooperation and increasing its effectiveness.

As to the essence of direct ties, the literature [on this topic] emphasizes that these are direct scientific-technological and production ties aimed at the acceleration of scientific-technological progress and the manufacture of advanced products that meet the best world standards; that is, that they are realized directly in the sphere of production. As far as foreign trade goes, commercial operations are, as a rule, the bailiwick of Soviet foreign trade associations which carry out foreign trade transactions.[1] As of 1 January 1987 several dozen industrial organizations also carry out such commercial operations.

With the goals of developing production and fostering cooperation, associations, enterprises, and organizations are authorized, independent of the existence of any agreements or protocols on direct ties, to conclude contracts for individual deliveries of manufactured products, product models, tools, fittings, instruments, and secondary resources not used in the production of materials, machinery, and equipment, as well as for the extension of services.

The existing system of contractual documents pertaining to direct ties includes intergovernmental agreements, interagency agreements, economic agreements, and foreign trade contracts.

Intergovernmental agreements are used primarily to launch large-scale undertakings in industrial cooperation and specialization, in the joint construction of industrial projects, and in the creation of interstate economic organizations, international economic associations, and joint enterprises. Recent years have seen the use of general intergovernmental agreements to further comprehensive cooperation in the most important areas of scientific-technological progress: in atomic-power machine building, electronics, robotics, and other areas. These agreements encompass both the development of new machinery and technology as well as the organization of specialized and cooperative production and the assimilation of new types of products. Such agreements identify the cooperating state agencies and economic organizations and their contractual relations.

Interagency agreements are used to coordinate the development of branches and to organize intrabranch cooperation in the production of specific products. The negotiations for and conclusion of such agreements are the joint responsibility of the administratively superior ministry—that is, the ministry primarily involved in the production of the relevant product group—and the Ministry of Foreign Trade. These agreements embrace such vital branches of machine building as shipbuilding, automotive engineering, machine-tool building, tractor building, and also the chemical, petrochemical, food, and pulp and paper industries, nonferrous metallurgy, etc.

Economic agreements are of an organizational nature and have as their aim the promotion of cooperation in the spheres of science, technology, and the production of specific types of products (including scientific research and experimental design projects), the assimilation by industry of new types of cooperatively manufactured products, and the subsequent inclusion of these products in foreign trade circulation.

The broadening of direct production and scientific-technological cooperation between Soviet organizations and those of the CMEA member countries led to the need for a definition of the procedures by which Soviet enterprises would estab-

1. For more detail, see V. Kuvshinov and E. Liakina-Frolova, "Pravovye aspekty priamykh sviazei" [The legal aspects of direct ties], *Vneshniaia torgovlia* 1985, No. 11, pp. 10–13.

lish direct ties. Two decrees of the Council of Ministers provided such definition: the Decree of 9 July 1981, "On the Improvement of Cooperation between USSR Ministries and Departments, Associations, Enterprises, and Organizations with Corresponding Departments, Enterprises, and Organizations of the Other CMEA Member Countries in the Fields of Science, Technology, and International Specialization and Cooperation in Production"[2]; and the Decree of 7 June 1984, "On Measures Aimed at Creating the Necessary Conditions for the Development of International Production and Scientific-Production Intrabranch Cooperation and at Improving Direct Ties between Ministries, Departments, Associations, Enterprises, and Organizations of the USSR and Those of the Other CMEA Member Countries."

Direct production and scientific-technological ties between associations, enterprises, and organizations of the USSR with those of the other CMEA member countries must become the most important vehicle for the establishment of stable and effective cooperation, for the exchange of advanced know-how, and for the according of mutual aid in the assimilation and introduction of new machinery and technology.

Another measure, Decree No. 992 of 19 August 1986, "On Measures for Improving the Management of Economic and Scientific-Technological Cooperation with the Socialist Countries," was especially designed to orient the further development of direct ties toward meeting the targets of the Comprehensive Program for Scientific-Technological Progress of the CMEA Member Countries, raising labor productivity, modernizing industrial plant, more completely utilizing production capacities, economizing on the use of resources, and increasing the manufacture of products that meet world technical and quality standards and that are capable of replacing economically unjustified imports from capitalist countries.

In order to create the economic and organizational conditions necessary for the all-around development of direct ties, the rights of associations, enterprises, and organizations were expanded, allowing them to assume an active role in international production and scientific-technological cooperation.

The ministries and departments must see to it that as large a number as possible of those enterprises enjoying real potential in the development of international production and scientific-technological cooperation participate in direct ties. They must help such enterprises in selecting partners for direct ties and create the necessary organizational and other conditions for the development of such ties.

Before going on to the rights accorded to enterprises and other organizations in the sphere of direct ties, we must say a few words about who may or who may not be parties to such direct relations.

*First*, these are production and science-production associations, enterprises, and organizations, to whom permission to participate in direct ties is given by the relevant ministry or department.

---

2. *Svod zakonov SSSR*, Vol. 9, pp. 51–63.

*Second*, these are associations, enterprises, and organizations that themselves enjoy the right to conduct export-import operations.

*Third*, these are organizations tapped as administratively superior organizations [for the purposes of coordinating work] on the problems listed in the Comprehensive Program for Scientific-Technological Progress of the CMEA Member Countries to the Year 2000.

*Fourth*, these are associations, enterprises, and other organizations that are participants in joint enterprises and international associations and organizations. This category of participants enters into direct ties with joint enterprises and their foreign participants.

Thus, in theory any Soviet enterprise may become a party to direct ties with enterprises from CMEA member countries, provided there is a production or other necessity for this and that it does not require a decision of the Soviet government (or its standing agency—the State Foreign Economic Commission) on extension of the right to conduct export-import operations.

An enterprise involved in direct ties has the right to decide independently all questions involved in cooperation and the exchange of advanced know-how.

In particular, it coordinates with its partner-enterprise in direct ties the list and volume of mutual deliveries involved in the cooperation agreement; it has the right to arrange for reciprocal supplies of cooperatively manufactured products, product models, tools, fittings, instruments, materials, individual machines, and equipment, and to exchange required services necessary to further cooperation and production development (including for mixed enterprises in the USSR); to rent out and rent from others tools, machines, and equipment; and to place single orders for the manufacture and delivery to the USSR of products that involve provision of the necessary material resources and technical documentation, and also to accept such orders.

In the sphere of scientific-technological cooperation, the realization of direct ties allows the Soviet enterprise to conduct scientific research, design, and experimental projects jointly, via cooperation, or in fulfilling orders placed by organizations of CMEA member countries; the enterprise may create toward this end joint collectives of experts and specialists to exchange on mutually agreed-upon terms scientific-technological documentation and to aid in the cooperative training of personnel.

Soviet enterprises maintaining direct ties with enterprises from CMEA member countries enter with the latter into economic agreements and contracts in their own name. If there is a need for immediate or short-term exchange, [the Soviet enterprise] may conclude one-year contracts for an agreed-upon sum without reference to the specific list of reciprocally delivered products or their prices provided that final accounts are settled before the end of the year. But these one-year contracts must define the time periods and procedures regulating contra accounts.

We should draw attention to the fact that, consonant with the principles of self-financing and self-recoupment of costs, the only variable limiting the volume of imported goods and services is the amount of foreign currency and also credit at the disposal of associations, enterprises, and organizations.

Inasmuch as enterprises have the right to enter into contractual relations with enterprises from other CMEA member countries, they may, if necessary, request foreign trade organizations, including their administratively superior ministries, to conclude such contracts; the enterprise would then pay such an organization appropriate remuneration. In essence, the reference is to a commission agreement between the enterprise and foreign trade organization.

In entering into economic agreements and contracts with enterprises from other CMEA member countries, Soviet enterprises are guided by the General Conditions for Production Deliveries between Organizations of CMEA Member Countries; the General Conditions for the Provision of Installation and Other Technical Services Connected with the Delivery of Machinery and Equipment between Organizations of Member Countries of the Council for Mutual Economic Assistance; and other normative documents and statutes, both of the CMEA and those drafted on a bilateral basis between the USSR and the other CMEA member countries.[3]

Thus, while prior to the restructuring in the sphere of foreign economic operations, all these normative documents governed primarily the relations of Soviet foreign trade organizations with their counterparts from the CMEA member countries, today the sphere of application of these documents has expanded considerably.

The legal aspects of direct ties have been defined in the Rules for the Realization of Direct Production and Scientific-Technological Ties between USSR Associations, Enterprises, and Organizations and Enterprises and Organizations of Other CMEA Member Countries. With this in mind, we will probably see in the future the introduction of the necessary changes and clarifications in the aforementioned 1981 and 1984 decrees.

---

3. See I. Szasz, *A Uniform Law on International Sales of Goods. The CMEA General Conditions*, Budapest 1980; *Handbuch der Aussenhandelsverträge*, Berlin 1986; and *ALB/RGW 1968. Kommentar*, Berlin 1975.

# 8

# LEGAL FORMS OF RELATIONS BETWEEN
# INDUSTRY AND FOREIGN TRADE

The question of the relations between industry and foreign trade appears to be of decisive importance against the background of the restructuring of the economic mechanism.

It was stated at the Twenty-seventh CPSU Congress that there are practically no branches today that could not be drawn into the sphere of foreign economic relations. But the traditional paths will not allow us to move forward rapidly here. We must redirect ministries, associations, and enterprises toward enhancing the nation's export potential, and we must increase the quality and competitiveness of machinery and equipment, as well as of other finished goods. The new demands also require a restructuring of the foreign economic departments. These departments must be more closely tied to the ministries and enterprises, they must search for ways to link their interests with the demands of the foreign market, and they must emerge not only as middlemen but as active participants in national economic decision making.[1]

The long-existing network of relations earlier had approximately the following configuration:

—relations between state administrative agencies (between the government and departments, between supra-economic departments and other agencies, between the Ministry of Foreign Trade and the State Committee for Foreign Economic Relations, on the one hand, and branch ministries and departments, etc., on the other);

—relations between foreign trade associations and industrial associations, enterprises, and organizations;

—relations between foreign trade associations, industrial associations, enterprises, and organizations, on the one hand, and state administrative agencies,

---

1. *Materialy XXVII s"ezda KPSS*, Moscow 1986, pp. 257–258.

both foreign economic and branch, on the other. These relations were regulated by a system of legal norms of both administrative-law and civil-law norms.

In principle, the structure of relations will remain, it appears, largely unaltered after the reorganization. But their content is to be provided in many respects with largely new forms, as these relations must become more developed, deeper, and more complex. After all, the principal trend in restructuring, as has been noted, is to expand the rights of industry in the sphere of foreign economic ties.

It is well known that as a result of the excessive centralization of foreign economic operations, the sphere of production was organizationally cut off from foreign markets, and it bore no immediate responsibility for, and had no direct interest in, the development of exports or the advantageous structuring of imports. Neither did it have much knowledge of foreign markets or a sense of its requirements. The organizational isolation of industry and foreign trade made it difficult to achieve the planned economic coordination of their interests. This situation became a brake on the mobilization of export resources, the rationalization of exports and imports, and the development of new, advanced forms and methods of foreign economic relations.

The need to improve the system of foreign economic operations is perceived all the more urgently now under the new conditions of management, inasmuch as the conversion to cost-accounting principles requires the maximum possible organizational, planning, and economic unity in all spheres of the economy.

Gaining greater access to foreign markets is vital for industry if it is to help in multiplying the nation's export resources, in forming and continuously replenishing stocks of competitive industrial products, in studying technical questions at a greater level of expertise, and at securing the commercial effectiveness of foreign trade contracts. Industry's closer proximity to foreign markets should help to overcome departmental barriers in the development of foreign trade and to increase the responsibility and interest of the productive sphere in achieving high quality for export products and in the economic results of foreign economic operations.

The redistribution of administrative functions in foreign trade among a number of ministries and departments should have a beneficial effect on the system of relations linking foreign trade with industry, and it should register a decisive breakthrough in bringing about the intensive development of foreign trade. In recent years, two factors have in large measure served as brakes on the latter:

—the potential for the extensive development of foreign trade circulation on the basis of the interbranch division of labor became exhausted as the economic soundness of physically increasing the volume of exports of raw materials and fuels approached its limit;

—the competitive standing of Soviet industrial products in world markets has gradually weakened against the background of accelerating scientific-technological progress.

A real possibility for overcoming these circumstances lies in the broader and more direct engagement of the production link in the foreign economic sphere. This means, on the one hand, raising the level of its activity, interest, and independence, and on the other, strengthening its responsibility for the development of economic ties with foreign countries.

Such a course will allow for demands that have arisen in the foreign economic sphere to be addressed. This primarily involves the creation of new export resources and the production of competitive industrial products via the mobilization of internal reserves, reserves that even with the progressive changes in the material and production base remain embedded in the very mechanism of the socialist economy and its foreign trade. The nature of relations between the production and foreign economic spheres are changing in a radical way. Before, the production link was asked to adapt its operations to the dictates and specific features of foreign markets; under the new conditions, foreign economic operations have taken on an altogether new character for the production sphere—they are becoming an organic and integral part of overall economic activity.

Along with the decentralization of foreign-trade administrative functions at the level of ministries and departments, and the simultaneous strengthening of the administration of the foreign economic complex at the governmental level through the State Foreign Economic Commission, there is one circumstance that will have a growing influence on the system of relations between foreign trade and industry. We are referring to changes in the methods of management. The center of gravity is shifting from command-administrative to economic methods and levers of management. A key direction in the reforms underway is the creation of a new economic mechanism for the nation's foreign economic ties, and bringing it into line with the new conditions and methods of management in the production sphere.

State agencies have at their disposal a "collection" of specific levers that they can utilize to ensure observance of general state interests in the sphere of foreign economic relations. This "collection" embraces a complex of different economic instruments: the foreign-currency earnings plan, long-term norms for the effectiveness of foreign trade operations, differentiated foreign-currency coefficients (used in accounting for exports and imports), transfers to foreign-currency funds of enterprises and associations, control over the substantiation of prices and the utilization of competition, the licensing of exports and imports, etc.

The essence of the new mechanism consists in the application of cost-accounting principles to the foreign economic operations of both foreign trade organizations and production enterprises. Joint Decree No. 991 of the CPSU Central Committee and the USSR Council of Ministers of 19 August 1986, "On Measures to Improve the Management of Foreign Economic Relations," provides that ministries and departments that have been empowered to supervise export and import operations must apply the principles of cost accounting, foreign-currency self-recoupment, and self-financing in carrying out their operations.[2]

One of the key issues is that of civil-law relations between industrial enterprises not yet having direct access to foreign markets and foreign trade associations. The manner in which this issue is resolved is capable of radically influencing the legal forms of relations between industry and foreign trade. As we know, Decree No. 991 provided for the conversion to a new contractual system in these relations. A new civil-law regime is to be drafted for this sphere.

As we know, earlier—beginning with 1940—agreements on the delivery of goods for export were not fixed in contractual procedure. They were based on assignments under the plan and supply orders, and they were regulated largely by special conditions confirmed by the USSR government. Characteristic of these relations, and this has been noted in the literature, was the fact that it was not necessary to secure the consent of the suppliers, that is, the manufacturers of the products, for [placement of] the supply orders and their execution, as long as the orders did not conflict with assignments stipulated in the plan. A one-sided transaction, the supply order expressed the will of only one party.[3]

The legal relationship in the case of imports had the character of a contract of commission and had the form of approved orders for import, and import procedures were regulated by special conditions confirmed by the USSR Council of Ministers.

Such a system could not be preserved under the new conditions of operation when industrial enterprises were being converted to full cost accounting, self-recoupment of costs, and self-financing. The 19 August 1986 Decree called for a full transition to contractual relations in deliveries of goods for export and purchases of imported goods.

The question arises, what type of contract should be adopted as the basis for the new contract system? Naturally, finding a solution to this question first requires clearly defining the general approach to be taken toward the contents of the relations between foreign trade associations and Soviet suppliers and customers.

In our opinion, these relations cannot in the future be defined by the rules which are characteristic for deliveries in the domestic market. Firstly, this would be in contradiction with the basic elements inherent in commission relations. Also, the Joint Decree No. 991 of 19 August 1986 of the CPSU Central Committee and the USSR Council of Ministers envisaged that foreign trade associations would operate as intermediaries. Consequently, the enterprise—supplier or customer—can set the conditions for export and import transactions, and the interest

---

2. For more detail, see Iu. Shamrai, "Perestroika vneshneekonomicheskikh sviazei i gosudarstvennaia monopoliia vneshnei torgovli," pp. 4–7.

3. See *Eksportno-importnye operatsii. Pravovoe regulirovanie* [Export-import operations. Their legal regulation], edited by V. S. Pozdniakov, Moscow 1970, pp. 112–113.

of the foreign trade association acting as intermediary would be secured by the payment of proportional commissions. Secondly, the specific features of foreign markets cannot be ignored, nor can the fact that the foreign trade associations are neither consumers nor producers of the goods and services involved.

It appears to us extremely important to find a resolution of all concrete questions that would safeguard the interests and proper balancing of the mutual rights and responsibilities of all Soviet organizations involved in export and import operations. The main thing is for the industrial enterprises to feel the full pressure of competition and be aware of the specific demands of foreign markets, even when they themselves do not have the right of direct access to it.

In drafting new regulations, another problem is bound to arise. The socialist countries account for a major share of the USSR's foreign trade turnover. In trade relations with these countries, the application of general conditions for delivery of goods (for example, the General Conditions for the Delivery of Goods of the CMEA, 1968–1975 [1979 edition]), having the force of USSR international treaties, is, as a rule, mandatory. Consequently, contracts concluded between foreign trade associations and foreign buyers and sellers from these countries are subject to the provisions of the relevant international acts, which in essence define the [foreign trade associations'] rights and obligations toward foreign contract partners. In view of the fact that foreign trade associations will operate as intermediaries, not only the specific features of foreign markets but also the relevant international treaties of the USSR must not be ignored in defining the rights, obligations, and responsibilities of foreign trade associations toward Soviet organizations; neither can be ignored the need to meet obligations for the supply and purchase of goods that have been undertaken at the intergovernmental level.

The establishment of foreign-currency-payment funds is the most important vehicle for increasing the interest of industrial enterprises in expanding exports. These funds may be used to acquire in foreign markets machinery, equipment, and materials that are necessary for the manufacture of industrial and other products, for the technical reconstruction of industrial plant, or for carrying out scientific research and other projects. In the event that enterprises fail to fulfill contractual obligations undertaken by them for the export or import of goods, they must pay compensation for the damage caused from their existing foreign-currency funds. Naturally, these principles must be duly reflected in normative acts on the new contract system regulating relations between industry and foreign trade.

Work is underway on the elaboration of new normative acts that will define the content of contractual relations of foreign trade associations with suppliers of goods for export and customers for imported goods. Of course, no one can be certain what form the final resolution will take. It is important to keep in mind, however, that the basic elements of the future contractual relations have been juridically predetermined in the 19 August 1986 decrees as well as in several other decisions adopted pursuant to these acts. Undoubtedly, the content of the future contractual relations between industry and foreign trade will reflect to an even greater extent the ideas and principles contained in the USSR Law on the State Enterprise (Association) and other normative acts which will codify the legal foundations of the country's new economic mechanism.

What can one say about this at the present time? Perhaps that in view of the provisions of the 19 August 1986 Decree and the principles of the new economic mechanism that is taking shape in the USSR (defined for the most part in the decisions of the Twenty-seventh CPSU Congress), there is every reason to expect that relations between foreign trade associations and their contractual partners in the USSR will normally be constructed according to the model of the contract of commission. In this case, the foreign trade association, acting as the comissioner, would conduct export-import operations in foreign markets in its own name but on commission from and for the account of the supplier or customer. In this situation, the principal can determine, for example, the optimal conditions for exporting his products. Other forms will probably also be applied along with this. We see on the whole the adoption of a flexible approach, the application of not one but perhaps several models, each of which would correspond to the specifics of the intermediary relations.

One can assume that the adoption of new normative acts dealing with the relations between industry and foreign trade is a matter of the not-too-distant future.

# 9

# SCIENTIFIC-TECHNOLOGICAL AND PRODUCTION COOPERATION

The development of the world economy and of international trade attest to the burgeoning participation of virtually all states in the international division of labor. To a large extent this is also a function of progress in science and technology and of the needs of production. Certainly, there is no country that is in the position to satisfy all its needs for goods and services from domestic production alone, to say nothing of the questionable economic wisdom and effectiveness of relying exclusively on domestic capacities. The latter can only lead to the irrational squandering of national labor and natural resources. Deepening the international division of labor is crucial if growth is to be achieved in national income and the volume of industrial and agricultural production, if the effectiveness of production is to be raised, and if the state of affairs in the economy is to improve.

The USSR's national economy maintains long-established and relatively developed economic ties with foreign countries. This applies first and foremost to the member countries of the CMEA. These ties are manifested in such widely known forms as buying and selling, contractor's agreements, barter transactions, licensing agreements, etc. As for science, technology, and production, cooperation in this sphere has not up to now developed to the extent necessary. Certainly, the prospects this form of cooperation offers are already visible in relations with the CMEA member countries as well as with a number of other countries, Finland, for example. However, it is generally recognized that cooperation in the sphere of foreign economic relations has been insufficiently utilized.

## The concept of cooperation

We traditionally conceive of international scientific-technological and production cooperation as long-term joint and coordinated activity, based on the principle of a division of labor, of two or more legal persons from different countries in the area of applied scientific research, experimental, design, and technological projects and processes of production, and/or the sale of goods and services carried out on a contractual basis and designed to produce for the partners an optimal economic result.

In modern social production, cooperation represents ties between associations, enterprises, and organizations involving the exchange of materials, semifinished products, parts, machine components, etc., necessary for the manufacture of the final product, and likewise involving the performance of various types of projects directed at achievement of an overall final result. Cooperation is considered to be close, long-term, and stable scientific-technological and production interaction between two or more partners, and their joint and coordinated activity.[1]

Depending on the nature of the ties involved, we can distinguish different forms of cooperation that vary in the depth of their integrational components. Nevertheless, they all have common features as well: a division of labor between the partners, and close interaction in the process of production and exchange on the basis of their extended and continuous technological interdependence.

Scientific-technological and production cooperation are closely intertwined. Their interdependence is manifested in several ways. The former may be considered a predecessor of the latter, as it quite often leads further on: cooperation at the stage of scientific research, experimental, design, and technological projects eventually becomes cooperation in production. Also, each form of cooperation is relatively independent and has its own specific features. Understanding this is important in analyzing legal relations in this area, defining the legal nature of the contracts, and resolving issues involving the liability of the parties for the nonexecution or inadequate execution of obligations, etc.

Relations in the sphere of cooperation are obligations regulated by norms of the law of obligations based on international treaties and on civil-law contracts that are established between two or more independent subjects; they are longterm, close, stable, and comprehensive ties of an organizational and property nature having the goal of creating and utilizing a final product (result) on the basis of a rational division of labor.

## The current status of cooperation

The practice of international trade shows that cooperation holds considerable potential as a means of expanding trade and is an important vehicle for updating technology, enhancing the economic effectiveness of production, for accelerating the exchange of machinery, equipment, and other industrial products and increasing their share in imports and exports.

---

1. See *Mezhdunarodnaia nauchno-tekhnicheskaia i proizvodstvennaia kooperatsiia* [International scientific-technological and production cooperation], edited by M. M. Boguslavsky *et al.*, Moscow 1982, p. 11.

As for the USSR's cooperation with other socialist countries, especially the member countries of the CMEA, its present scale is such that it has become a substantial determinant of the volume and structure of mutual trade, particularly in finished products.

The history of scientific-technological and production cooperation between Soviet organizations and firms from capitalist and developing countries is rather short: the first transactions here date from the end of 1960s and the beginning of the 1970s. At present we have several dozen cooperation agreements with firms from Austria, Great Britain, Italy, Finland, France, the FRG, Switzerland, Sweden, and Japan. They involve, in particular, joint research and development of a specific product, development of the technology for its production, manufacture of the product in one or both of the countries, and coordinated marketing efforts, including marketing in third countries. Approximately half of production cooperation ventures involve primarily technology transfer within the framework of licensing agreements and have as their goal reducing the assimilation period for the manufacture of the licensed products involved.

Past experience in scientific-technological and production cooperation between Soviet organizations and firms from capitalist and developing countries has revealed fundamental obstacles to its further development (of course, cooperation with each individual country has its own dynamics): the relative narrowness of sales markets abroad and their saturation with competing goods works against the development and manufacture of products under cooperation agreements with the USSR; the differing standards and differing methods of quality control entail the need for more precise definitions of the technical documentation of the cooperatively manufactured product and the technology used in its manufacture, which requires additional time and expense; and, of course, the most important are the factors related to trade policy. A number of outstanding internal problems have also limited its utilization: the absence of a clear definition of the group of organizations that are empowered to take part in scientific-technological and production cooperation with firms from capitalist and developing countries, and their mutual rights and responsibilities; unsatisfactory planning for the establishment and utilization of this form of foreign economic relations; the absence of an adequate legal regime for the financial and foreign-currency aspects of cooperation; and the insufficient economic stake for Soviet organizations in participating in this sphere.

Soviet organizations' experience in cooperation with companies from capitalist and developing countries attests to the potentialities and expediency of its further expansion and intensification both in science and technology and in production. Scientific-technological cooperation can in principle involve joint projects in the sphere of applied research; experimental, design, and technological projects; and the creation of product prototypes. Production cooperation holds particular promise for the spheres of machine building, instrument making, computer technology, manufacture of medical equipment, and in the chemical, petrochemical, light, and food branches of industry. Cooperation should promote the mastering and assimilation of new and technologically advanced products and new types of services, and it should play a large role in helping the USSR to achieve the goals charted for its foreign economic operations.

## The general approach to cooperation

Scientific-technological and production cooperation with the socialist countries and with firms from capitalist and developing countries is looked upon as one of the means that must achieve a genuine breakthrough in foreign economic relations, helping to meet the demands in this sphere and to accelerate its development. Obviously, effective cooperation is hardly possible without direct ties.

In the USSR's relations with other socialist countries, with many developing countries, and with some capitalist countries, there are no obstacles or factors of a political nature that serve to hinder or negatively influence the development of scientific-technological and production cooperation. Consequently, the emphasis here is on the resolution of economic, organizational, and legal issues and the creation of preconditions for the successful development of cooperation. Joint Decree No. 992 of the CPSU Central Committee and the USSR Council of Ministers of 19 August 1986,* "On Measures to Improve the Management of Economic and Scientific-Technological Cooperation with the Socialist Countries," contains the following directives:

—to deem the priority development of economic ties with the socialist countries, guided by the principles of socialist internationalism, as the most important political and national goal; to bring about a radical restructuring of the system of cooperation with these countries, making the move from predominantly trade relations to intensive specialization and cooperation in production, and placing at the foundation of all work the Comprehensive Program for Scientific-Technological Progress of the CMEA Member Countries to the Year 2000;

—to bring about a substantial change in the forms and methods of realizing foreign economic ties with the socialist countries; in improving the centralized planning of economic relations, the primary stress must be placed on the active and comprehensive introduction of new and advanced forms of interaction, and the creation of the requisite economic and organizational conditions that would facilitate the activity of cooperating associations, enterprises, and organizations on the basis of full cost accounting and mutual advantage (clause 1).

With many other countries, scientific-technological and production cooperation takes place in unfavorable conditions that are of a noneconomic nature. This is first and foremost the case with some capitalist countries.

The USSR's general approach to economic ties with capitalist countries finds it definition in the USSR Constitution and a whole series of normative and other

*Editor's note—See SP SSSR 1986, No. 33, item 172, pp. 587–591 (summary).

legal acts, including the USSR's international treaties. For example, policy on economic relations with various groups of states is covered in the Guidelines for the Social and Economic Development of the USSR, which are approved for extended periods, and in laws on the state plans of economic and social development of the nation for five-year periods. These relations are constructed in the spirit of the United Nations Charter and the 1975 Final Act of the Conference on Security and Cooperation in Europe.

The USSR stands firmly for the normalization of international relations in the spheres of trade, science, and technology, for the removal of all artificial barriers and restrictions, for the implementation of measures that strengthen mutual trust in international economic relations, for the elimination of all forms and manifestations of economic aggression, including in the area of technology, for the restructuring of the entire system of international economic and scientific-technological relations on a just and democratic basis, and the establishment of a new international economic order.

In line with their policy of peaceful coexistence and in the interest of social progress, and convinced that the international socialist division of labor is constructed from the perspective of a global division of labor, the USSR and the other CMEA member countries intend to continue developing economic and scientific-technological ties with other states on the foundations of equality, mutual advantage, and respect for sovereignty, independent of the other states' social systems.

In their production cooperation with firms from capitalist countries, Soviet organizations observe the relevant principles of the Final Act of the Conference on Security and Cooperation in Europe covering industrial cooperation, and rely on the experience of such cooperation, taking into account both its positive and negative aspects.

**The goals and forms of cooperation**

Achieving a genuine breakthrough in the entire system of cooperation through intensive scientific-technological and economic integration is the single most important goal of cooperation between the USSR and the other socialist countries. Moreover, cooperation is aimed at the resolution of the major economic and technical problems of their national economies (clause 2 of Decree No. 992 of 19 August 1986).

Less global but no less important goals are the development, mastering, and assimilation of progressive technology, the creation of new and reconstruction of existing capacities, etc. (clause 6).

The principal goals of Soviet organizations in their cooperation with firms from capitalist countries are the following:

—improving the organization and raising the technical level and effectiveness of production;

—manufacturing qualitatively new and more competitive products, and expanding their sales possibilities in the domestic and foreign markets;

—achieving maximal utilization of scientific-technological achievements and the more productive exchange of technical and technological knowhow;

—restructuring and modernizing the material and technical base of industry and securing the full utilization of its capacities.

The forms of cooperation might be the following:

1) specialization in joint production. In this form of cooperation, each of the partners specializes in the manufacture of certain products within the framework of coordinated production programs, so that the demand for products not manufactured by one partner are satisfied through purchases from the other partner. There is also another variant, when one of the partners manufactures individual elements and components and the other completes the assembly and production of the final cooperative product; and yet another variant has it that each partner manufactures individual elements and components of the final cooperative product, and its final assembly and production takes place at both partners' enterprises via mutual deliveries of these elements and components. The technology utilized in these forms of cooperation may be supplied by one partner or both partners, or it may be specially developed;

2) cooperation in licensing. Cooperation here involves joint production and sales of products manufactured by one or both of the partners under a license arrangement which may be accompanied by deliveries of equipment and/or component parts. Moreover, this form of cooperation may presuppose another variant, when one of the partners manufactures the final cooperative product under a license arrangement; this may also involve deliveries of equipment and/or semifinished products, just as it may provide for the licensing partner to acquire a part of the cooperatively manufactured products;

3) any other forms related to specialization, joint production, or license cooperation, including specialization in joint scientific-technological projects; deliveries of assembled products and/or equipment; the exchange of products with a view toward improving their mix; and joint efforts in the markets of third countries.

### International legal regulation of cooperation

The role of international cooperative relations is to unite the [common] interests of states with identical or different socioeconomic systems. In so doing, they must take into account similarities and distinctions in economic systems and management mechanisms and the organization of science and production; the features of the legal status of state administrative agencies and other participants in [cooperative] relations; and the specific features of other countries' legal regulation of cooperative relations.

International cooperation, particularly if it involves large-scale projects, often requires changes in the structure of production, large capital investments, the use of foreign manpower, and a host of other measures.

Questions of this character, inasmuch as they touch upon the overall interests of states, cannot be resolved at the level of individual economic units. Cooperative relations therefore require an interstate character, with the parties to them being states in the persons of administrative agencies. These relations are regulated by international law and take on the relevant international legal forms.

The foundations of international cooperative relations issue from international treaties, including long-term programs, which guide the cooperative activity of associations, enterprises, and organizations. International treaties that provide for cooperation differ in accordance with the government or administrative agency in whose name they have been concluded, and also in accordance with the degree of detail in which the obligations of the partners are defined. The common denominator, however, is that they are designed to resolve the most important issues of cooperation. In particular, they define the spheres of cooperation, the principles of financing, and the legal and organizational forms of cooperation. Upon entering into such treaties, states become organizers of cooperation between enterprises, and thus assume the obligation of ensuring and promoting that cooperation.

Many of the USSR's international treaties include provisions dealing with scientific-technological and production cooperation. With capitalist countries, for example, by the end of the 1970s the USSR maintained over sixty intergovernmental agreements on scientific-technological and economic cooperation and more than ten long-term programs.[2]

## The Soviet legislation

Before 1981 Soviet associations, enterprises, and organizations did not enjoy the right to enter into cooperation agreements, although in certain cases they did become participants in them with special authorization. Such agreements—like all civil-law economic transactions with a foreign element—were concluded by foreign trade associations or state administrative agencies (ministries and departments) together with foreign trade organizations.

For the Soviet Union, international scientific-technological and production cooperation emerged and developed largely on the basis of its international treaties and ad hoc legal acts of state administrative agencies. It is natural that under such conditions this practice was not marked by consistency in its forms or by uniformity; indeed, it was in a certain sense contradictory and suffered from shortcomings.

We will take the example of scientific-technological ties and examine the past organization of cooperation.

2. See V. L. Mal'kevich, *Vostok-Zapad: ekonomicheskoe sotrudnichestvo. Tekhnologicheskii obmen* [East–West economic cooperation. Technology exchange], Moscow 1981, pp. 29–30.

As a rule, international cooperation in science and technology flowed from international interagency, or so-called "diagonal," agreements and contracts on cooperation in specific areas. From the Soviet side, these agreements were negotiated either by the USSR State Committee for Science and Technology, or by this state administrative agency together with branch ministries and departments, or by the latter themselves.

These contracts and agreements provided for two basic forms of their realization: the implementation of individual projects on the basis of working plans without the signing of contracts, and the conclusion of contracts by foreign trade organizations calling for research and development on the basis of cooperation. These two forms were retained even after the adoption by the USSR Council of Ministers on 9 July 1981 of Decree No. 652, "On the Further Improvement of Cooperation between USSR Ministries and Departments, Associations, Enterprises, and Organizations with Corresponding Departments, Enterprises, and Organizations of the Other CMEA Member Countries in the Area of Science, Technology, and International Specialization and Cooperation in Production."[3] This Decree supplemented the previously mentioned two decrees by establishing another means of realizing interagency agreements with the CMEA member countries—the conclusion of direct economic contracts by the organizations involved in the projects.

Consonant with the emergence of these three forms of realizing interagency and "diagonal" contracts and agreements on scientific-technological cooperation, there developed in the USSR three categories of legal relations between Soviet state agencies and organizations—parties to cooperative agreements.

*In the first instance*, the state agency that signed the contract or agreement directed its subordinate Soviet organization-cooperative partner to draft a working plan jointly with the foreign partner that was subject to confirmation by the appropriate agency. The one-year plans for scientific research and design projects of the Soviet organizations-cooperative partners included measures for the realization of the confirmed working plans. The inclusion of projects in the plan provided in fact the basis for the Soviet organization's participation in international scientific-technological cooperation. As a rule, the Soviet organization maintained contact with the foreign partner (correspondence, transfer and receipt of results, etc.) through the higher agency, which monitored the fulfillment by the Soviet side of the contracted obligations. The Soviet organization-cooperative partner could establish direct contact with the foreign partner with the permission of the higher agency. Thus outlined, the relationship between Soviet agencies and organizations had an administrative, nonproperty character.

*In the second instance*, in the fulfillment of interagency agreements, Soviet organizations-cooperative partners concluded civil-law (economic) contracts with foreign partners from the CMEA member countries. Here, all activities of

---

3. *Svod zakonov SSSR*, Vol. 9, pp. 51–63.

Soviet organizations connected with these contracts had to receive authorization. The Soviet partner's obligations issuing from its contracts were included in the five- and one-year plans of development of the branch and in the plans of the Soviet organizations involved.

There were no substantial differences between the first and second variants of the realization of agreements on international scientific-technological cooperation, even though in the second variant it was not only the plan act but also the economic venture with the foreign partner that underlay the corresponding internal relationships. Even in the second variant, the relationship between the administrative agency and the organization-cooperative partner had an administrative character.

*In the third variant,* where cooperation was effected on the basis of contracts for scientific-technological projects (which was largely the province of the All-Union Association *"Vneshtekhnika"*), relations between Soviet organizations had a qualitatively different, indeed property, character. The aforementioned foreign trade association entered into economic agreements with organizations-cooperative partners in order to ensure fulfillment of the foreign economic obligations assumed by it. The organizations-cooperative partners usually entered into these contracts with *V/O "Vneshtekhnika"* as a function of their confirmed plans. Thus, a complex juridical category lay at the root of internal relationships in this variant of the realization of international scientific-technological cooperation: the plan act and the economic (civil-law) contract.

To this day there is no one normative act designed to regulate the relations between Soviet agencies and organizations in the negotiation, conclusion, and execution of contracts for scientific-technological and production cooperation.

Questions concerning cooperation with the CMEA member countries were largely resolved in the abovementioned Decree of 9 July 1981. It established which Soviet agencies and organizations had the right (and in what procedure) to effect scientific-technological and production cooperation with the corresponding agencies and organizations from the CMEA countries, in the process severely limiting the rights of ministries and departments, on the one hand, and enterprises on the other. It provided that state administrative agencies organize scientific-technological and production cooperation on the basis of the USSR's international treaties that were entered into by them and that were concluded in conformity with Decree No. 743 of the USSR Council of Ministers of 28 August 1980, "On the Procedures for Concluding, Executing, and Denouncing International Treaties of the USSR of an Interagency Character."[4] We should note that changes will probably be effected in this Decree in light of the adoption of the decrees of 19 August 1986.

As regards scientific-technological and production cooperation with capitalist and developing countries, up to the present there is no general normative act that

4. *Svod zakonov SSSR,* Vol. 9, pp. 20–22.

defines the authority of ministries and departments, as well as associations, enterprises, and organizations, and the procedures for concluding, ensuring execution, and executing such contracts and agreements. On the Soviet side, as we know, such agreements were made either by branch ministries or departments together with the Ministry of Foreign Trade, or jointly with foreign trade organizations, or only by the latter. Internal relationships—between the Soviet parties to foreign economic contracts for scientific-technological and production cooperation and the Soviet partner-organizations—were constructed on the basis of the USSR's international treaties, assignments under the plan, and in conformity with normative acts that established the procedures for delivery of products for export and the fulfillment of orders for imports.

## What is new in Soviet legislation

Joint Decrees No. 991 and 992 of the CPSU Central Committee and the USSR Council of Ministers of 19 August 1986 contain a series of overarching and important provisions on scientific-technological and production cooperation. These first of all concern cooperation with the socialist countries.

A series of specific provisions pertain to cooperation with all countries:

—associations and enterprises must include in their plans indicators characterizing the development of production cooperation (clause 15 of Decree No. 991). Consequently, with due regard to clause 4 of Decree No. 992, assignments on the development of production cooperation are not established by administratively superior agencies. Nevertheless, the relevant branches' plans of economic and social development must include the volumes of cooperative deliveries (clause 15 of Decree No. 991);

—all earnings from deliveries carried out within the framework of cooperation must be paid into the foreign-currency funds of associations, enterprises, and organizations (clause 21 of Decree No. 991).

Decree No. 991 extended to associations, enterprises, and organizations the right to establish direct ties with enterprises and organizations from other CMEA member countries in the interests of securing their active involvement in foreign economic operations. It also accorded them independent decision-making powers in questions involving scientific-technological and production cooperation, including the conclusion of economic (civil-law) contracts and contracts for the delivery of products and services connected with cooperation and the development of production, as well as [the authority] to determine the economic terms of cooperation (clause 11).

Decree No. 992 provides that associations, enterprises, and organizations have the independent authority:

—to determine the direction and specific goals of cooperation, to select the enterprises and organizations from CMEA member countries with whom it would be expedient to establish direct ties, and to coordinate with them lists and volumes of mutual deliveries connected with cooperation;

—to carry out mutual deliveries of cooperatively produced products, product models, tools, fittings, instruments, materials, and individual machines and equipment and to exchange the necessary services in connection with the realization of cooperation and with the development of production (including for joint enterprises in the USSR); to lease out and lease tools, machinery, and equipment; to place one-time orders for the manufacture and delivery of products to the USSR and to transfer for this the necessary material resources and technical documentation, and also to accept such orders;

—to carry out scientific research, design, and experimental projects with organizations from CMEA member countries, to establish joint collectives of specialists toward these ends, to exchange scientific-technological documentation—exclusive of discoveries, inventions, and "know-how"—on mutually agreed-upon terms, and to provide mutual assistance in the training of personnel (clause 9).

In order to achieve coordination of the general results of their economic operations with the results of their work involving direct ties, associations, enterprises, and organizations have the right (clause 10):

—to coordinate prices on component parts produced for cooperation, as well as on services provided. The prices on these products must be coordinated with the price on the final product; the latter must be determined in accordance with the existing principles of price formation in trade between CMEA member countries.

To ensure that associations, enterprises, and organizations maintain an interest in the development of economically effective cooperation, in enhancing the technical level and quality of the products, and in reducing production costs, foreign trade (contract) prices may be recalculated in internal prices using foreign-currency coefficients;

—to enter into economic agreements and contracts with cooperating enterprises and organizations on their own behalf. If there is a need for short-term exchange, they may conclude one-year contracts for an agreed-upon sum without spelling out the specific list of the agreed-upon products or the prices on them, agreeing only to settle accounts by the end of the year.

The only limitation on the volumes of imported goods and services may be the lack of the necessary foreign-currency funds and credit on the part of the association, enterprise, or organization;

—to leave all earnings from cooperative deliveries at the complete disposal of the work collectives, in transferable rubles. These earnings and remaining foreign-currency transfers from the sale of finished products and services are deposited into the foreign-currency fund of associations, enterprises, and organizations on terms determined by stable, long-term schedules, and they are not subject to withdrawal by higher-level agencies or limitation in their utilization.

Associations, enterprises, and organizations maintaining direct ties with enterprises and organizations of the CMEA member countries, are authorized (clause 11):

—to acquire on credit from the USSR Foreign Trade Bank* transferable rubles and [sums in] the national currencies of the countries of the socialist commonwealth for the purposes of conducting scientific-technological projects and developing effective production processes connected with cooperation;

—to use monies from their foreign-currency funds to purchase in CMEA member countries goods to meet the needs of their work collectives: industrial goods, medical equipment, and consumer, sporting, and other goods.

In compiling budgets and plans for the distribution of material resources, the USSR State Planning Committee and the State Committee for Material and Technical Supply may designate under a special target category part of the products imported from socialist countries, especially machinery, equipment, and materials, to be purchased with the existing foreign-currency funds of associations, enterprises, organizations, ministries, departments, and union-republic councils of ministers.

Pursuant to clause 12 of Decree No. 992, products manufactured under cooperation must be offered for sale in the USSR at wholesale or contract prices that reflect their technical level, consumer properties, and their utility.

Clause 18 provides that USSR branch ministries, departments, and union republics interact directly with the corresponding agencies of other CMEA member countries and enter with them into international bilateral or multilateral agreements of an interagency character. USSR ministries, departments, and union-republic councils of ministers submit proposals to the State Planning Committee for the export and import of products in agreement with the list included in the state plan of economic and social development.

Branch ministries and departments as well as union-republic councils of ministers are held responsible (clause 19) for the implementation of direct ties by their subordinate associations, enterprises, and organizations, and the former must create for them the requisite economic and organizational conditions for such implementation.

As for the legal regime regulating scientific-technological and production cooperation with capitalist and developing countries, with the exception of the abovementioned new provisions, it has not been supplemented as yet with new norms. Obviously, there is need for systematic and sufficiently detailed regulation of relations in this sphere, and in the future the necessary normative acts will in all likelihood be drafted.

We ought to emphasize, however, that the existing economic, organizational, and legal conditions do offer broad possibilities for developing and deepening mutually advantageous cooperation between Soviet organizations and firms from capitalist and developing countries.

---

*Editor's note*—Now the USSR Bank for Foreign Economic Relations.

We must recognize first and foremost that Decree No. 991 provides almost seventy associations, enterprises, and organizations of industry direct access to foreign markets. All suppliers of goods and services for export will have their own foreign-currency funds into which will flow earnings from cooperative deliveries. Higher agencies can neither remove these funds nor limit their utilization, and they will accumulate if their holders so wish. Delivery volumes under cooperation must be included in the plans of the relevant branches. Associations, enterprises, and organizations also have the right to acquire foreign-currency credits from the USSR Foreign Trade Bank.

From the Soviet side, enterprises, associations, and other organizations enjoying the rights of legal entities may become participants in scientific-technological and production cooperation. In addition, those industrial organizations enjoying direct access to foreign markets may themselves—directly, without intermediaries—enter into cooperative ventures with firms from capitalist countries. Those industrial organizations not having direct access may participate in cooperative foreign economic ventures jointly with foreign trade organizations.

Thus, in their general contours the key issues involved in cooperation with firms from capitalist and developing countries have already been resolved.

**Contracts of cooperation**

In laying the groundwork for and implementing scientific-technological and production cooperation, defining its content and terms, and making use of its results, an important role belongs to civil-law (economic) foreign economic contracts concluded by the associations, enterprises, and organizations involved. This is a widely known fact, and the attention accorded it derives from the fact that international agreements and Soviet legislation address only the most general questions involving cooperation between Soviet organizations and firms of capitalist and developing countries. Thus, these contracts must provide answers to a myriad of other concrete questions. As a rule, Soviet organizations address these questions in the preliminary stages of cooperation. Let us dwell on some of the general features of contracts of cooperation.

Prior to embarking upon cooperative ventures, Soviet organizations carefully study the issues, the resolution of which will determine the harmony of the cooperation and its effectiveness under favorable economic and legal conditions. This involves, in particular, gathering information on potential foreign partners attesting to their economic and financial situation, the scale of their operations in the market, the technical level of their production, etc., and it also involves careful study of the various forms of potential cooperation. In addition, questions concerning the objectives of cooperation are studied, including:

—production costs of goods and services that may be produced and provided under the terms of the cooperative venture, as compared with the products of potential competitors;

—the price on the cooperatively manufactured product;

—the market potential (particularly in the long term) of the cooperatively manufactured product;

Studies of these and other relevant questions address such variables as the economic situation and the legal regime governing foreign economic activity in the relevant countries, the regime there governing cooperative ventures (including privileges granted to partners and the potential influence of customs and tax rates and regulations), international treaties and trade and political conditions, and any limitations and obstacles.

In approaching these questions, Soviet organizations that are potential participants in cooperative production must in principle assure the certainty of foreign-currency balance in the reciprocal deliveries covered by the venture. This derives from the importance of maintaining for the USSR a normal balance of payments.

After studying the questions of potential scientific-technological and production cooperation, the Soviet agencies and organizations involved enter into negotiations with the firms that they have targeted as desired partners in cooperation, they obtain the approval of the competent state agencies, if necessary, for one or another aspect of the future venture, and, finally, they sign the contracts of cooperation. Often, the adoption of letters of intent and/or protocols of understanding on cooperation will precede the conclusion of contracts.

In concluding contracts calling for cooperative production, particular attention is paid to questions of quality and standardization, prices, financing and marketing of the cooperatively manufactured product; customs and taxes; the duration obligations will remain in force; confidentiality, etc.

The contracts normally define the general parameters for the manufacture of products and components under the terms of the cooperative venture; the determinant factors in achieving quality of the products and components (available technology, blueprints, specifications, specimens, international and/or national standards, etc.); methods for quality control and product classification; and questions pertaining to trademark utilization. In addition, the contracts usually obligate the parties to improve constantly on the technical level and quality of the cooperatively manufactured product using the latest advances in science and technology and world experience in the manufacture of the given type of product.

Of course, the effectiveness of cooperation in large measure depends on the price that is set on the cooperatively manufactured product and its elements and components. Prices are usually set down in the contracts; many contracts, however, contain not prices but the principles, time periods, and procedures for their formulation, with due regard to the specific features of the ventures and the long-term character of the cooperation. In taking note of the general approach to this question, it should be recognized that Soviet organizations may independently come to understandings on price with their partners. They take into consideration prices on analogous products as well as competition in the market, making use of data contained mostly in price lists, proposals, and contracts of third-party firms.

It is important to secure contract prices that accord with prices in the world market for analoguous products, inasmuch as the principle of using "world market prices" as a benchmark is strongly emphasized in many of the USSR's international treaties, it is a prerequisite for the cost-accounting operations of Soviet organizations, and it is one the elements of economic policy in this area.

Two crucial questions are locating sources of financing and credit for cooperative ventures, and determining the methods of receiving payments and the procedures for settling accounts. To finance a venture, contracts may envisage, for example, the utilization of both the in-house capital of the partners (one or all) as well as loans, and it may provide for such forms of payment for received goods as deliveries of elements and components or of other, specialized products; cash payments; or deliveries of goods toward the liquidation of loan debts.

In settling questions involving marketing in contracts of cooperation, Soviet organizations and their partners endeavor to coordinate marketing and risk strategies, volumes and time frames of deliveries, sales strategies, and terms for the provision of technical services.

Soviet organizations review the customs and tax regulations existing in partner and third countries, as well as existing international treaties in this area, in order to avoid unforeseen expenses that could have a powerful negative effect on the effectiveness of the entire venture.

An important feature of contracts providing for production cooperation is their long-term nature. The latter makes possible, and the interests of Soviet organizations may require, flexibility in resolving problems that likely will arise eventually in cooperative ventures. Such questions may involve the scientific-technological aspects of cooperation, conditions of production, prices, marketing, etc. At the same time, this is also attractive for Soviet organizations' partners in cooperation, inasmuch as it allows them to plan the scale of their production capacities, to finance research and other projects, to expand projected sales volumes, etc. To make possible a flexible approach toward the resolution of issues arising in cooperative ventures, the contracts normally provide for conditions for changes in individual obligations and for the holding of talks on a regular basis involving questions of interest to one or both sides.

Soviet organizations strive to ensure the confidentiality of any of their operations and information that, if revealed, could impair the operations or otherwise have a deleterious effect on their partners or on the situation in the market. This is all the more important if we are talking about cooperative ventures. Preparation for and realization of such ventures necessarily involve the exchange of technical and commercial information by the partners. Therefore, questions of confidentiality are given particular attention in the contracts, and even in the preliminary obligations.

As for the terms that Soviet organizations apply to contracts of cooperation, one [recent] document will suffice to characterize them: Recommendations for Conditions of Agreement for Production Cooperation between Soviet Organizations and Finnish Companies, which were drawn up in 1984 under the auspices of the Standing Soviet-Finnish Intergovernmental Commission on Economic Cooperation.[5] While this document formally relates to production cooperation in Soviet-Finnish economic relations, the terms recommended in it contain no fundamental differences from the practice regarding contracts for production cooperation with firms from other capitalist countries. Certainly, it also contains specific provisions [germane to Soviet-Finnish economic relations]. On the whole, however, the aforementioned Recommendations can serve as a source of information on the present-day contractual practices of Soviet organizations in many areas of production cooperation.

5. See P. S. Smirnov, "Dogovor proizvodstvennoi kooperatsii" [The production cooperation agreement], in the compendium *Materialy sektsii prava* [Materials on aspects of law], vol. 37, Moscow: USSR Chamber of Commerce and Industry, 1986, pp. 14–24.

# 10

# JOINT ENTERPRISES ON THE TERRITORY OF THE USSR

Joint enterprises (hereinafter JEs) represent a form of economic, industrial, and scientific-technological relations between organizations and firms of different countries, and the USSR, too, employs this form in its foreign economic operations. Thus, Soviet organizations have participated in JEs since the 1920s, primarily in the shape of trading companies established in a number of capitalist and developing countries; in the 1960s and 1970s, the number of such companies grew and their range of activities broadened to some extent. During the period of the New Economic Policy and up until the 1930s, several joint-stock companies operated in the USSR that were partially constituted with foreign capital.[1] Therefore, we are not referring, in the strict sense of the word, to the utilization of a thoroughly new form, but to reactivating and recreating the joint enterprise on the territory of the USSR and of significantly broadening its scope, in order to adapt it to a radically altered political and economic landscape. Naturally, the use of JEs has other goals today as well.

It is a known fact that prior to 1983, the necessary legal preconditions did not exist in the USSR for the creation of JEs. It should be mentioned in this regard that the CMEA sponsored studies in the first half of the 1970s, the goal of which was to determine the legal foundations for creating joint ventures involving

---

1. See N. N. Voznesenskaia, ''Pravovye formy sovmestnogo predprinimatel'stva i praktika SSSR'' [Legal forms of joint ventures and the USSR practice], *Sovetskoe gosudarstvo i pravo* [Soviet state and law] 1985, No. 3, pp. 59–66; N. V. Mironov, ''Pravovoi status sovmestnykh khoziaistvennykh organizatsii stran-chlenov SEV na territorii SSSR'' [The legal status of joint economic organizations of CMEA member countries on the territory of the USSR], *Sovetskoe gosudarstvo i pravo* 1985, No. 3, pp. 45–51; *Pravovye formy nauchno-tekhnicheskogo i promyshlenno-ekonomicheskogo sotrudnichestva SSSR s kapitalisticheskimi stranami* [Legal forms of scientific-technological and industrial cooperation between the USSR and capitalist countries], edited by M. M. Boguslavsky, Moscow 1980, pp. 19–24, 200–207, 227–277.

organizations from the CMEA member countries; this led to the adoption by the CMEA Executive Committee on 16 January 1976 of the Uniform Statutes on the Establishment and Activity of International Economic Organizations.[2] Problems related to international economic organizations (hereinafter IEOs) became the subject of intensive theoretical research.[3] Yet, not one such organization came into being in the Soviet Union. As for the socialist countries, on the other hand, the great majority (Bulgaria, Hungary, China, North Korea, Cuba, Poland, Romania, Czechoslovakia, and Yugoslavia) already have legislation on the books dealing with JEs and to varying extents are already making use of this form of cooperation.[4] Soviet specialists have noted that economists from the socialist countries hold this form of cooperation to have promise.[5]

Even before the first international associations were created in the USSR, the literature on IEOs operating in CMEA member countries pointed out that the employment of this form of economic ties represents quite a new problem that raises a host of complicated and less than clear-cut issues for theory and practice. By their nature, these issues are as much legal as they are economic. Without finding correct solutions to them, the successful functioning, indeed the very establishment and development of IEOs, will be impossible.[6] This applies in full measure to JEs, including those involving firms from capitalist and developing countries.

The reactions of the foreign media have been quite diverse toward the USSR's decision to adopt such a complicated, sometimes termed highest, form of cooperation as the joint enterprise [formed] on USSR territory. We should note that almost everyone who has addressed this issue has stressed the need for coming up with a legal regime to govern the creation and operations of JEs, and that the outstanding questions are quite numerous.

An important step toward laying the legal foundations for the establishment and operation of JEs in the USSR was the adoption, on 13 January 1987, of a series of normative acts. These resolved a whole group of fundamental questions

---

2. *Osnovnye dokumenty Soveta Ekonomicheskoi Vzaimopomoshchi* [Basic documents of the Council for Mutual Economic Assistance], Vol. 2, Moscow 1983, pp. 227–277.

3. See, for example, I. A. Gringol'ts, "Mezhdunarodnye khoziaistvennye organiza-tsii v stranakh-chlenakh SEV (teoriia i praktika pravovogo regulirovaniia)" [International economic organizations in CMEA member countries (theory and practice of legal regula-tion)], Author's dissertation submitted in fulfillment of requirements for the degree of Doctor of Juridical Sciences, Moscow 1977; *Pravovye formy organizatsii sovmestnykh proizvodstv stran-chlenov SEV* [Legal forms of the organization of joint production in-volving CMEA member countries], edited by E. T. Usenko, Moscow 1985.

4. Data on the basic legislative provisions of the European socialist countries. See *Documents of the United Nations Joint Economic Commission—Trade/G.E. 1/R. 37,* 4 July 1986.

5. *Moskovskie novosti* [Moscow news] 1987, No. 3, p. 7.

6. See E. T. Usenko, ed., *Pravovye formy organizatsii sovmestnykh proiz-vodstv*, pp. 4–5.

related to JEs. We will summarize the provisions of these acts below, and we will comment on some of them. Since JEs consisting of Soviet organizations and firms from all different countries enjoy a host of common features, we will focus our attention here on JEs bringing together Soviet organizations and firms from capitalist and developing countries. We will also illuminate the primary differences between such JEs and those formed with organizations from CMEA member countries as well as international associations and organizations.

**Sources for the legal regime***

The norms covering JEs are contained in the Edict of the Presidium of the USSR Supreme Soviet of 13 January 1987, "On Questions Relating to the Creation and Activity on USSR Territory of Joint Enterprises, International Associations and Organizations Involving Soviet and Foreign Organizations, Firms, and Administrative Agencies" (hereinafter, the Edict of 1987). This Edict is a relatively short document, consisting only of five items.

Published along with the Edict on the same date were two rather voluminous decrees of the Council of Ministers: No. 48, "On Procedures Governing the Creation and Operation on the Territory of the USSR of Joint Enterprises, International Associations and Organizations of the USSR and Other CMEA Member Countries," and No. 49, "On Procedures Governing the Creation and Operation on the Territory of the USSR of Joint Enterprises Involving Soviet Organizations and Firms from Capitalist and Developing Countries" (hereinafter, Decrees No. 48 and 49, respectively).

Decree No. 48 issued from the relevant provisions of Decree No. 992 of the CPSU Central Committee and the USSR Council of Ministers of 19 August 1986, "On Measures to Improve the Management of Economic and Scientific-Technological Cooperation with the Socialist Countries" (clauses 14–17).

In addition, on a number of issues the Edict of 1987 and both decrees refer to other normative acts: the Statute on Exaction of Overdue Taxes and Nontax Payments, Approved by Edict of the Presidium of the USSR Supreme Soviet on 26 January 1981[7]; the Law of the USSR of 30 November 1979, "On State Arbitration in the USSR"[8]; and the Edict of the Presidium of the USSR of 12 May 1978, "On the Payment of Income Tax by Foreign Juridical and Physical Persons."[9] Substantial changes and additions to these Decrees are contained in Decree No. 1074 of the USSR Council of Ministers of 17 September 1987, "On Additional Measures for Improving Foreign Economic Operations Under the New Conditions of Management."

---

*Editor's note*—The complete texts of the most important Soviet legislation on joint ventures are reproduced below in English translation, in Appendices IV, V, and VII.

7. *Vedomosti Verkhovnogo Soveta SSSR* 1981, No. 5, item 122.
8. *Vedomosti Verkhovnogo Soveta SSSR* 1979, No. 49, item 844.
9. *Vedomosti Verkhovnogo Soveta SSSR* 1978, No. 20, item 313.

We should note that another edict also remains in force, that of the Presidium of the USSR Supreme Soviet of 26 May 1983, "On Operating Procedures of Joint Economic Organizations of the USSR and Other CMEA Member Countries Existing on USSR Territory"[10] (hereinafter, the Edict of 1983).

In addition to all this, on a number of questions Decrees No. 48 and 49 stipulate adoption of special legal acts, which issue from the following:

—pursuant to clause 31 of Decree No. 48 and clause 34 of Decree No. 49, construction projects for JE sites are subject, prior to their confirmation, to approval according to the procedures established by the USSR State Construction Committee;

—pursuant to clause 23 of Decree No. 48 and clause 45 of Decree No. 49, the USSR Ministry of Finance together with the Central Statistical Administration of the USSR Council of Ministers* confirm the forms of operational, bookkeeping, and statistical accounting and accountability of JEs;

—pursuant to clause 48 of Decree No. 49, the USSR State Committee for Labor and Social Problems and the All-Union Central Council of Trade Unions are empowered to determine the specific features of application of Soviet legislation on social insurance to foreign citizens employed by JEs;

—pursuant to clause 50 of Decree No. 48 and clause 43 of Decree No. 49, the USSR Ministry of Finance is empowered to issue directives on the taxation of JEs;

—pursuant to clause 64 of Decree No. 48, the State Foreign Economic Commission of the USSR Council of Ministers has the right to determine the specific features of the application of this Decree to the creation on the territory of the USSR of JEs, international associations and organizations involving non-CMEA socialist countries.

Apparently, however, special normative acts will be adopted not only on the above-mentioned questions dealing with JEs, but on a number of others as well, even though this is not provided for expressly and does not follow from Decrees No. 48 and 49. Thus, some individual provisions of these decrees will probably require clarification and greater detail, and the actual creation and activity of JEs will reveal gaps in the legal regime. In time, the exigencies of the USSR's foreign economic relations as embodied in JEs may lead to the formation of an extensive, developed, and complex system of legal norms which will include sources of diverse levels of legal norms, the basis for which, at the contemporary stage, has been established by the Edict of 1983. The first act, the adoption of which did not issue from the provisions of Decrees No. 48 and 49 but from practical considerations, is Directive No. 34 of the USSR Ministry of Finance of 12 February 1987, "On the Procedures for Registration of Joint Enterprises, International

---

10. *Vedomosti Verkhovnogo Soveta SSSR* 1983, No. 22, item 330.

*Editor's note*—Now the USSR State Committee for Statistics (*Goskomstat*), created in August 1987. (Its Statute can be found in *SP SSSR* 1987, No. 29, item 101.)

Associations and Organizations Created on the Territory of the USSR and Involving Soviet and Foreign Organizations, Firms, and Administrative Agencies.''

The USSR's international treaties can become important sources for the legal
regime of JEs. Decrees No. 48 and 49 (clauses 3 and 1, respectively) provide that
the operations of JEs are governed by all-union and union-republic legislation,
and that the procedure for the withdrawal of funds is established by the USSR's
interstate and intergovernmental agreements. JEs formed from Soviet organizations and organizations of other CMEA countries in principle should be constituted by international treaties of the USSR or at least on their basis. The experience
of legal regulation of JEs in other countries suggests that international treaties
may have to be concluded in the future on, for example, the question of mutual
protection of investments. We should point out that already now the possibility of
coordinating legal norms on the basis of interstate or intergovernmental agreements has been expressly provided for on specific questions concerning JEs.
Thus, clause 22 of Decree No. 48 provides that the USSR Ministry of Finance
determines the procedures and conditions for the recalculation of foreign currency involved in JE operations with the concurrence of the competent agencies of
the interested (socialist) countries.

By 13 January 1987, intergovernmental agreements on the creation and basic
operating principles of joint enterprises, international associations and organizations had been signed with Bulgaria (4 November 1986), Hungary (4 November
1986), the GDR (17 December 1986), Poland (15 October 1986), and Czechoslovakia (4 November 1986).

Of course, not only the norms contained in the USSR's international treaties
will be extended to JEs in the established procedure, but also the aforementioned
normative acts as well as those that are or may be planned for adoption in the
future. In view of the fact that, in areas not covered by the USSR's international
treaties or by special norms, the JEs will be legal entities under Soviet law, the
general norms of Soviet law will beyond any doubt apply to them as they apply to
all other legal entities. In some areas indicated in Decrees No. 48 and 49, norms
that extend only to individual categories of legal entities under Soviet law will
also apply to JEs.

### Goals of creation and spheres of operation

Consonant with the preamble to Decree No. 49, the general goals leading to the
creation of JEs should be considered the progressive development of trade,
economic, and scientific-technological cooperation between the USSR and capitalist and developing states on a stable and mutually advantageous foundation.

Decree No. 49 spells out the goals of Soviet ministries, departments, and state
committees. In creating JEs, they must posit their goals to be securing the fuller
satisfaction of the nation's needs for certain types of industrial products, raw
materials, and food products; acquiring for the Soviet economy advanced foreign

machinery and technology, managerial know-how, and additional material and financial resources; developing the nation's export base; and reducing the number of ineffective imports (clause 3). Clearly, the specific situations will determine which goal will have the greater or lesser importance, which will be at the forefront and which will play the secondary role. There may, moreover, be other goals, for example: expanding the supply of goods for export, more fully saturating the domestic market with different types of services and making them available to foreign organizations and firms, consistently renovating the equipment and technology used in manufacturing specific products with the goal of securing the growth of production efficiency, etc.

Decree No. 49 does not directly define the goals of the participants in JEs. That it does not do this for foreign firms is entirely natural. Without a doubt, however, the latter's goals at the least should not run counter to the goals ascribed to JEs in the general plan for Soviet ministries, departments, and state committees, nor should they run counter to the USSR's legal order. As regards the goals of Soviet organizations, one should think that they must coincide fully with the tasks in this area assigned to the state administrative agencies to which the given organizations are subordinate. Moreover, Soviet organizations must have a direct interest in participating in specific JEs. It is no accident that Decree No. 49 establishes a procedure for examining the feasibility of creating JEs in which the initiative for submitting specific proposals must belong to the Soviet organizations.

Decree No. 49 does not directly identify in which branches of the economy JEs may be constituted and may operate. At the same time, it should be noted that this Decree places no limits on them, either. The Edict of 1983 (clause 1), which applies to JEs involving Soviet organizations and organizations of other CMEA member countries, provides an exhaustive and quite broad list of activities permitted to JEs. In light of the above as well as of the provisions of the Edict of 1987 and Decree No. 48, we can posit that even though Decree No. 49 contains no concrete provision on this question, JEs involving Soviet organizations and firms from capitalist and developing countries may be established and operated in all areas of the economy. Required are the presence of interest on the part of all prospective participants and the mutually advantageous nature of the cooperation.

### Participants

Decree No. 49 extends to all Soviet enterprises, associations, and other organizations that are legal entities, the right to participate in JEs, regardless of whether or not they may directly carry on foreign economic operations, including export-import operations (clause 4).

One or more Soviet organizations may take part in a JE. There may also be one or more foreign participants, but they must have the status of a legal entity.

Decree No. 49 does not specify the types of organizations (in their nature and spheres of operations) that are more preferable or appropriate for participation in JEs. In view of the overall goals of JEs and judging from the experience of other countries, we can say that JEs should take in not only production enterprises and associations, but it would be helpful also to include organizations specializing in scientific research, experimental-design, drafting, and technological work, or organizations containing such subdivisions, as well as trade organizations that are sufficiently experienced in operating in foreign markets, that maintain the necessary channels to sell the manufactured products and services, and that are skilled in providing marketing and technical support for the products offered by them. Such organizations may be Soviet or foreign participants in JEs, or may come from both sides.

Taking note of the fact that in the literature, ministries, departments, and state committees are considered to have the characteristics of legal entities,[11] the question arises as to whether they can also be participants in JEs. While Decree No. 49 does not expressly answer this, we can assume that they are not authorized to participate in JEs. We ought, nevertheless, to recognize here that by contrast Decree No. 48 does expressly assume the right of ministries, departments, and state committees to become participants in JEs. This provision was probably included to provide for the possibility of participation at equal level in a JE in the event a CMEA member country expressed the wish to carry out cooperation within the JE directly on behalf of an administrative agency. Decree No. 48 essentially takes into account a possible variant for resolution of the given question in the CMEA member countries. We should note that the literature generally takes a negative view on the possibility of direct participation of administrative agencies in JEs.[12]

While Decree No. 49 established the procedures for the transfer of participants' shares in JE charter capital to third parties, the question of whether or not any sort of formality should be observed in taking on a new partner in a JE remains open. In our opinion, the nature of the procedure by authorization for the creation of JEs demands, if not the approval of the Council of Ministers, then [at least] the sanction of the State Foreign Economic Commission for expanding the number of participants in any JE.

---

11. *Sovetskoe grazhdanskogo pravo* [Soviet civil law], Vol. 1, edited by V. P. Gribanov and S. M. Korneev, Moscow 1979, p. 157.

12. See Z. A. Tkach, "Sovmestnye khoziaistvennye organizatsii stran SEV: poriadok uchrezhdeniia i deiatel'nosti" [Joint economic organizations involving CMEA countries: procedures for establishment and operations], *Trudy VNIISZ* [Papers of the All-Union Scientific Research Institute for Soviet Legislation] 26: *Problemy sovershenstvovaniia sovetskogo zakonodatel'stva* [Problems in improving Soviet legislation], Moscow 1983, pp. 164–165.

## Creation of JEs

Soviet organizations interested in setting up JEs must submit their proposals for such, along with the technical and economic documentation and draft articles of incorporation, to their administratively superior ministries, departments, and state committees (clause 2 of Decree No. 49).

These administrative agencies review submitted proposals along with the State Planning Committee, the Ministry of Finance, and other state agencies. In so doing, they must act in conformity, in particular, with the Statute on the Procedures for Establishing, Reorganizing, and Liquidating Enterprises, Associations, Organizations, and Establishments, confirmed by Decree No. 816 of the USSR Council of Ministers of 2 September 1982.[13]

Among the ministries, departments, and state committees having an interest in JEs is, without a doubt, the Ministry of Foreign Trade, one of the chief responsibilities of which, moreover, is to assist the operation of JEs (see clause 2 of the Statute of this Ministry).

In practice, the creation of a JE—or, more accurately, the execution of the necessary contracts by the participants—is in practice often preceded by the signing of so-called protocols, or understandings, or letters of intent. More often than not, these documents merely establish the intent of the parties to create a JE in the future; they contain only organizational provisions and place no property obligations on the parties other than that of maintaining confidentiality. Sometimes they set time periods for the performance of specific activities of the parties and the time frame in which the intent to create the JE will remain in force.

Decree No. 49 sets out the authorization procedure for the creation of JEs. Its core is the condition that a legal entity may only come into being with the authorization of a competent body which verifies the legality and expediency of creating such an organization.[14] Decree No. 49 also established that authorization for the creation of JEs must come from the USSR Council of Ministers. But the Decree of 17 September 1987 provides that USSR ministries and departments and union-republic councils of ministers have the right independently to adopt decisions on the creation in the USSR of joint enterprises involving organizations and firms from all countries, including capitalist countries.

JEs will be established on the basis of the agreements signed by the participants. Since such agreements (along with JE charters) constitute articles of incorporation (clause 8), the drafts of which must be submitted to the appropriate agency in order to receive authorization, the question arises as to whether these may be merely the texts of agreements initialed by the prospective partners, or they must be formally signed contractual agreements that are to enter into force upon fulfillment of a specified condition (the Council of Ministers' positive

---

13. *Svod zakonov SSSR*, Vol. 5, pp. 379–383.
14. See *Sovetskoe grazhdanskoe pravo*, Vol. 1, p. 150.

decision concerning the creation of the JE). Obviously, only agreements signed by legally empowered persons may be submitted to an empowered agency, since only this variant will prevent the parties to JEs from pulling out of the transaction, and the agency will not review statements of intent that do not place obligations on the parties. Of course, in this variant, the agreement may provide for a specified period (for example, six months) within which the aforementioned condition must be fulfilled, and if authorization is not granted, then the parties may consider themselves freed from the obligation to establish the JE.

Every JE must have a charter, which is approved by the participants. In particular, the charter should define the goals and spheres of operation of the JE; its domicile, a list of participants, size of the charter capital and the procedures for its formation, the participants' shares in it, procedure for establishing the amount of yearly transfers of sums from profits into the reserve capital fund and for establishing a list of other funds, and the procedure for forming and spending these funds, if such questions were not addressed in the agreement creating the JE; the structure, staff, authority, and formation procedures of management bodies and of the auditing commission; decision-making procedures by JE management bodies, and questions the resolution of which requires the unanimous approval of the participants; the JE's procedures for reporting to its constituent partners on its operations; [required] elements of the content of collective agreements between the JE and its trade union organization; and circumstances and procedures of liquidation (clauses 7, 21, 30, 44, 47, 51). Clearly, the charter may be approved, or be considered to be as such by the participants, only after authorization for the creation of the JE is granted.

Among the questions that could and should be addressed in the articles of incorporation (besides those mentioned above), we ought to mention the following: the specific principles and valuation procedures for the participants' contributions to the JE charter capital, which naturally should accord with the principle ''based on contract prices, and with due regard to world market prices''; the dates by which the participants must pay in their contributions; the participants' liability for failing to make, or failing to make in full measure, the agreed-upon contributions; the overall and the exclusive powers of the JE board, frequency of board meetings and procedures for their convocation, decision-making and voting procedures, quorum, consequences of the failure to notify a participant of the date and place of a board meeting, the powers and tenure of the director general; the participants' obligation to assist the JE in its operations; and the right of the JE board to issue documents regulating intra-JE relations.

An agreement creating a JE could also stipulate that the Soviet participants assume the obligation of taking care of all the necessary formalities in the USSR for obtaining approval of the creation of the JE; that the parties will maintain confidentiality of information exchanged between them; and that each of the participants will separately (or proportionally to its share in the charter capital) cover expenses associated with the creation of the JE up to the time the agreement enters into force (or the JE is registered), and expenditures incurred thereafter will be covered by the JE.

A question of some importance is the right of the participants to introduce changes into the JE charter. The normative acts adopted on 13 January 1987 do not address this question directly. There is no doubt that the need to make changes may arise in practice. One possible solution would be to include in the text of the agreement creating the JE a clause providing for the right of the participants to introduce by mutual agreement necessary changes in the charter that would not affect the objectives and basic operational goals of the JE.

The normative acts only partially define the relation between the provisions of the agreement creating the JE and its charter, inasmuch as Decree No. 49 spelled out requirements only in regard to the content of the charter. Obviously, duplication of these documents would be harmful. At the same time, the charter could elaborate on the provisions included in the agreement. It would seem to be more expedient for the agreement to resolve the general questions and to define the mutual rights and obligations of the parties, while the charter dealt with the actual operations of the JE.

After authorization of the creation of the JE has been received and the articles of incorporation have entered into force, the latter must be registered with the Ministry of Finance. The JE's rights as a legal entity originate "from the moment" (obviously, the date) of registration. Notice of the creation of the JE must be published in the press (clause 9).

## The signing of transactions

Nothing is said in the operative normative acts governing JEs about the procedures that JEs must observe when signing foreign economic transactions on their own behalf. Mindful of the crucial importance this question holds, we should focus attention on Articles 14 and 125 of the Principles of Civil Legislation of the USSR and the Union Republics of 1961[15] and Decree No. 122 of the USSR Council of Ministers of 14 February 1978, "On Procedures for Signing Foreign Trade Transactions."[16] Importantly, a legal concept is lacking not only of what constitutes a foreign economic transaction but also a foreign trade transaction.[17] In practice the interpretations of the concepts of these transactions may vary widely, which to a certain extent is made inevitable by the differing approaches to this problem found in juridical literature.[18]

---

15. *Svod zakonov SSSR*, Vol. 2, pp. 6–42.

16. *Svod zakonov SSSR*, Vol. 9, p. 92.

17. In the literature, views have been expressed for quite sometime suggesting clarification of the group of transactions to which special procedures for the signing of foreign trade transactions could be applied. See V. S. Pozdniakov, *Sovetskoe gosudarstvo i vneshniaia torgovlia*, p. 103.

18. See V. A. Musin, *Mezhdunarodnye torgovye kontakty* [International commercial contacts], Leningrad 1986, pp. 5–16.

In view of the extremely grave consequences that would ensue from nonobservance, one would hope that JEs will observe the procedures provided for in Soviet legislation for signing foreign trade transactions, even if there is some doubt as to whether or not a specific transaction falls under the foreign trade category.

Having said this, there also arises the question as to whether or not the agreement to establish a JE itself should be considered a foreign trade transaction, and thus, whether the special procedures for signing foreign trade transactions should apply to it. The literature provides an affirmative answer to this question.[19]

## Legal status

JEs will constitute legal entities under Soviet legislation (legal entities in Soviet law). By inclusion of this provision, clause 6 of Decree No. 49 extends to JEs all the general provisions of Soviet civil legislation applying to legal entities (see, for example, Articles 11–13 of the Fundamental Principles of Civil Legislation of 1961, and also Articles 23, 26, and 29–31 of the Civil Code of the RSFSR). Some of these are simply reproduced in Decree No. 49 (see clauses 6, 15, and 19) while some others were tailored to apply specifically to JEs. Thus, clause 18 of Decree No. 49 allows for the creation by JEs of subsidiaries which, constituting legal entities in their own right, will not be liable for the obligations of JEs, just as the JEs will not be liable for those of their subsidiaries. By contrast, the general civil legislation does not expressly indicate whether or not the subsidiary is a legal entity (Article 31 of the Civil Code of the RSFSR, for example, provides that the subsidiary manager acts with power of attorney conferred by the relevant legal entity).

Decree No. 49 defines a number of important elements of the legal status of JEs differently than the civil legislation does for Soviet legal entities in general. For example, Article 13 of the Fundamental Principles of Civil Legislation of 1961 provides that a legal entity answers for its obligations with its property which, according to Soviet legislation, is subject to attachment. As we know, the latter normally does not and cannot apply to fixed assets, and working capital is subject to attachment only within reasonable limits. By contrast, the JE is liable with all its property for its obligations (clause 18 of Decree No. 49).

Moreover, Decree No. 49 resolved some questions bearing on the legal status of JEs that are not addressed in the general civil legislation. Thus, the Decree provides that the Soviet state and the parties to the JE are not liable for its obligations and that the JE, in turn, is not responsible for the obligations of the Soviet state and the parties (clause 18). To this we can add that being vested with

---

19. See M. M. Boguslavsky, ed., *Pravovye formy nauchno-tekhnicheskogo i promyshlenno-ekonomicheskogo sotrudnichestva*, p. 219.

the rights of a legal entity should exclude the JE from any liability for the obligations of other Soviet legal entities (state, cooperative, public, or any combination thereof), and *vice versa*.

The JE is unquestionably a new type of legal entity in Soviet law, the legal status of which possesses characteristic features definitely its own. Some of the JE's features are not found in any other legal entities (the presence of the foreign element), while in some areas the legal regime governing them has features common to all Soviet organizations (for example, in the carriage of cargo). In several areas, their legal regime is endowed with features utilized by Soviet state organizations (particularly in the areas of property rights and depreciation allowances). Other features are typical of Soviet nonstate organizations (particularly collective farms) and state organizations engaged in agricultural production (state farms), or in the discharge of specific activities (reference here is especially to the observance of the rule of mandatory property insurance of the JEs by USSR insurance agencies). Finally, in one important area, to JEs—this new type of legal entity in Soviet law—are extended norms that had earlier been intended to apply to foreign legal entities: the exaction from JEs of overdue taxes must occur in conformity with procedures established for foreign legal entities established by the Statute on the Exaction of Overdue Taxes and Other Nontax Payments, confirmed by Edict of the Presidium of the USSR Supreme Soviet on 26 January 1981 (clause 2 of the Edict of 1987).

Soviet law shall be the *lex corporationis* of the JE.[20]

**Enterprise name**

The normative acts adopted on 13 January 1987 contain no concrete provision on such an important matter as the names of JEs. Consequently, here must also be extended to JEs the relevant general norms: for example, Article 29 of the RSFSR Civil Code, as well as the Statute of the Firm, confirmed by the Joint Decree of the Central Executive Committee and the USSR Council of People's Commissars of 22 June 1927,[21] and the Statute on the Procedure for Naming and Renaming State Facilities of Union Subordination and Physical-Geographic Units, confirmed by Decree No. 914 of the USSR Council of Ministers of 29 November 1966.[22]

But a closer examination of the norms contained in these statutes shows that they can be applied to JEs only by analogy, with due regard to JEs' specific features. Thus, the norms governing the naming of legal entities follow the policy that the name of every organization should refer to the body under whose jurisdic-

---

20. See E. T. Usenko, ed., *Pravovye formy organizatsii sovmestnykh proizvodstv*, pp. 123–129.

21. *Sobranie Zakonov i Rasporiazhenii SSSR* [Collections of laws and decrees of the USSR] 1927, No. 40, pp. 394–395.

22. *Svod zakonov SSSR*, Vol. 1, pp. 407–413.

tion it operates. But while JEs will be legal entities, they will not fall under the jurisdiction of any ministry, department, or state committee.

In selecting a special name for a JE, it would be desirable in our opinion to ascertain beforehand the possibility of using it in the USSR and abroad as a tradename (service mark) of the JE. An important factor here is that in the USSR, trademarks and trade names may be used and enjoy legal protection only after they have been registered with the USSR State Committee for Inventions and Discoveries. But a corresponding search is required prior to registration. Conseqently, preparatory work undertaken in good time will allow for the choice of a well-sounding as well as protectable (as a trade name) special name for the JE (see the Statute on Trademarks of 1974, which was confirmed by the USSR State Committee for Inventions and Discoveries*).

## Assets

Each JE will have charter capital, in which the share of the Soviet participants must be at least 51 percent (clause 5 of Decree No. 49).

The charter capital is comprised of contributions from the JE participants, and it may be augmented from profits resulting from the JE's economic operations as well as from additional contributions (clause 10). Contributions may consist of buildings, structures, equipment, and other material valuables; rights to the use of land, water, and other natural resources, as well as buildings, structures, and equipment; other types of property rights, as well as rights to industrial and other intellectual property; or cash funds in both the currencies of the partner countries in the JE and in freely convertible currency (clause 11).

The contributions are calculated in rubles according to contract prices on the relevant types of assets with due regard to world market prices; contributions in foreign currency are recalculated in rubles according to the official exchange rate of the USSR State Bank existing on the day the agreement constituting the JE is signed, or on any other date agreed upon by the participants. In the absence of applicable world market prices, the value of the said assets is determined by agreement between the parties (clause 12). If the participants in a joint enterprise agree, their contributions to the reserve fund may be valued in both Soviet and in foreign currency.

In practice, questions may very well arise regarding the methods of valuating the rights to the use of land, water, and other natural resources, as well as of buildings, structures, and equipment. Operations involving the utilization of land, for example, in principle are of a very special nature. In this instance it would be well to refer to clause 28 of the aforementioned Uniform Statutes on

---

*Editor's note—This was amended to 11 June 1987 by decrees of the USSR State Committee for Inventions and Discoveries (most recently by Decree No. 6 [15]). The amended text is reproduced in Biulleten' Normativnykh Aktov Ministerstv i Vedomstv SSSR [Bulletin of normative acts of USSR ministries and departments] 1988, No. 1, pp. 11–20.

International Economic Organizations, which states that utilization rights may be valued by a capitalization of rents and/or incomes resulting from the use of natural resources during the term of operation of the agreement constituting the JE. A similar view has been expressed in the literature.[23]

As regards recalculation in rubles of foreign participants' contributions, Decree No. 49 does not prohibit the use of, for example, an average exchange rate over a specified period of time for the purpose of adjusting the real value of the contributed assets for any fluctuations in currency markets.

The assets of JEs must be insured by USSR insurance agencies (clause 14).

## Management

The participants in a JE must conduct its management on a joint basis. The adoption of decisions on certain issues—specified beforehand in the articles of incorporation—require a unanimous vote, while on others it requires an absolute or a simple majority of votes.

The participants will carry out the management of JEs through management boards. At the same time, the participants may reserve the right to resolve by themselves certain questions related to the operations of the JEs. In such cases, the boards will, if necessary, draft proposals and submit them to the participants for examination.

An extremely important issue here not addressed in the documents adopted on 13 January 1987 is that of the participation of employees of JEs in the management of their affairs. A rich source of legal norms on this question is the Law of the USSR of 17 June 1983, "On Work Collectives and Enhancing Their Role in the Management of Enterprises, Establishments, and Organizations."[24]

The highest body of a JE is its board, which consists of persons appointed by the participants (clause 21 of Decree No. 49). Obviously, the number of representatives each participant may appoint to the board of a JE should be proportional to its share in the charter capital, but this question may also be resolved at the discretion of the parties. Naturally, each of the participants is free to choose as its representatives whomever it desires. The only determining factors should be the goals of the JE's operations and the need to provide competent management of its affairs. Another question that remains open is whether staff appointments require the approval of all of the JE's participants.

The authority of the JE's board would likely extend to the following areas: defining the basic directions of the JE's activity in accordance with its goals; drafting documents to govern intra-JE relations; taking on new participants;

23. See N. V. Mironov, "Pravovoi status sovmestnykh khoziaistvennykh organizatsii," pp. 50–51; E. T. Usenko, ed., *Pravovye formy organizatsii sovmestnykh proizvodstv*, p. 132.

24. *Svod zakonov SSSR*, Vol. 1, p. 370-I-II.

defining the size and time periods for payment of monies owed to a withdrawing participant, with the agreement of the latter; setting up new bodies for the JE and defining their staffs and authorities; electing or appointing, and also recalling the general director and members of the auditing commission; confirming the JE's programs and reports on their implementation; determining the amounts, uses, and use procedures for the JE's finance capital; approving budgets, distributing funds acquired in the capacity of finance, and adopting decisions on coverage of the JE's losses; determining the total complement of personnel of the JE and approving the staff list, including salaries; taking decisions on the acquisition and sale of individual fixed assets and licenses; establishing and closing subsidiaries; introducing changes into the JE charter; appointing and dismissing members of the liquidation commission and approving the final report on the liquidation of the JE.

In determining the board's authority and the areas in which decisions do not require unanimous approval, the parties to the JE may reserve special guarantees in order to protect the rights of those participants who in a specific situation may comprise a minority.

Day-to-day management of the JE will be the responsibility of the executive board of directors [*direktsiia*], which is comprised of Soviet and foreign citizens. The chairman of the executive board and the general director of the JE must be Soviet citizens (clause 21).

As regards the general director, the parties to the JE might stipulate in the charter, for example, that he is accountable to the board for his activities, that he manages the day-to-day economic operations of the JE and ensures fulfillment of its program as well as of board decisions; prepares drafts of decisions to be submitted to the board; represents the JE externally; and appoints and dismisses JE employees. The general director must have the right to ask for and obtain from the participants the materials and information necessary to him.

The charter may also state that the auditing commission monitors the economic operations of the JE and is accountable for its activities to the board, to which it submits reports on audits carried out, as well as conclusions on the annual reports of the JE. Obviously, its members should not be staff employees of the JE. Nevertheless, the duration of the appointment and the size of the auditing commission should be defined, as well as its operating procedures.

**Personnel**

JEs must be staffed primarily by Soviet citizens (clause 47). The terms of remuneration of labor, work and rest schedules, and social insurance and social security for JE employees are determined by Soviet legislation, with the exception of questions related to wage remuneration and awarding of vacations and pensions to JE employees who are foreign citizens, which may be resolved in agreements between the JEs and these employees (clause 48).

The JE management is obliged to conclude collective contracts with the trade union organization created at the JE (clause 47).

Questions relating to the conclusion of collective contracts are covered, in particular, in chapter 2 of the 1970 Fundamental Principles of Labor Legislation of 1970 as amended,[25] as well as in the labor codes of the union republics, a number of decrees of the USSR Council of Ministers, and in the Statute on Procedures for Concluding Collective Contracts, which was confirmed by a Decree of the All-Union Central Council of Trade Unions and the USSR State Committee on Labor and Social Problems dating from 28 September 1984.[26]

On the whole, the rights of the enterprise's management and trade union committee in determining the content of the collective contract appear not to be circumscribed (see Article 7 of the Fundamental Principles of Labor Legislation, and also the Edict of the Presidium of the USSR Supreme Soviet of 27 September 1971, "On Confirmation of the Statute on the Rights of the Trade Union Committee of an Enterprise, Establishment, and Organization," and the Joint Decree No. 177 of the USSR Council of Ministers and the All-Union Central Council of Trade Unions of 6 March 1966, "On the Conclusion of Collective Contracts at Enterprises and in Organizations"[27]). Nevertheless, clause 47 of Decree No. 49 provides that the content of collective contracts arrived at between the management of a JE and its trade union organization is determined not only by Soviet legislation but also by the articles of incorporation. The question arises here, how does this item accord with the relevant articles in the labor codes of the union republics, which establish that the provisions of a collective contract must not run counter to labor legislation (see, for example, Article 8 of the RSFSR Labor Code)? Keeping in mind that authorization for the creation of the JE will come from the USSR Council of Ministers, the intent of clause 47 is to enable the participants in the JE to come to an agreement on provisions relating to labor that, while diverging from general norms approved by the USSR government or at the departmental level, nevertheless meet the requirements of the legislation. The authorizations issued by the Council of Ministers will constitute approval of those provisions in the articles of incorporation that relate to collective contracts, and will invest them with the necessary legal authority.

For questions relating to the residence and status of foreign citizens in the USSR, a matter of importance for future JE employees, we should refer to the Law of the USSR of 24 June 1981, "On the Legal Status of Foreign Citizens in the USSR," and Decree No. 433 of the USSR Council of Ministers of 10 May 1984, which confirmed the Residence Requirements for Foreign Citizens in the USSR.[28]

---

25. *Svod zakonov SSSR*, Vol. 2, pp. 184–213.

26. See *Kommentarii k zakonodatel'stvu o trude* [Commentary on labor legislation], Moscow 1986, pp. 14–23.

27. *Svod zakonov SSSR*, Vol. 1, pp. 347–354; Vol. 2, pp. 218–220.

28. *Svod zakonov SSSR*, Vol. 3, pp. 778–784; Vol. 10, pp. 329–336.

## Rights of the participants

Participants enjoy, in particular, the following rights:

—to transfer, under mutual agreement, either in full or in part its shares in the JE to third parties. In each individual case the State Foreign Economic Commission of the USSR Council of Ministers must authorize such a transfer. The Soviet partners have preferential right to acquire the shares of foreign partners (clause 16 of Decree No. 49). Of course, authorization for the transfer of shares is not required in the case of universal legal succession or if such a transfer is mandated by competent state agencies (addressed to participants that are state organizations). In such instances, obtaining the agreement of other participants is also not required. However, in instances where one of the participants undergoes reorganization, the other participants in the JE may demand a guarantee from it that the new participant will fulfill its obligations. It would be wise to include provisions on such questions in the articles of incorporation;

—to receive that part of the JE's profits remaining after deduction of sums to be transferred to the USSR state budget and sums earmarked for the creation and augmentation of the JE's capital, and that is distributed between the participants proportional to their shares in the charter capital (clause 31);

—to obtain data relating to the operations of the JE, the condition of its assets, and to its profits and losses (clause 44);

—to appeal to the JE board the decisions of the general director (even though this right is not expressly provided for in Decree No. 49).

The normative acts adopted on 13 January 1987 guarantee to foreign participants in a JE the right to reclaim their contributions in the event the JE is liquidated. In this connection, we should note that the value of the assets may exceed the size of the charter capital, since this will have been augmented with income from the JE's own economic activity. The participants in any JE unarguably have legal interests in all of its assets, and in the event of liquidation (or their withdrawal from it) the participants must have the right to claim not only their shares in the charter capital but also their proportionate shares in the total assets of the JE. Valuating the assets of the JE in the event of its liquidation (or the withdrawal of one of its participants) could be carried out on the basis of the same principles which guide the valuation of the contributions.

## Rights of joint enterprises

In addition to the rights extended by Soviet legislation to all legal entities, JEs have the right, in particular:

—to enjoy protection of their industrial property in conformity with Soviet legislation; this includes the acquisition in the USSR of both the inventors' certificates and of patents for the protection of the inventions of their personnel (clause 17 of Decree No. 49).

It is established that the articles of incorporation should set down the procedures for the transfer of industrial property rights to the JE from its participants and from the JE to the participants, and also for their commercial use and protection abroad. Obviously, questions relating to the transfer by the participants of industrial property rights in the form of contributions to the charter capital, as well as to their utilization and protection, in principle can and should be resolved in the agreement to create the JE or (less realistically) in its charter. There will probably not be a need during the drafting of the articles of incorporation to address questions related to other forms of transferring industrial property. After the JE is constituted, the transfer of industrial property rights to it by its participants and by it to them will have to be effected, it would seem, as a foreign economic transaction, and with observance of the relevant requirements of Soviet law.

Regarding the protection and transfer abroad of technology belonging to the JE, including that belonging to its foreign participants, we should draw attention to Article 110 of the Fundamental Principles of Civil Legislation of 1961, which refer to transfer procedures established by the USSR Council of Minister[29];

—to enter into relations with central state administrative agencies of the USSR and the union republics through bodies administratively superior to the Soviet participants in the JE, and directly with local administrative agencies and other Soviet organizations (clause 22);

—to conduct export and import operations necessary to its economic activities independently or through Soviet foreign trade organizations, or through the marketing networks of the foreign participants in the JE (clause 24);

—to carry on correspondence and telegraph, teletype, and telephone communications with organizations of foreign countries (clause 24).

As we know, the civil-law and dispositive capacity of legal entities has a special, rather than a general, character (unlike that of other persons—Soviet citizens): while citizens may retain any rights and obligations that do not run counter to law, legal entities retain only those that accord with the established goals of their activity (Article 12 of the Fundamental Principles of Civil Legislation of 1961).

## Operating principles

The most important operating principles of JEs are cost accounting, self-recoupment of costs, and self-financing (clause 6 of Decree No. 49).

Along with this we should note that JEs will independently draft and confirm programs of their economic activities (clause 23). JEs must cover all their for-

29. See M. M. Boguslavsky, ed., *Pravovye formy nauchno-tekhnicheskogo i promyshlenno-ekonomicheskogo sotrudnichestva*, pp. 238–239, 246–247; *Mezhdunarodnaia peredacha tekhnologii: pravovoe regulirovanie*, edited by M. M. Boguslavsky, Moscow 1985, pp. 103–119.

eign-currency outlays, including payments of profits and other sums owed to participants and foreign specialists, from earnings resulting from the sale of their products (goods and/or services) in foreign markets (clause 25). Sales in foreign markets should be understood to mean the performance of transactions expressed in foreign currency or in special accounting units. The Soviet state does not guarantee JEs the sale of their products (clause 23).

It is important to keep in mind that several of the operating principles of JEs are intrinsic to all legal entities under Soviet legislation and are directly provided for by general provisions or those which follow from the Soviet legal system. Here are some of them: the observance of legality, the good-faith fulfillment of assumed obligations, and the implementation of operations by the most economic means.

In the conduct of export-import operations, JEs' operating principles can but coincide with those upon which Soviet foreign trade associations and organizations having direct access to foreign markets carry out similar operations. The latter principles can, in our opinion, be characterized in the following manner:

—relations between the relevant Soviet organizations and their foreign partners are based on the international treaties of the USSR and the applicable norms of law;

—in buying and selling goods and acquiring and providing services in foreign markets, Soviet organizations act in accordance with their plans and are guided by the generally recognized principle of nondiscrimination. Morover, any foreign economic transaction is based only on commercial considerations: price, quality, and availability of goods and services, sales potential, and shipping and other conditions;

—to organizations and firms of countries with whom the USSR maintains normal trade and economic relations on the basis of the most favored nation status, Soviet organizations strive to offer appropriate opportunities to participate in the conclusion and performance of export and import transactions for goods and services, in accordance with normal business practice.

JEs are guided in their operations by Soviet legislation, and exceptions thereto are established by the USSR's interstate and intergovernmental agreements (clause 1 of Decree No. 49).

## Regulations on economic activity

Decree No. 49 provides that deliveries of Soviet equipment, raw and other materials, component parts, fuel, energy, and other products to JEs, as well as the sale of their products in the USSR, are carried out, with payment in rubles, through Soviet foreign trade organizations at contract prices with due regard to world market prices (clause 26). The Decree of 17 September 1987 provides that, in coordination with Soviet enterprises and organizations, JEs determine the type of currency to be used in charging for the manufactured products and in paying for purchased goods, and it sets down the procedures JEs are to follow in selling their products in, and obtaining supplies of goods from, the Soviet market.

If a Soviet party to a JE is an organization having direct access to foreign markets, questions relating to supply of the JE with goods of Soviet origin and selling its products in the USSR may be resolved in the agreement to create the JE.

Preferably, the agreement should also set out the procedures for marketing the JE's products abroad; including, for example, delineating possible obligations of the Soviet and foreign participants.

Prior to their confirmation, construction drafts for JE facilities should be approved in the procedure established by the USSR State Construction Committee* (clause 34 of Decree No. 49).

JEs' cargo is carried in accordance with the procedures established for Soviet organizations (clause 35).

The funds of a JE must be held in its ruble and foreign-currency accounts in the USSR State Bank and the USSR Foreign Trade Bank, respectively. Monies deposited in the JE's bank account will earn interest: in foreign currency—based on world money market rates; and in rubles—under terms and in procedures determined by the USSR State Bank. Differences in exchange rates that affect JEs' foreign-currency accounts and their operations in foreign currency must be reflected in their balance sheet (clause 29).

JEs may obtain credit on commercial terms—in foreign currency, from the USSR Foreign Trade Bank or, with the approval of the latter, from foreign banks and companies; and in rubles, from the USSR State Bank or the USSR Foreign Trade Bank (clause 27). These Soviet banks have the right to verify that credits extended to JEs are used for their intended purpose and are repaid promptly and in full (clause 28).

Each JE will maintain a reserve fund and other funds essential to its operations and to the social development of its collective. Deductions from profits should be deposited in the reserve fund until the size of the fund reaches 25 percent of the charter capital of the JE (clause 30).

Decree No. 49 does not spell out the uses of the reserve fund. Consequently, this is a matter that should be decided upon by the participants in the JE. In this connection, we should note that the aforementioned Uniform Statutes on International Economic Organizations (para. 34) describe the reserve fund as a source from which the JE's losses can be covered from balances at the end of the financial year.

JEs make depreciation deductions in accordance with the directives applicable

---

*Editor's note—The USSR State Construction Committee is the name of the reorganized USSR State Committee for Construction Affairs (*Vedomosti SSSR* 1986, No. 35, item 730. The new Statute can be found in *SP SSSR* 1987, No. 3, item 15). The abbreviated name remains *Gosstroi*.

to Soviet state organizations, unless otherwise specified in the articles of incorporation (clause 33).

JEs must remit to the USSR state budget payments for its employees' state social insurance coverage as well as contributions to the pensions of Soviet employees, at the rates established for Soviet state organizations (clause 49).

## Taxation

JEs must pay a tax on profits, although they are exempt from paying taxes during the first two years after starting to declare a profit (clause 1 of the Edict of 1987).* In subsequent years JEs must pay a tax in the amount of 30 percent of the portion of profits remaining after payments have been made to the reserve fund and other funds earmarked for the development of production, science and technology (clause 36 of Decree No. 49). The Ministry of Finance has the right to reduce the amount of the tax or to exempt individual JEs altogether from tax payments (clause 1 of the Edict of 1987).

Unless otherwise specified by an international treaty of the USSR, the portion of profits due the foreign participant in a joint enterprise is assessed a tax in the amount of 20 percent upon transfer of the said profits abroad (clause 41 of Decree No. 49). It is a known fact that a number of international treaties signed by the USSR concerning issues of taxation provide for reduced tax rates on such incomes.[30]

Clause 2 of the Edict of 1987 and Decree No. 49 (clauses 37–40, 42) establish that JEs must pay a tax on income deriving from operations not only on the territory, continental shelf, or in the economic zone of the USSR, but also on the territory of other countries. These acts also determine procedures for computation and payment of both taxes and overpayment refunds, the liability for overdue tax payments, and procedures for exaction and for appealing the actions of financial agencies in exacting the tax.

Wages of foreign employees are subject to taxation in the procedures and amounts specified in the Edict of the Presidium of the USSR Supreme Soviet of 12 May 1978, "On Income Tax from Foreign Legal and Physical Persons" (clause 50).

---

*Editor's note—This passage in the authors' original manuscript read "during the first two years of their operations," reflecting the initial legislation of January 1987 governing the creation of joint enterprises with capitalist and developing countries (Appendix 4, clause 36). A subsequent Joint Decree of the CPSU Central Committee and the USSR Council of Ministers issued in September 1987 (Appendix IX) included a new condition for taxation, and the Editor has revised the wording in the present text accordingly.

30. See M. M. Boguslavsky, ed., *Pravovye formy nauchno-tekhnicheskogo i promyshlenno-ekonomicheskogo sotrudnichestva*, pp. 257–270; V. A. Kashin, *Mezhdunarodnye nalogovye soglasheniia* [International tax agreements], Moscow 1983, pp. 157–165.

## Oversight over operations

JEs must maintain operating, accounting, and statistical records in conformity with the procedures in effect in the USSR for Soviet state enterprises, and they will bear responsibility for observing the procedures governing the maintenance of records and reports and their accuracy (clause 45).

Clause 45 refers to "the procedures in effect in the USSR for Soviet state enterprises," and in this connection particular relevance attaches to Decree No. 633 of the USSR Council of Ministers of 29 June 1979, "On the Confirmation of the Statute on Accounting Reports and Balances."[31]

JEs may not provide reports or information to state or other agencies of foreign states (clause 45).

Supervision and audits of JEs' activities may be performed by the participants themselves, the auditing commission, or, for a fee, by a Soviet auditing organization operating on a cost-accounting basis (clauses 44, 46). Such an organization—*"Inaudit"*—was established in Moscow on 24 September 1987.

## Reorganization

Norms contained in the civil codes of the union republics provide the basis for legal regulation of the reorganization of legal entities at the statutory level. Pursuant to Article 37 of the RSFSR Civil Code, reorganization is one of two forms in which a legal entity is terminated, the other being liquidation. It is considered that reorganization is the termination of the legal entity without termination of its operations, the subject of the latter becomes another juristic person.[32]

The reorganization of legal entities entails, as we know, a universal legal succession. For example, the partners in a legal entity undergoing reorganization in this case retain the entire complement of civil-law rights and obligations. However, some changes take place on the other end of the corresponding obligations.

Reorganization is marked by a number of specific features that considerably set it apart from liquidation, and in some cases—reorganization of a legal entity with the preservation of its name, for example—it is rather tenuous to look upon it as a variety of termination of a legal entity. It should be noted that decrees of the Council of Ministers that deal with the status of different types of legal entities, including foreign trade organizations, usually treat reorganization differently from liquidation, and in any event they do not as a rule refer to reorganization as termination.

---

31. *Svod zakonov SSSR*, Vol. 5, pp. 292–307.

32. *Kommentarii k Grazhdanskomu kodeksu RSFSR* [Commentary on the Civil Code of the RSFSR], edited by S. N. Bratus' and O. N. Sadikov, Moscow 1982, p. 65.

Decree No. 49 contains one provision dealing with reorganization of JEs; this is included in Part II, "Participants, Assets, and Rights of Joint Enterprises" (clause 16). In addition, there is a Part VII in the Decree which deals exclusively with liquidation of JEs.

It is established that in the event of reorganization of a JE, its rights and obligations will be transferred to its legal successors. We should note that the RSFSR Civil Code distinguishes three varieties of reorganization: merger, partition, and annexation (Article 37). In the event of merger or division, the legal entity's assets (rights and obligations) are transferred to the newly constituted legal entities. In the event of annexation to another legal entity, its assets are transferred to the latter.

In view of the fact that reorganization of JEs and of other legal entities under Soviet law is governed only under the most general rules, and that the need to reorganize a JE, especially to partition it or divest it of part of its operations, may obviously arise in practice, the participants in JEs should give these questions special attention in drafting the articles of incorporation.

**Term of operation**

Decree No. 49 leaves the determination of this important issue to the decision of the participants in a JE, stipulating, however, that the term of operation must be expressly mentioned either in the agreement to create the JE or in its charter (clause 8).

Judging from its meaning and language, one can assume that clause 8 precludes the creation of a JE with an indefinite (unlimited) term of operation. While they must be specified, the terms of operation can vary widely, depending on the interests of the parties. The periods needed for recoupment of contributions to JE assets may serve as a point of reference in deciding on terms of operation (at least for approval of their minimum duration).

Determining the term of operation of a JE is of immense importance. In particular, none of the participants will have the right to withdraw from the JE prior to the expiration of the agreed-upon term, except in cases where the norms of applicable law allow for the unilateral termination of obligations.

The articles of incorporation, especially the agreement to create the JE, could establish the right of each party to early termination of its participation in the JE, spelling out the procedures for exercise of this right and the time period within which prior notice of withdrawal should be given. Among the grounds for early withdrawal that might be included in the agreement, the following hardly raise any argument: if a participant seriously and systematically violates its obligations to the other participants or to the JE, and also if its conduct of activities is detrimental to the interests of the JE. A period of time might also be agreed upon here, upon the expiration of which (after a warning following a violation) the other participants may withdraw from the JE if the participant does not cease the offending actions.

## Liquidation

The JE can be liquidated under the circumstances and according to the procedure specified in the articles of incorporation. It can also be liquidated by decision of the USSR Council of Ministers if its activities are in conflict with the objectives and tasks set forth in the articles of incorporation (clause 51 of Decree No. 49).

Among the grounds for liquidating a JE, its participants may include in the articles of incorporation, for example, the occurrence of unforeseen events constituting insurmountable obstacles to the JE's further operations (*force majeure*).

An announcement of the liquidation of a JE must be published in the press. The liquidation of a JE must also be registered with the Ministry of Finance (clause 51, 53).

The JE's charter could contain provisions regarding liquidation such as the following:

—for the purpose of liquidating the JE, the board (or the general director, if so empowered) must create a commission accountable to it;

—the JE board may dismiss or replace members of the liquidation commission at its discretion at any time;

—upon appointment of a commission, the legal powers of the general director (or his previous functions) are terminated. The commission exercises the rights of the general director, but only toward the goal of liquidating the JE. The commission is charged with winding up the current dealings of the JE, seeing, if possible, to the sale of its assets (to the participants, among others, if they are so inclined), and satisfying the demands of creditors. Upon conclusion of its work, the commission must submit a report to the board.

## Settlement of disagreements and disputes

The Edict of 1987 (clause 5) and Decree No. 49 (clause 20) provide that disputes arising between a JE and Soviet organizations, between a JE and another JE, and also between participants in a JE regarding its activities must be submitted to the courts of the USSR or, with the agreement of the parties, to an arbitration court. Thus, a mandatory judicial settlement of a whole group of potential disagreements and disputes relating to JEs has been established. The examination of disputes in a nonjudicial procedure is covered by the Statute of the Arbitration Court (Supplement No. 3 to the RSFSR Code of Civil Procedure of 1964), which provides the normative basis for establishing a body empowered to resolve disagreements and disputes between interested parties. This Statute, however, was intended principally to cover relations between citizens, and seemingly could be applied to relations involving JEs only by analogy.

There are two permanently sitting arbitration courts in the USSR, and both of them are charged (one exclusively) with examining disagreements and disputes arising from foreign economic relations. The Maritime Arbitration Commission of the USSR Chamber of Commerce and Industry, in accordance with its Statute, confirmed by Edict of the Presidium of the USSR on 9 October 1980, resolves civil-law disputes arising out of maritime commercial shipping.[33]

The other permanently operating arbitration court—the USSR Foreign Trade Abritration Commission of the USSR Chamber of Commerce and Industry—in accordance with its Statute, confirmed by Edict of the Presidium of the USSR Supreme Soviet on 16 April 1975,* may only resolve civil-law disputes arising between subjects of law from different countries in the course of realizing foreign trade and other international economic and scientific-technological ties.[34] In view of the fact that JEs will be legal entities under Soviet law, their disputes with Soviet organizations or among themselves cannot be submitted to the Foreign Trade Arbitration Commission. Disputes arising between participants in JEs regarding their operations may, obviously, be submitted, with the agreement of the parties, to this Arbitration Commission for resolution, if the interested parties desire not to have them examined in a court of the USSR or in another arbitration court on USSR territory.

There are no obstacles in the USSR to having disputes between JE participants examined in an *ad hoc* arbitration. Since, however, Soviet legislation presently contains no regulations on this form of foreign trade arbitration, such provisions must be included in the articles of incorporation or in some other form of written agreement between JE participants.

Neither the Edict of 1987 nor Decree No. 49 contain any reference to the resolution of disagreements and disputes arising between JEs and their foreign participants or with other foreign organizations and firms, nor do they refer to a body of law that is applicable to relations between participants in JEs, between JEs and their participants, and between JEs and other parties. Procedures followed on these questions should accord with the USSR's international treaties and Soviet legislation.

As to which body of law could, with the agreement of the parties, be applied to the agreement to create a JE, the view has been expressed in the literature that in its economic essence the JE represents a form of industrial, scientific-technological, and other economic cooperation, albeit a much more complex form, to be sure.[35] It has also been emphasized in the aforementioned Uniform Statutes on

---

*Editor's note*—The name of the USSR Foreign Trade Arbitration Commission has been changed to Arbitration Court, by Edict of the Presidium of the USSR Supreme Soviet of 14 December 1987, with simultaneous adoption of a new Statute (*Vedomosti Verkhovnogo Soveta SSSR* 1987, No. 50, item 806). According to clause 8 of the new Statute, new *Rules of Procedure (Replacement)* are to be approved for the new Arbitration Court by the Presidium of the USSR Chamber of Commerce and Industry. The name of the USSR Maritime Arbitration Commission of the USSR Chamber of Commerce and Industry remains unchanged.

33. *Svod zakonov SSSR*, Vol. 9, pp. 137–139.

34. *Svod zakonov SSSR*, Vol. 9, pp. 135–137.

35. See N. V. Mironov, "Pravovoi status sovmestnykh khoziaistvennykh organizatsii," p. 46.

the International Economic Organization (para. 89) and in the literature that a body of law different than that applied to the JE itself cannot be applied to the agreement to create the JE.[36] As we know, JEs constituted on the territory of the USSR will be legal entities under Soviet law. Soviet civil legislation has no provisions pertaining directly to the creation of JEs. Provisions dealing with agreements on joint activity, as those found, for example, in Articles 434–438 of the RSFSR Civil Code, might formally be extended here, but it should be kept in mind that these provisions naturally were not intended to govern relations arising with the creation of JEs involving foreign organizations and firms.[37]

## Privileges and guarantees

Decree No. 49 provides that in the event of liquidation of joint enterprises or withdrawal from them, foreign participants have the right to the return of their contributions in the form of cash or goods, on the basis of the residual value of their contributions at the time of withdrawal or liquidation, and after their obligations to the Soviet participants and third parties are repaid (clause 52). Naturally, obligations to the JE as well as to the Soviet state (for example, for taxes due) must also be repaid.

Moreover, the foreign participants in a JE are guaranteed the right to transfer abroad, in foreign currency, monies allotted to them in the distribution of profits from the operations of the JE (clause 32). The foreign employees of the JE may also transfer abroad and in foreign currency any unexpended wages (clause 50).

Any equipment, materials, or other property that foreign participants in a JE have shipped into the USSR as their contributions to charter capital are exempt from customs duties (clause 13).

The property rights of joint enterprises in the USSR enjoy protection in accordance with the provisions of Soviet legislation established for Soviet state organizations (clause 15). The property of JEs is not subject to requisition or confiscation by administrative procedure, and claims may be assessed against such property only by decision of the relevant court or arbitration court chosen or established by the parties, or in the procedure agreed upon by them (clauses 15 and 20). It should be noted that decisions of foreign courts or arbitration tribunals that have been applied in other countries can as a rule only be executed in the USSR in conformity with the USSR's international agreements. Property may be requisitioned, but only with compensation of the value of the said property (Article 31 of the Fundamental Principles of Civil Legislation of 1961[38]).

---

36. See E. T. Usenko, ed., *Pravovye formy organizatsii sovmestnykh proizvodstv*, p. 129.

37. M. G. Masevich, "Dogovor o sovmestnoi deiatel'nosti" [The joint venture contract], *Sovetskoe gosudarstvo i pravo*, Moscow 1979, No. 6, p. 135.

38. *Kommentarii k Grazhdanskomu kodeksu RSFSR*, pp. 188–189.

Construction and installation work to be performed for JEs by Soviet organizations, and the material resources needed for the construction of their facilities must be allocated to JEs on a priority basis (clause 34).

Land, its depths, waters, and forests may be made available to JEs both for a fee and free of charge (clause 4 of the Edict of 1987).

Of what importance is it to JEs that their property enjoys the same protection in the USSR that Soviet state organizations enjoy (see clause 15 of Decree No. 49)? Part of the answer can be found by referring to Article 153 of the RSFSR Civil Code, which establishes the unlimited claim of ownership to socialist property regardless of the good faith of the acquirer (see also Article 152 of the Civil Code), as well as to Article 90, which exempts from a period of limitation demands of state organizations for the return of state property on the grounds of its unlawful possession by nonstate organizations.

**Principal differences in the legal regime governing joint enterprises formed with firms from capitalist and developing countries from that governing joint enterprises formed with organizations from CMEA member countries**

Decree No. 48 (as it is stated in the preamble) was adopted with the goals of deepening socialist economic integration and binding more closely the scientific-technological and production potential of the countries of the socialist community. At the same time, Decree No. 49, as reads its preamble, was adopted with the goals of furthering the development of commercial, economic, and scientific-technological cooperation between the USSR and capitalist and developing countries on a stable and mutually advantageous basis. Herein we find expressed a difference not only in goals but in the already existing level of legal relations.

Decree No. 49 contains no direct references to a policy of utilizing JEs as a form of economic cooperation in relations with capitalist and developing countries. In contrast, Decree No. 48 (in clause 1) directs the standing agencies of the USSR Council of Ministers and ministries to mount broad efforts toward creating in the USSR JEs with the participation of organizations from CMEA member countries.

Both Decree No. 48 (clause 2) and the Edict of 1983 (clause 1) clearly identify the types of possible activities open to JEs and the economic spheres in which they may be constituted: production, scientific-production, scientific-technological, and other types of economic activity in industry, science, agriculture, construction, trade, transportation, and other spheres. No such delineation was provided for JEs formed with companies from capitalist and developing countries.

JEs formed with organizations from the CMEA member countries will be established on the basis of interstate or intergovernmental agreements concluded by the USSR. In cases provided for by international agreements concluded by the USSR at this level, a foundation for the establishment of JEs may be international agreements of an interdepartmental character or economic (civil-law) contracts (clause 3 of Decree No. 48 and the Edict of 1983.)

While JEs involving firms from capitalist and developing countries may be constituted by organizations and firms having the status of legal entities and that are not state administrative agencies, participants in JEs created on the territory of the USSR with organizations from CMEA member countries may, in necessary cases, be administrative agencies of the USSR and the CMEA member countries (clause 6).

The Edict of 1983 (clause 2) classifies the property of JEs as the common socialist property of the USSR and the relevant CMEA member countries (see also clauses 2 and 25 of Decree No. 48). Classifying the property belonging to JEs formed with Soviet state organizations and firms from capitalist and developing countries is a much more complex matter in the theoretical sense, and this is a question that remains open.

In JEs formed with organizations from CMEA member countries, the minimum share of the Soviet partner is not stipulated. Clause 27 of Decree No. 48 provides that the size of the participants' shares in the JE are defined in the articles of incorporation. It also establishes that the participants' contributions should be valued in rubles according to foreign trade prices that are determined on the basis of existing CMEA arrangements.

The general director of a JE formed with organizations from CMEA member countries must also be a citizen of the USSR (clause 16), while the nationality of the board chairman will be decided either in the international treaty concluded by the USSR or by the JE participants.

JEs formed with organizations from the CMEA member countries can obtain credit not only from such Soviet banks as the USSR State Bank and the USSR Foreign Trade Bank, but also from the USSR Bank for Financing Capital Investments. In obtaining credit, JEs must enjoy credit terms no less favorable than those extended to the relevant Soviet state organizations (clause 34 of Decree No. 48).

For this form of JE, material and technical supply and the sale of its products should be effected on a priority basis through the system of wholesale trade and through the supply network of the relevant branch of the USSR national economy, or through foreign trade organizations (clause 30). Herein it is established that products manufactured by a JE are distributed between its partners proportional to their shares in the charter capital or by mutual agreement (clause 36). Upon being included in the network of material and technical supply in the USSR, such JEs will acquire their supplies and sell their products in the USSR at wholesale or contract prices, and in being supplied through foreign trade organizations—at foreign trade prices (clause 30 of Decree No. 48).

Proportional to the participants' *pro rata* participation in the charter capital, the JE's earnings from the sale of its products may, by decision of its managing body, be distributed in freely convertible currency in amounts that exceed its current needs, provided compensation is made in transferable rubles (clause 39 of Decree No. 48).

Disputes arising between JEs formed with organizations from CMEA member countries and Soviet organizations, between such JEs themselves, and between their participants on questions having to do with JE operations, are submitted for examination not to courts of the USSR or to arbitration courts, with the agreement of the parties, but, as a rule, to state arbitration agencies of the USSR (clause 15).

## The principal features distinguishing international associations and joint organizations from joint enterprises

International associations are created for the purpose of coordinating the production, science-production, and other forms of economic activity carried out by their participants (clause 2 of Decree No. 48). While the right to conduct independent economic activity (clause 56) is not excluded, this function nevertheless is viewed as supplementary to coordination.

Joint organizations (scientific research, design, and others) are constituted with the intent of carrying out scientific research, design, and other types of activity in the interests of their participants (clause 2). Joint organizations thus differ from JEs in the type of activity they are engaged in. It should be noted that while the chief goal of international associations is coordination of their participants' activities, for both joint organizations as well as for JEs the primary goal is independent economic activity.

The specific features of the objectives and goals of the activity of international associations and joint organizations have likewise affected the manner in which some aspects of their status have been resolved (see, in particular, clauses 51–56 of Decree No. 48). Thus, the intent is that the principles underlying the creation of international associations will be preservation of national ownership of the property of the participants and conduct of their operations in accordance with the coordinated plans of the participants and the general plans of the relevant international associations (clause 2).[39]

---

39. See I. D. Ivanov, "Joint Ventures in the Soviet Union," *The CTC Reporter* 1987, No. 23, pp. 48–49.

# CONCLUSION

We have examined above the principal features of the new structure and management of foreign economic operations in the USSR. It should be kept in mind, and we hope this is clear from our discussion, that this new system is still in the formative stages. Joint Decrees No. 991 and 992 of the CPSU Central Committee and the USSR Council of Ministers, of 19 August 1986, have placed enormous tasks before the state administrative agencies and organizations engaged in foreign economic operations, and coping with these tasks will demand from them much effort and time. On a number of issues the groundwork has yet to be completed for the new normative acts.

In what directions should we expect to see the legal regime governing the foreign economic relations of the USSR develop? In this regard it would be well to keep in mind that restructuring foreign economic operations flows logically from the tasks of effecting radical changes in the entire economic mechanism of the USSR; indeed, it is a component part and a precondition to the success of the latter.

The Twenty-seventh Congress of the CPSU posited as strategic policy the acceleration of the nation's socioeconomic development, a policy that is oriented to the long term. What this means is that a goal has been formulated and an entire array of means have been identified with the help of which the posited goal may be achieved. The ultimate goal of the strategy of acceleration is the advancement of Soviet society to qualitatively new frontiers in all spheres of life: economic, social, political, and intellectual.

Such a new quality of growth assumes dynamism, qualitative reforms in the economy, structural reorganization, changes in the technical base of production, and the fostering of a special climate in the economy that is conducive to achieving progress in science and technology. These are the principal features of the strategy of acceleration.

The development of theory is a no less important task. In this sphere, such a situation should be created in which long-held assumptions cease to be viewed as eternal and immutable, not subject to the influence of a changing situation. It follows from the strategy of accelerating the USSR's socioeconomic development that general formulas and assumptions must be translated into the language of concrete policy and adapted to the practical tasks that lie ahead.

It is clear that the mechanism of management must be improved, not in fits and starts, but continuously, so as to preclude even the possibility that tendencies toward stagnation may arise. In this connection, the management mechanism will be constantly improved upon, and obsolescent forms that are obstructing movement forward will be shed and discarded.

What is the essence of the new mechanism? When we talk of restructuring, as in the radical restructuring of the economic mechanism, we have in mind the whole system, in its totality: planning, cost accounting, prices, credit, wholesale trade in the means of production, and much more.

The primary measure seized upon to achieve this following the 1987 Plenum of the CPSU Central Committee was the utilization of the wellspring of potential that is the human factor: creating conditions that foster the showing of initiative and enterprise, encouraging the desire to work, and enhancing the independence and responsibility of workers.

At the same time, one of the crucial links in the economic mechanism became a target of restructuring: the operating conditions of enterprises, associations, and other organizations. Prices, finance, and the activity of state administrative agencies were not affected at this stage. The main thrust was expanding the rights of enterprises and according them the possibility of independently deciding many questions while at the same time strengthening their economic responsibility for the quality and technical level of their manufactured products and for prompt fulfillment of their obligations. By and large, adoption of the Law of the USSR "On the State Enterprise (Association)" marked —from the legal point of view— the completion of this stage.

The second stage, much more radical than the first, should bring wholesale changes in the interrelations of enterprises, associations, and other organizations with the state budget and the agencies of state power and administration. This stage will see a reexamination of the tasks and functions of the USSR State Planning Committee and other supra-economic agencies, branch ministries, and industrial departments. And we should expect to see broad utilization of market levers of economic management (cost, price, finance, and credit), as opposed to the earlier almost exclusive use of administrative methods.

The agenda calls for comprehensive reform, the introduction of an integrated system, which naturally requires a certain amount of time. Restructuring does not involve attempts, scientifically futile, to find *the* one universal means to resolve the existing problems. Strengthening commodity-money relations is an important means, but it cannot be the only one. What is endeavored is an active, very flexible, mobile, and ever-searching policy, not a onetime palliative but a system of measures, a policy dictated by taking a new look at the reality of economic and political life. The upshot must be a new, rational economic regime that functions, in the ideal, on automatic pilot.

The changes wrought in the nation's foreign economic relations should be judged against the backdrop of just such an understanding of the nature of restructuring in the USSR. It must be clear that only the very first steps have been taken so far. A number of measures remain to be carried through, and the structure and management of foreign economic operations will be altered, clarified, and developed as a function of the restructuring of the entire economic mechanism. In particular, the legal regime governing the USSR's foreign economic relations must undergo improvement not only on the national level (where it remains to adopt a Law of the USSR on Foreign Economic Relations and a whole series of other normative acts), but also on the international level. Steps are already being undertaken to change the legal regime underlying bilateral relations with individual countries, and the USSR has advanced a series of proposals on upgrading cooperation within the CMEA. It is intended to normalize relations with clusters of individual states, for example, with the "Common Market." The USSR, as is known, participates in international trade on the basis of universally recognized principles and standards of international law, regulations, and customs existing in this sphere of international intercourse. Along with this, the USSR is endeavoring to play a role in the activities of organizations engaged in issues of international trade, such as GATT, for example.

As we know, the decisions adopted in August 1986, laying as they did the foundation for the wholesale restructuring of the USSR's foreign economic operations, generated a variety of reactions. We'll not dwell on these here or analyze the evaluations and judgments expressed. One could hardly expect that any changes would be interpreted uniformly, all the more so long-awaited changes of such enormous import. There will be difficulties and there will be successes. Time will arrange everything in its proper place. The main thing is to surmount any difficulties in good time, then success will be secured. The success sought after—this is the creation of a new structure and system of management for the USSR's foreign economic operations that has the capacity to cope with modern demands.

# APPENDICES

# I

# LAW OF THE UNION OF SOVIET SOCIALIST REPUBLICS ON THE STATE ENTERPRISE (ASSOCIATION)*

## 30 June 1987;
### Vedomosti Verkhovnogo Soveta SSSR 1987, No. 26, item 385

In accordance with the USSR Constitution, this law determines the economic and legal basis of the economic activity of socialist state enterprises (associations), strengthens state (public) ownership of the means of production in industry, construction, the agro-industrial complex and other branches, and expands opportunities for the participation of work collectives in the efficient use of this property, in the management of enterprises and associations, and in handling state and public affairs. The law deepens the principle of centralization in the accomplishment of the highly important task of the development of the national economy as a single whole, provides for the strengthening of economic methods of management, the use of full cost accounting and self-financing, the expansion of democratic principles and the development of self-management, and defines the relationship between enterprises (associations) and bodies of state power and administration.

## I. The enterprise (association) is the basic unit of the national economy

*Article 1. The State Enterprise (Association) and its tasks*

1. State enterprises (associations), along with cooperative enterprises, comprise the basic unit of the single national-economic complex. Enterprises (associations) play a principal role in the development of the country's economic poten-

---

*English translation © 1987 by Current Digest of the Soviet Press. "The Law on the State Enterprise," *Current Digest of the Soviet Press*, Vol. 39 (1987), Nos. 30–31. Printed with permission.

The *CDSP* translation originally included, in brackets, substantive passages that had been dropped from the earlier Draft Law. The Editor has deleted those passages here.

tial and in the achievement of the supreme goal of social production under socialism—the fullest possible satisfaction of people's growing material and spiritual requirements.

This law defines the principles of the organization and activity and the legal status of state enterprises and associations (hereinafter referred to as enterprises, except in instances that deal with the special features of associations).

2. At the state enterprise, the work collective, using public property as its proprietor, creates and augments the people's wealth and ensures the combination of the interests of society, the collective, and each worker. The enterprise is the socialist commodity producer; it produces and sells output, performs work and provides services in accordance with the plan and contracts and on the basis of full cost accounting, self-financing and self-management and the combination of centralized management and the independence of the enterprise.

The enterprise carries out its activity in industry, agriculture, construction, transportation, communications, science and scientific services, trade, material and technical supply, the service sphere and other branches of the national economy. Regardless of its particular specialty, the enterprise carries out the production of consumer goods and provides paid services to the population. It may conduct several types of activity (agro-industrial, industrial-and-trade, in-dustrial-and-construction, science-production* and others) simultaneously.

The enterprise is a juridical person, it enjoys the rights and performs the duties connected with its activity, and it possesses a specific part of public property and has its own balance sheet.

3. The enterprise's chief task is satisfying in every way the social require-ments of the national economy and of citizens for its output (work, services), which should have high consumer properties and be of high quality, and doing so with the smallest possible outlays, as well as increasing its contribution to the acceleration of the country's social and economic development and, on this basis, ensuring growth in the well-being of its collective and of its members.

The consumer's demands are binding on the enterprise, and their complete and timely satisfaction is the supreme meaning and norm of the activity of every work collective.

To carry out its chief task, the enterprise ensures:

the development and increased efficiency of production, its all-around intensi-fication, the acceleration of scientific-technological progress, growth in labor productivity, resource conservation, and an increase in profits (income);

the social development of the collective, the formation of an up-to-date materi-al base for the social sphere, the creation of favorable possibilities for highly productive labor, the consistent implementation of the principle of distribution

---

*Editor's note—In the original *CDSP* translation this term [*nauchno-proizvodstvennoe*] was rendered as ''research-and-production.'' It has been changed here and throughout this text in order to maintain consistency with the translation of the manuscript.

according to labor, social justice, and the protection and improvement of the human environment;

the self-management of the work collective, which creates for each worker a deep personal interest in the thrifty utilization of public property and his organic participation in the affairs of the collective and the state.

## Article 2. Principles of the enterprise's activity

1. The enterprise's activity is built on the basis of the state plan of economic and social development as a highly important instrument of implementing the economic policy of the Communist Party and the Soviet state. Guided by control figures, state orders, long-term scientifically substantiated economic normatives and ceilings, as well as customers' orders, the enterprise independently works out and confirms its own plans and concludes contracts.

2. The enterprise operates on the principles of full cost accounting and self-financing. The production and social activity of the enterprise and payment for labor are carried out using money earned by the work collective. The enterprise recovers its material outlays through receipts obtained from the sale of output (work, services). Profit or income is the generalizing index of the enterprise's economic activity. The enterprise must use part of the profit (income) to fulfill commitments to the budget, to banks and to the higher-level agency. The other part is left completely at its disposal and, together with money for the payment of labor, forms the collective's cost-accounting income and is the source of the enterprise's vital activity.

3. The enterprise's activity in conditions of full cost accounting and self-financing is carried out in accordance with the principle of socialist self-management. The work collective, as the full-fledged master of the enterprise, independently resolves all questions of production and social development. Achievements and losses in the enterprise's work have a direct effect on the level of the collective's cost-accounting income and on the well-being of each worker.

4. Enterprises operate in conditions of economic competition among themselves, a highly important form of socialist competition, for the fullest possible satisfaction of consumer demand for efficient, high-quality, and competitive output (work, services) with the smallest possible outlays. The enterprise, which ensures the production and sale of the best output (work, services) with the smallest possible costs, obtains a large cost-accounting income and an advantage in its production and social development and in pay for its employees.

The state uses planning and employs competitive designing and production, financial and credit levers and prices for the all-around development of economic competition among enterprises, while restricting their monopoly position as producers of a certain type of output (work, services).

5. The enterprise operates on the basis of socialist legality. In conditions of full cost accounting and self-financing, it is endowed with extensive rights the

observance of which is guaranteed by the state. In the interests of carrying out the tasks and exercising the powers established by this law, the enterprise has the right, at its own initiative, to make all decisions, if they are not at variance with existing legislation.

The enterprise bears complete responsibility for the observance of the interests of the state and the rights of citizens, the safekeeping and augmentation of socialist property, the fulfillment of commitments that it has made, and ensuring a level of profitability necessary for work in conditions of full cost accounting and self-financing, and it strengthens state, production and labor discipline.

The enterprise's activity must not disrupt the normal working conditions of other enterprises and organizations or worsen the living conditions of citizens.

6. The state is not responsible for the commitments made by the enterprise. The enterprise is not responsible for the commitments of the state, nor for those of other enterprises, organizations and institutions.

### Article 3. The collective's cost-accounting income, its distribution and use

1. The collective's cost-accounting income is the source of the enterprise's production and social development and of payment for labor, it is at the enterprise's disposal, it is used independently, and it is not subject to withdrawal.

With the authorization of the higher-level agency, the enterprise may use the following forms of cost accounting:

based on the normative distribution of profits. Settlements are made with the budget and the higher-level agency, and interest on credits is paid, out of profits. The residual profit formed after these settlements is at the disposal of the work collective. Based on normatives, the following funds are formed from the residual profit: the fund for the development of production, science and technology; the fund for social development; and the material incentive fund or other similar funds. The wage fund may be formed on the basis of the net output normative or another measure of output. In this case, the collective's cost-accounting income is formed out of the wage fund and the residual profit;

based on the normative distribution of income obtained after the recovery of material outlays out of receipts. Settlements are made with the budget and the higher-level agency, and interest on credits is paid, out of income, after which the collective's cost-accounting income is formed. The single pay fund is formed as the remainder of the collective's cost-accounting income after the formation from it of the following funds: the fund for the development of production, science and technology; and the fund for social development or other similar funds, determined on the basis of normatives applied to the cost-accounting income.

A financial reserve and a foreign-currency payments fund may be formed at the enterprise.

2. The enterprise uses the wage fund to pay employees according to their labor contribution.

The material incentive fund is expended for the payment of bonuses, monetary rewards, and other forms of incentives and for material assistance.

The enterprise may, instead of a wage fund and a material incentive fund, form a pay fund, which serves as the sole source of all payments to workers for the results of their labor.

3. The enterprise uses the fund for the development of production, science and technology for the financing of research and experimental-design projects, for the renewal and expansion of fixed assets on an up-to-date technical basis, for increasing the enterprise's working capital, and also for other purposes of production development.

The enterprise independently uses depreciation allowances, channeling them, according to the established normative, into the fund for the development of production, science and technology or into another similar fund.

4. The work collective uses the fund for social development for housing construction, the all-around strengthening of the material and technical base of the social and cultural sphere, the maintenance of its facilities, the implementation of health-improvement and mass-cultural measures, and the satisfaction of other social requirements.

5. The enterprise has the right, with the consent of the work collective, to channel part of the money in the material incentive fund (the pay fund) into the fund for social development and to channel part of the money in the fund for the development of production, science and technology into housing construction, within the limits established by legislation.

6. The enterprise forms, out of the unit cost of output (work, services) and according to a normative, a repair fund, the money in which is used to carry out all types of repairs on fixed assets.

### Article 4. The enterprise's material and technical base and monies

1. The enterprise's material and technical base and monies—i.e., its property—consists of fixed assets and working capital, as well as other physical assets and financial resources. The enterprise exercises the rights of possession, use, and administration of this property.

The enterprise must constantly ensure the reproduction of the material and technical base on a progressive basis and make efficient use of production capacities and fixed assets.

2. With a view to achieving a full return from its production potential, the enterprise establishes a two-shift—and, for one-of-a-kind or expensive equipment or when production conditions make it necessary—a three- or four-shift schedule of operation. The employment of a different schedule of operation by an enter-

prise requires the permission of the higher-level agency and the consent of the local soviet and the appropriate trade union agency.

3. The enterprise's working capital is completely at its disposal and is not subject to withdrawal. A shortage in an enterprise's working capital is covered using the collective's cost-accounting income, and the enterprise replenishes its working capital out of its own resources. The enterprise must ensure the safe-keeping, rational utilization, and accelerated turnover of working capital.

4. The enterprise has the right:

to transfer to other enterprises and organizations and to sell, exchange, rent, make available free of charge for temporary use or loan buildings, structures, equipment, means of transportation, implements, raw materials, and other phys-ical assets, as well as to write them off the books if they wear out or become obsolete;

to transfer material and monetary resources, including money from the mate-rial incentive fund, with the consent of the work collective, to other enterprises and organizations that perform work or services for the enterprise.

Receipts from the sale of unused property and rent payments (if the rental of property is not the enterprise's basic activity) in the indicated instances are channeled into the fund for the development of production, science and technol-ogy, while losses resulting from transfers to other enterprises and organizations, as well as from the sale and writing off of property, are covered by the enterprise using the appropriate economic incentive funds of the enterprise.

## II. Management of the enterprise (association) and self-management of the work collective

### Article 5. The structure of the association and the enterprise

1. In accordance with the goals and tasks of economic activity and the special activity and special features of the structure and organization of management, various types of associations and independent enterprises operate in the branches of the national economy. The basic types of associations are production and science-production associations. The association, regardless of the territorial location of its structural units and the independent enterprises that are part of it, functions as a single production-and-economic complex and ensures the organic combination of the interests of the development of branches and territories. It carries out its activity on the basis of a single plan and balance sheet.

The enterprise and the association organize factory-based service for their output and factory-outlet trade and create, where needed, the appropriate subdi-visions for this.

2. The production association is created for the production of certain types of output (work, services) on the basis of the more efficient use of scientific-technological potential, developed article-specific specialization, and production

cooperation and combination. It consists of structural units that carry out industrial, construction, transportation, trade and other activities. Research, design, and technological organizations and other structural units may also be parts of the association.

3. The science-production association is created for the development and production, in the shortest possible time, of highly efficient sets of machinery, equipment, instruments, technological processes, and materials that determine scientific and technical progress in the relevant areas of great national economic importance. It is created on the basis of research (design, technological) organizations or enterprises (production associations) that possess a developed design and experimental base, and it functions as a single science-production complex.

4. The enterprise consists of subdivisions that operate on the principles of internal cost accounting or a collective contract: production facilities, shops, divisions, sectors, livestock sections, brigades, teams, bureaus, laboratories, and others.

Part of the material incentive fund and the fund for social development, the amount depending on the results of the activity of the enterprise's subdivisions, may be allocated, according to a procedure established by the enterprise, to those subdivisions.

5. In the association, its structural units operate on the basis of cost-accounting principles and in accordance with the provisions concerning these principles as confirmed by the association, and these units consist of subdivisions. A structural unit may have a separate balance sheet and bank account.

The association allocates the necessary fixed assets and working capital to the structural unit and determines procedures for carrying out relations within the association and resolving disputes among structural units, as well as the responsibility for nonfulfillment of their commitments.

The structural unit, within the bounds of the rights granted to it by legislation and the association, is in charge of the property allocated to it and concludes economic contracts with other organizations on behalf of the association.

The association may grant the structural unit the right to conclude economic contracts on behalf of the structural unit and to bear responsibility for the property allocated to it under such contracts. When the property allocated is insufficient, the association bears responsibility for the structural unit's commitments.

The structural unit forms the material incentive fund and the fund for social development according to the procedure established by the association and depending on the results of its activity. The money in these funds may not be withdrawn by the association without the consent of the structural unit's work collective. The association has the right to put part of the fund for the development of production, science and technology, as well as of other funds, at the disposal of the structural unit.

6. The composition of the association is established by the higher-level agency, the structure of the structural units that are parts of the association is

established by the association, and the structure of the enterprise and its subdivisions is established by the enterprise.

The management of the association is carried out, as a rule, by the executive and the management of the head structural unit (head enterprise) of the association and is organized, in the main, according to a two-level system with direct subordination to the ministry, state committee, or department.

Independent enterprises that enjoy rights in accordance with this law may be a part of the association. The association directs such enterprises, performing the function of a higher-level agency with respect to them, and has the right to centralize, fully or partially, the performance of their individual production-and-economic functions. In doing so, enterprises' resources that are necessary for performing the indicated functions may be centralized with the enterprises' consent.

7. To effect a further rise in the level of production concentration, enterprises, associations, or organizations may be included in the makeup of major organizational structures—state production associations. Enterprises, associations, and organizations that are part of such associations retain their economic independence and operate in accordance with this law.

## Article 6. Management of the enterprise

1. The management of the enterprise is carried out on the basis of the principle of democratic centralism and the combination of centralized management and the socialist self-management of the work collective.

Socialist self-management is realized in conditions of broad openness through the participation of the entire collective and its public organizations in working out highly important decisions and monitoring their fulfillment, the election of executives, and one-man management in the administration of the enterprise. The pooling of the working people's efforts and the development of their initiative for achieving high work results, the instilling of good organization and discipline in personnel and an increase in their political consciousness are ensured on the basis of self-management.

The enterprise's party organization, as the political nucleus of the collective, operates within the framework of the USSR Constitution, directs the work of the entire collective, its self-management agencies and the trade union, Komsomol, and other public organizations, and monitors the activities of the management.

Social and economic decisions affecting the enterprise's activity are worked out and adopted by the executive with the participation of the work collective, with party organizations, as well as trade union, Komsomol, and other public organizations operating in the collective in accordance with their charters and legislation.

2. The enterprise carries out the election of executives (as a rule, on a competitive basis), which ensures an improvement in the qualitative composition

of leadership cadres and the strengthening of their responsibility for the results of their activity. The elective principle applies to the heads of enterprises, structural units of associations, production facilities, shops, divisions, sectors, livestock sections, and teams, as well as to foremen and brigade leaders.

3. The executive of an enterprise or a structural unit of an association expresses the interests of the state and the work collective. He is elected by a general meeting (conference) of the work collective by secret or open ballot (at the discretion of the meeting or conference) for a term of five years and is confirmed by the higher-level agency. If the candidate elected by the work collective is not confirmed by the higher-level agency, a new election is held. In doing so, the higher-level agency must explain to the work collective its reasons for refusing to confirm the results of the election.

The executive of an enterprise or a structural unit of an association may be relieved of his duties by the higher-level agency on the basis of a decision of the general meeting (conference) of the work collective or, with the authorization of the collective, by the council of the work collective.

The executive of a head structural unit (head enterprise) elected by the work collective is confirmed by the higher-level agency as the executive of the association. If the management of an association is exercised by an isolated apparatus, the association's executive is elected at a conference of representatives of the work collectives of its structural units and associations. The executive of an association is relieved of his duties ahead of schedule according to the same procedure.

The executive of subdivisions—production facilities, shops, divisions, sectors, livestock sections, and teams, as well as foremen and brigade leaders, are elected by the appropriate collectives by secret or open ballot for a term of up to five years and are confirmed by the enterprise's executive. The aforementioned executives may be relieved of their duties ahead of time by the enterprise's executive, on the basis of a decision by the collective of the appropriate subdivision.

The executives of enterprises, the structural units of associations and subdivisions, as well as foremen and brigade leaders, who are relieved of their duties before the expiration of their terms may be reelected or assigned to other work according to a procedure established by legislation with respect to persons removed from elective office.

Deputy executives and executives of the legal and bookkeeping services and the quality-control services of enterprises are appointed to their posts and removed from them by the executive, according to established procedure.

4. One-man management in the system of the enterprise's self-management is carried out by the executive of the enterprise and by the executives of the structural units of associations and subdivisions.

The executive (general director, director, manager) of the enterprise directs all the enterprise's activity and organizes its work. He is responsible to the state and the work collective for the results of the enterprise's work.

The executive of an enterprise acts on behalf of the enterprise without authorization, represents the enterprise before all other enterprises, institutions, and organizations, disposes of the enterprise's property, concludes contracts, issues authorizations, and opens settlement and other bank accounts for the enterprise.

Within the bounds of the enterprise's jurisdiction, its executive issues orders and instructions that are binding for all employees of the enterprise. The decisions of executives of structural units and subdivisions and of foremen and brigade leaders are binding for all employees subordinate to them.

5. The general meeting (conference) is the basic form of exercising the work collective's authority.

The general meeting (conference) of the work collective:

elects the executive of the enterprise and the council of the work collective and hears reports on their activity;

examines and confirms plans for the social and economic development of the enterprise and determines ways of increasing labor productivity and profit (income), improving production efficiency and output quality, preserving and augmenting public property, and strengthening the material and technical base of production as the foundation of the collective's vital activity;

approves the collective contract and authorizes the trade union committee to sign it with the enterprise's management on behalf of the work collective; makes socialist pledges; approves factory labor regulations submitted by the management and the trade union committee; and

examines other very important questions of the enterprise's activity.

6. A meeting (conference) of the enterprise's work collective is convened by the council of the work collective as needed, but at least twice a year. Questions are submitted for examination by the meeting (conference) at the initiative of the council of the work collective, the management, party, trade union, Komsomol and other public organizations, People's Control agencies and individual members of the collective, as well as of the higher-level agency.

### Article 7. *The council of the enterprise's work collective*

1. In the period between meetings (conferences), the council of the work collective of the enterprise (the structural unit of the association) exercises the powers of the work collective. The council concentrates primary attention on developing the working people's initiative and increasing each employee's contribution to the common cause, and it carries out measures to achieve high final results of the enterprise's activity and to obtain cost-accounting income for the collective.

The council of the work collective:

monitors the fulfillment of the decisions of general meetings (conferences) of the work collective and the implementation of critical comments and proposals by workers and office employees, and provides the work collective with information on their fulfillment;

hears reports from the management on progress in the fulfillment of plans and contractual commitments and on the results of production-and-economic activity, and maps out measures to facilitate more efficient work by the enterprise and the observance of the principle of social justice;

in conjunction with the elected agencies of party, trade union, and Komsomol organizations, confirms the conditions of socialist competition and sums up its results;

handles questions of improving the management and organizational structure of the enterprise, seeing to it that employees' pay corresponds to their personal contribution, and effecting the just distribution of social benefits;

adopts decisions on the use of the fund for the development of production, science and technology, the material incentive fund and the fund for social development, on channeling money into the construction of residential buildings, children's institutions, and public catering facilities and on the improvement of working conditions and job safety and of medical, consumer, and cultural services to workers and office employees, and handles other questions of the social development of the collective;

handles questions of the training and advanced training of cadres, the observance of factory labor regulations and of state, labor, and production discipline at the enterprise, and maps out measures to strengthen it;

monitors the granting of benefits and privileges to innovators, front-ranking production workers, and war and labor veterans using money in the material incentive fund and the fund for social development;

hears reports from representatives of the collectives of subdivisions, submits proposals concerning the use of moral and material incentives for labor successes, and examines questions of granting state awards;

handles questions of electing the councils of collectives of production facilities, shops, divisions, sectors, and other subdivisions, and determines their rights within the bounds of the powers of the council of the work collective of the enterprise (structural unit of the association);

handles other questions of production and social development, if they do not fall within the jurisdiction of the meeting (conference) of the work collective.

The council of the work collective works in close contact with the management and with party, trade union, Komsomol, and other public organizations.

2. Decisions of the council of the work collective that are adopted within the bounds of its authority and in accordance with legislation are binding for management and the members of the collective.

If there is disagreement between the management of the enterprise and the council of the work collective, the question is resolved at a general meeting (conference) of the work collective.

3. The council of the work collective is elected by a general meeting (confer-

ence) of the collective of the enterprise (structural unit of the association) by secret or open ballot for a term of two or three years. Workers, brigade leaders, foremen, specialists, and representatives of management and of party, trade union, Komsomol, and other public organizations may be elected to the council. The council's size is determined by a general meeting (conference) of the work collective. Management representatives must not exceed one-fourth of the total membership of the council of the work collective. In regularly scheduled elections, at least one-third of the council's members, as a rule, are newly elected.

The council of the work collective elects a chairman, vice-chairmen, and a secretary of the council from among its members. Council sessions are held as needed, but at least once a quarter. The members of the work collective's council perform their duties on a voluntary basis.

A member of the council of a work collective may not be dismissed or subjected to any other disciplinary penalty without the consent of the council of the work collective.

A member of a council who has not justified the collective's trust may be removed from the council by decision of a general meeting (conference) of the work collective.

The enterprise's management creates the necessary conditions for the effective activity of the council of the work collective.

## Article 8. The enterprise's personnel

1. Work in the selection, placement, and upbringing of personnel at the enterprise is conducted by the management and the party organization, with the active participation of the council of the work collective and trade union, Komsomol, and other public organizations.

The enterprise forms a stable work collective that is capable of achieving high final results in conditions of full cost accounting and self-financing and on the basis of self-management. It sees to it that personnel correspond to the growing demands of present-day production; it develops in employees businesslike efficiency and responsibility for the accomplishment of the enterprise's tasks, instills the best labor traditions and a spirit of pride in their collective in personnel, and increases their stake in attaining the highest possible labor productivity; and it strives to ensure that each employee values his job.

2. The enterprise displays a constant concern for the steady growth of the vocational skills and a continual rise in the political, general-education, and cultural level of its personnel, and for the transfer of employees with an eye to their skills and the interests of production. For this purpose, the enterprise conducts the training and retraining of personnel, organically combining vocational and economic studies, ensures growth in the skills of employees directly on the job and in educational institutions, reinforces the physical plant of education facilities, organizes training combines, courses and centers and schools for the

study of advanced labor methods, and develops mentorship.

The enterprise creates the necessary conditions for combining instruction with work and grants the benefits stipulated by existing legislation. With their consent, employees may be sent by enterprises for instruction in specialized secondary and higher educational institutions, as well as to graduate school, with the payment of a stipend. The enterprise makes payments, in established amounts, for the training of specialists for the enterprise in higher educational institutions and for the advanced training of employees.

The enterprise provides assistance to educational institutions in training young people for work and in molding their vocational interests.

3. The enterprise's leadership cadres should possess lofty business, political, and moral qualities, socialist enterprise and devotion to principle, and should be able to create a united collective and to ensure the combination of the interests of work collective with the public interest. Today's executive needs lofty professionalism and knowledge of the fundamentals of management science and economic thinking, qualities that make it possible to see long-term prospects and to manage efficiently.

The enterprise creates a reserve of leadership cadres and conducts constant work with them.

4. With a view to improving the selection, placement, and training of personnel, improving their business skills and the quality and efficiency of their work and ensuring closer ties between wages and the results of labor, the enterprise is to conduct the certification of executive personnel and of specialists.

On the basis of the certification results, the executive of the enterprise makes a decision on raising or lowering employees in grade title and skill category, raising or lowering their salaries, establishing, changing, or abolishing salary increments, and promoting them or relieving them of their duties. If subdivision executives who have been elected by collectives are, on the basis of certification results, deemed unfit to hold their posts, they may be relieved of their duties on the basis of a decision by the executive of the relevant subdivision.

*Article 9. The enterprise's relations with the higher-level*
*agency and the local soviet*

1. Relations between the enterprise and the higher-level agency (ministry, state committee, department, or other higher-level agency) are built on the basis of planned management and observance of the principles of full cost accounting, self-financing, and self-management at the enterprise.

All bodies of state power and administration are to facilitate in every way the development of economic independence, initiative, and socialist enterprise on the part of enterprises and their work collectives.

Management of the enterprise is carried out primarily by economic methods on the basis of control figures, state orders, long-term economic normatives, and ceilings. The list of control figures, economic normatives, and ceilings established for the enterprise is confirmed by the USSR Council of Ministers. The higher-level agency does not have the right to transmit to the enterprise control figures, economic normatives, and ceilings over and above the confirmed list. The composition of state orders is confirmed by the USSR State Planning Committee and USSR ministries (departments). For enterprises under the jurisdiction of republic ministries and departments, as well as for consumer goods and paid services (except for state orders of the USSR State Planning Committee and USSR ministries and departments), the composition of state orders is confirmed by the union-republic council of ministers. The basic planning data established for the enterprise are to be strictly coordinated.

The enterprise is guided by the demands of the uniform technical policy conducted in the branch by the ministry or department, and it obtains assistance from the ministry or department in the training and retraining of personnel and in the implementation of foreign economic ties.

In all its activity, the higher-level agency must ensure conditions for efficient work by the enterprise, strictly observe the enterprises's rights, further their complete implementation, [and] not interfere in the enterprise's day-to-day economic activity, and also provide information on its activity to the enterprise's work collective.

The higher-level agency counteracts the monopoly tendencies of individual enterprises, to this end carrying out measures to overcome the overstating of unit cost and prices, stagnation in the technical development of production, and artificial restrictions on the production and marketing of output enjoying consumer demand.

2. The enterprise, on the basis of an established normative, transfers to the higher agency part of its profit (income) for the creation of centralized funds and reserves. The higher-level agency may use these funds and reserves to allocate money to the enterprise for the implementation of measures necessary for the development of the branch.

3. The higher-level agency must monitor the enterprise's activity, its observance of legislation, and the safekeeping of socialist property. A comprehensive audit of the production and financial-and-economic activity of the enterprise is conducted by the higher-level agency not more often than once a year, with the involvement of interested organizations.

The ministry, department, or other higher-level agency may transmit instructions to the enterprise only in accordance with its jurisdiction as established by legislation. If a ministry, department, or other higher-level agency issues an act not in accordance with its jurisdiction or that violates legislative requirements, the enterprise has the right to appeal to a state court of arbitration to have the act in question declared invalid, in full or in part.

Losses inflicted on an enterprise as a result of the fulfillment of a higher-level agency's instructions that violate the rights of the enterprise, as well as losses that are a consequence of the improper exercise of the higher-level agency's duties with respect to the enterprise, are subject to compensation by that agency. Disputes over the question of compensation for losses are settled by a state court of arbitration.

4. In accordance with legislation, the enterprise actively participates in work conducted by the soviet of people's deputies to ensure the comprehensive social and economic development of the area in question and the best possible satisfaction of the population's requirements, and also in the formation of the local budget according to established normatives.

The enterprise interacts with the soviet of people's deputies in its work to find and put into operation reserves for accelerating the development of production and improving its efficiency. Part of the money saved by the enterprise through the implementation of measures organized by the soviets to use reserves for production growth and resource savings is transferred to the union-republic (in republics not divided into provinces) and autonomous-republic councils of ministers and local soviet executive committees to be used for the economic and social development of the respective areas.

The enterprise clears technical and economic feasibility studies and technical and economic estimates for the construction of facilities and lists of authorized construction projects, with respect to established indices, with the appropriate union-republic (in republics not divided into provinces) and autonomous-republic councils of ministers and local soviet executive committees.

The local soviets of people's deputies facilitate the efficient activity of enterprises in their areas and adopt measures for the creation of operating schedules favorable to these enterprises' employees for trade, public catering, consumer service, public health, and cultural organizations and municipal transportation, as well as convenient operating schedules for children's institutions.

5. The enterprise performs work or services not envisaged by the plan but stipulated in assignments from a higher-level agency or the soviet's decisions on the basis of economic contracts, with outlays reimbursed by the enterprises and organizations for which the work or services are performed (with the exception of outlays on eliminating the consequences of natural disasters and accidents).

## III. The enterprise's production and social activity

### Article 10.  Planning

1. The planning of the enterprise's activity is carried out in accordance with the principle of democratic centralism on a scientific basis, with the broad participation of the work collective in the drafting and discussion of plans. It proceeds from the need to satisfy consumers' growing demand for high-quality output (work, services) with the smallest possible outlays and to ensure growth in the collective's cost-accounting income as the main source of the self-financing

of its production and social development and of pay.

2. Proceeding from the long-term tasks of the branch and taking into account plans for the comprehensive development of the area, the enterprise works out the prospects for its production and social development. It provides for measures for expanding production and raising its technical level, updating output and improving its quality in accordance with the requirements of the domestic and world markets, making the fullest possible use of scientific-technological achievements, and actively participating in nationwide, branch, and scientific-technological programs and joint programs with CMEA member countries.

3. The principal form of the planning and organization of the enterprise's activity is the five-year plan of economic and social development (with breakdowns by year). The enterprise works out and confirms the five-year plan independently. It uses initial planning data as the basis for forming the five-year plan: control figures, state orders, long-term economic normatives, and ceilings, as well as direct orders from customers and material-and-technical supply agencies for output (work, services).

In doing so, the enterprise proceeds from the fact that:

control figures reflect social requirements for the output produced by the enterprise and minimal levels of production efficiency. They are not directive in nature, they should not fetter the work collective in drafting the plan, and they should leave it broad scope to choose solutions and partners when concluding economic contracts. Control figures include an index of output (work, services) in value terms (adjusted) for the conclusion of contracts, profit (income), foreign-currency receipts, the most important general indices of scientific-technological progress, and indices for the development of the social sphere. During the period that the new economic mechanism is being mastered and the changeover to full cost accounting, unsubsidized operations, and self-financing is being completed, control figures may also include indices of labor productivity and the materials-intensiveness of output;

state orders guarantee the satisfaction of top-priority social requirements and are issued to enterprises for the commissioning of production capacities and facilities in the social sphere using state centralized capital investments, as well as for the delivery of certain types of output that are necessary above all for the accomplishment of nationwide social tasks, the fulfillment of scientific-techno-logical programs, the strengthening of defense capability and ensuring the country's economic independence, and for deliveries of agricultural output. State orders are issued to the enterprise by the higher-level agency and may be placed on a competitive basis; they must be included in the plan. When state orders are issued, provision should be made for the mutual responsibility of the two parties—the executor and the customer;

long-term economic normatives are stable throughout the five-year plan and ensure close coordination between state interests and the cost-accounting interests of the enterprise and the material interest of employees. Economic normatives determine relations with the budget, the formation of the wage fund, economic incentive funds and other aspects of the economic activity of the enterprise, and are established with a view to special regional features;

ceilings establish the maximum size of state centralized capital investments for the development of interbranch production facilities, new construction, and the accomplishment of especially important tasks in accordance with a list of enterprises and facilities included in the state plan, of amounts of construction-and-installation and contract work, and of centrally allocated material resources to provide for the requirements of production and construction.

4. The enterprise works out and confirms its annual plans independently, proceeding from its five-year plan and concluded economic contracts. In doing so, the enterprise plans output (work, services) and other indices of economic and social development, putting the five-year plan's assignments into concrete form; with the appropriate organizations and enterprises, it resolves questions of the provision of material and technical resources and of contract construction-and-installation work. During the drafting of plans, the ministry, department, or other higher-level agency, in conjunction with the enterprises, ensures the comprehensive coordination of their proposals.

Contracts for the production and delivery of consumer goods are concluded as a result of the free sale of articles at wholesale fairs, which are the basis for planning the product mix, improving the quality of goods, and raising the indices that determine the production and social development of the enterprise.

5. During the drafting of the five-year plan, the enterprise provides for the complete utilization of production capacities, employs progressive and scientifically substantiated norms for labor outlays and the consumption of raw and other materials, power and fuel, makes substitutions for materials and articles in short supply, draws secondary resources into economic turnover on a broad basis, and strives to reduce production costs and increase profits.

The enterprise must strictly observe plan discipline and completely fulfill plans and contractual commitments.

6. The enterprise of union (republic) subordination must clear its draft plans with the appropriate union-republic (in republics not divided into provinces) or autonomous-republic council of ministers and with the local soviet executive committee on questions of the development of the social sphere, services to the population, the production of consumer goods, construction, number of employees, the utilization of labor resources, local types of raw and other materials, secondary resources, environmental protection, and land, water, and forest use. Measures to implement the voters' mandates are taken into consideration in the enterprise's draft plans.

## Article 11. Scientific-technological progress and improving quality

1. The enterprise's activity in the field of scientific-technological progress should be geared to a continuous rise in the technical level and organization of

production, the improvement of technological processes, turning out products of the highest quality that are competitive on the world market, the timely updating of output, and the fullest possible satisfaction of consumers' needs and demands. The enterprise develops the production of specialized technological equipment. Scientific-technological development projects are carried out by the enterprise, using its own forces and research and design organizations whose services it enlists.

The quality of output (work, services) is decisive in the public assessment of the results of each work collective's activity. Concern for the reputation of their enterprise should be a subject of professional and patriotic pride for workers, engineers, designers, and executives.

2. The large-scale, comprehensive and timely employment of achievements of science and technology and the production of efficient and high-quality output are a highly important means of increasing the enterprise's profit (income) and ensuring the self-financing of its production and social development. The enterprise sells output the parameters of which meet or exceed the highest world achievements at higher prices. For the production of obsolete articles and poor-quality output, the enterprise gives discounts from wholesale prices and incurs material responsibility and inescapable losses in the collective's cost-accounting income, wages, and social benefits.

3. The enterprise must ensure the strict observance of technological discipline, standards, and technical specifications and reliability, trouble-free operation, and operational safety for the equipment it produces. It monitors the quality of output (work, services), strengthens its own quality-control services, provides assistance to the work of the state product acceptance system, and organizes warranty and post-warranty repairs, as well as factory-based service for the equipment it produces.

4. For the purpose of accelerating scientific-technological development projects and raising the level of the integration of research and production, the production association and the enterprise:

ensure the top-priority development of their own research and experimental facilities; may create scientific-technological and design subdivisions and strengthen them with cadres of research personnel and specialists;

set up stable direct ties with research, design, and technological organizations;

conclude contracts, on the basis of cost accounting, for the performance of research and development projects by scientific institutions, higher educational institutions, the organizations of scientific-technological societies, inventors and rationalizers, and other enterprises, regardless of their departmental subordination.

5. The science-production association must take a leading position in the creation and wide-scale introduction in the production of highly efficient equipment, technological processes, and new-generation materials. It is responsible

for the scientific-technological level of the output (work, services) produced in the national economy on the basis of its speciality.

Research, design, and technological organizations must ensure a high level of research and development work and the implementation in this work of long-range demands for the quality of output (work, services), develop output on the highest world level and progressive basic technologies and fundamentally new ones, and actively promote their broad application in the national economy. The indicated organizations bear material responsibility for transmitting to production development projects that do not meet the highest world level in terms of basic indices, and when this is the case their executives and development personnel are subject to disciplinary liability and may incur losses in wages and material incentives.

6. Enterprises, production, and science-production associations and research organizations are to make wide use of various forms of scientific-technological competition in their activity and are to create an atmosphere of creativity in work collectives. With a view to selecting the most efficient solutions to scientific-technological problems and developing the initiative of scientists, specialists, and workers, contests and parallel design projects are conducted, and temporary scientific collectives are created. The development of the most important national economic output is carried out, as a rule, on a competitive basis. Enterprises, associations, and organizations that have achieved successes as a result of scientific-technological competition and that have won contests receive priority in material and moral incentives and increase their profits (income).

Interbranch scientific-technological complexes unite the efforts of enterprises and carry out the coordination of the research, experimental-design, and technological work that they perform in the main areas of scientific-technological progress, as well as work relating to the manufacture of experimental models and bringing them to series production.

7. The enterprise must strive to involve all members of the work collective in the accomplishment of tasks of accelerating scientific-technological progress, improving output quality, and raising the level of production organization and standards, and it encourages the working people's scientific-technological creativity in every way. The enterprise organizes work relating to invention and rationalization at the enterprise and exchanges of experience and conducts reviews; it creates quality groups and employs other forms of the working people's creative participation in improving quality; and it ensures the safekeeping of technological, patent, and license information.

## Article 12. Technical reequipment and reconstruction

1. The enterprise must make efficient use of production potential, increase the shift index of equipment operation, carry out the continuous updating of equipment on an advanced technical and technological basis, and strive for all-out

growth in labor productivity. It draws up a program for the uninterrupted modernization of its material and technical base and concentrates efforts and resources on the technical reequipment and reconstruction of production on the basis of progressive designs.

2. The enterprise carries out technical reequipment, reconstruction, and expansion using the fund for the development of production, science and technology and other analogous funds, as well as bank credits, and, as a top priority, makes provision for the necessary resources and contract work.

Centralized financing is allocated to the enterprise for conducting large-scale measures for the reconstruction and expansion of existing production facilities, as well as for the construction of social facilities, in special cases. The list of appropriate enterprises and facilities is confirmed in the state plan.

3. The enterprise has the right:

to work out, using its own forces or on a contractual basis, design-and-estimate documentation for carrying out work related to the technical reequipment, reconstruction, and expansion of existing production facilities, as well as for the construction of nonproduction facilities;

to confirm design-and-estimate documentation and lists of authorized construction projects for production and nonproduction facilities, the construction of which is carried out using the cost-accounting income of the enterprise's collective and bank credits;

to confirm production schedules for construction-and-installation work, coordinating them with contractors;

to refuse to accept obsolete designs from developers of design documentation.

4. The enterprise carries out the technical reequipment, reconstruction, and expansion of existing production facilities by efficiently combining the do-it-yourself and contract methods of construction. It ensures the observance of normative construction schedules, norms for putting production capacities into operation, and the rate of return on investments.

For the performance of construction-and-installation work by the contract method, the enterprise concludes a contract for the entire period of construction.

The contracting enterprise, in conjunction with the client and subcontracting organizations, ensures the commissioning of facilities under construction by the established deadlines and is responsible for their quality.

### Article 13. The social development of the work collective

1. The implementation of an active social policy as a powerful means of increasing production and efficiency, developing the labor and public-political activeness of the enterprise's employees, instilling collectivism in them and establishing a socialist way of life should be a very important area of the enterprise's activity. The enterprise must show concern for improving working and living conditions and for satisfying the interests and needs of its employees,

their families, and war and labor veterans.

The enterprise's work collective and each of its employees earns the money for social development through their highly productive labor. Possibilities for satisfying the collective's requirements for social benefits are determined by the final results of the enterprise's work and the collective's cost-accounting income. Questions of social development are resolved by the work collective.

The enterprise carries on its social activity in close cooperation with the local soviet of people's deputies.

2. The enterprise must assign paramount importance to activating the human factor, improving working conditions, increasing the creative content of work, and gradually transforming labor into a prime necessity. To this end, the enterprise:

strives for a sharp reduction, and in the long run the elimination, of heavy physical, monotonous, and low-skill labor;

employs technological production processes that are safe for workers and the population and meet the requirements of sanitary norms and safety measures, and ensures the prevention of accidents and the elimination of on-the-job injuries;

introduces automation and mechanization on a broad scale, and improves the organization of workplaces and the organization of labor;

creates more favorable conditions for working women;

provides comprehensive assistance to young people in improving their vocational training and raising their general-education and cultural level.

3. In order to create favorable social conditions for employees directly on the job, the enterprise:

organizes public catering, provides hot meals for all employees, uses—when necessary—money in the fund for social development to lower the cost of meals in its cafeterias and snack bars, and actively develops its own auxiliary farming operations;

improves medical services to employees, strives to reduce the incidence of disease while ensuring a comprehensive approach to preventive-medicine and medical-treatment activity, provides premises to public health institutions free of charge, and expands and strengthens treatment and preventive-medicine facilities;

actively develops diversified paid services, striving for the fullest possible satisfaction of employees' needs, and facilitates the efficient use of their free time.

4. With a view to the accelerated development of the material base of the social sphere and the creation of conditions for a healthy everyday life and recreation for employees and their families, the enterprise:

channels the bulk of the money in the fund for social development into the construction of residential buildings, children's institutions, and other social facilities;

strives to provide the family of each employee with its own apartment or individual home as quickly as possible, carries out the construction and operation of, and timely repairs on, the residential buildings belonging to it using its fund for social development and bank credits, organizes cooperative construction, provides employees with all possible assistance in individual housing construction, and issues loans for this purpose;

develops a network of kindergartens, day-care centers, Young Pioneer camps, and other children's institutions;

carries out the construction of, repairs on, and the operation of sanatoria and rehabilitation centers, boardinghouses, houses of culture, tourist and athletic facilities, and other recreational facilities;

develops in every way physical culture, sports, and the amateur creative activities of employees and members of their families;

promotes the development of collective orchard and vegetable growing;

carries out the distribution of housing, accommodations in vacations homes and sanatoria, orchard and garden plots, and other social benefits.

The enterprise's management and trade union committee, with the consent of the council of the work collective, are authorized to allocate housing out of turn to certain highly skilled specialists and other employees in view of their labor contribution. The enterprise may provide material incentives to employees of medical, children's cultural-enlightenment, and athletic institutions, public catering organizations and organizations that provide services to the work collective but are not part of it.

5. The enterprise's work collective promotes the strengthening of the family and creates favorable conditions for women that allow them to successfully combine motherhood with participation in labor and public activity. Questions involving women's working and living conditions are to be resolved with the active participation of the women's council.

6. Work collectives show constant concern for war and labor veterans, pensioners, disabled persons, and children, surround them with attention, provide them with the necessary assistance, create conditions for enlisting able-bodied pensioners and disabled persons in work that they are able to do, involve them in the public life of the collective, and make available to them the possibilities that the enterprise has for medical and other services, recreation, and leisure-time activities. The enterprise takes part in the construction of homes for the elderly and the disabled, exercises sponsorship of these homes, as well as of children's homes, boarding schools and infants' homes, and provides them with material and financial assistance.

7. The enterprise actively promotes the efficient work of schools, educational and medical-treatment institutions and it may finance, using its own money, appropriate measures.

The enterprise that is assigned to a general-education school or vocational-technical school as its base enterprise organizes the labor training of the school's pupils and creates the necessary conditions for this.

*Article 14. Labor and wages*

1. At the enterprise, the USSR citizen realizes his constitutional right to work and to be paid in accordance with the results of his work and its quantity and quality.

It is the duty of every employee to work honestly and conscientiously, to increase labor productivity, to improve output quality, to take care of and augment public property, and to observe labor discipline.

The enterprise must make effective use of the labor of employees and, on this basis, strive to improve the collective's well-being and to successfully accomplish tasks of its production and social development. It should, along with material incentives, make extensive use of diverse forms of moral incentives to employees for high achievements in work.

The wages of each employee are determined by the final results of work and by the employee's personal labor contribution and are limited to a maximum amount.

2. For the fullest possible utilization of labor potential and the creation of conditions for the highly productive activity of every employee, the enterprise:

establishes technically substantiated labor norms and revises them in step with the improvement of the organization of labor and production and the implementation of technical measures;

strives for the performance of growing amounts of work with a relatively smaller number of personnel;

conducts the certification and rationalization of workplaces, determines the necessary number of them, and abolishes superfluous workplaces;

establishes forms of the organization of employees' labor, sets wage scales, assigns workers to wage categories and specialists to salary categories, and organizes the introduction of advanced methods of labor;

establishes a schedule of working time and rest time, clearing it with the local soviet of people's deputies, introduces flexible schedules, authorizes short workdays and short work weeks, organizes homework, and also determines the length of additional vacation time, in accordance with legislation.

The enterprise provides, on the basis of openness, an objective assessment of the employee's personal labor contribution to the results of economic activity, encourages conscientious labor, creates an atmosphere of intolerance toward violators of discipline and shoddy workers, and employs strict material, disciplinary, and public sanctions against them.

3. With a view to increasing the efficiency of labor, strengthening the collective interest in and responsibility for the results of work, and molding in employees a proprietary attitude toward the use of means of production, the enterprise:

uses brigade cost accounting and the brigade contract as the basic collective forms of the organization of labor and of incentives for it. When necessary, engineering and technical personnel and other specialists are included in the brigade;

converts sections, shops, and other subdivisions to the contract form. The work of these subdivisions is organized on the basis of a contract between the collective and the management, with the necessary property assigned to the subdivision in question and pay based on long-term normatives;

when necessary, employs the family contract.

4. The enterprise forms, according to the established normative, a wage fund (pay fund) based on the final results of work. It must ensure, in accordance with confirmed normatives, priority growth for labor productivity in comparison with growth in average wages.

Within the limits of the wage fund, determined according to the normative, the enterprise, taking into account the specific nature of the production facility and the tasks confronting it, independently establishes the wage fund for certain categories of employee—designers, technologists, research personnel—and for employees of quality-control services. The enterprise must ensure a relative reduction in the number of managerial personnel and in the percentage of money channeled into its maintenance.

The enterprise determines the total number of employees and their composition by occupation and skill, and it confirms the staffing.

5. The enterprise must use pay as a highly important means of stimulating growth in labor productivity, accelerating scientific-technological progress, improving output quality, increasing production efficiency, and strengthening discipline. It ensures the introduction of new base wage rates and salary scales, using money earned by the work collective.

The enterprise has the right:

to determine forms and systems of employees' pay, while preventing wage-leveling;

to determine jobs for which remuneration is paid according to higher wage rates, and also to provide additional benefits to workers and office employees in light of specific working conditions;

to introduce premium pay for combining occupations (positions), expanding service zones, or increasing the amount of work performed, including for positions and occupations regarded as different categories of employees, without restrictions on the amounts of this premium pay, using, and within the limits of, savings in the wage fund that are formed on the basis of the base wage rates (salaries) of released employees;

to establish, using savings in the wage fund, pay increments for each category of employee: for workers, for occupational skill; for executives, specialists and office employees, for high achievements in work and the on-schedule performance of especially important jobs;

to establish salaries for subdivision executives, specialists, and office employees without keeping to the average salaries according to the table of organization and without taking the relationship among their numbers into account;

to determine specific areas for using the material incentive fund;

to work out and confirm procedures for paying bonuses to workers, executives, designers, technologists, and office employees of structural units and subdivisions;

to ensure preference in providing labor incentives for designers, technologists, and other employees who are directly involved in the development and introduction in production of the latest equipment and technologies, inventions, and rationalization proposals.

6. Improvements in the organization of labor and in pay, measures for the social development of the work collective and the distribution of social benefits, and monitoring of the correct application of established systems of pay and of settling accounts with the working people are carried out at the enterprise in conjunction with or with the consent of the trade union committee.

### Article 15.  Material and technical supply

1. The material and technical supply of the enterprise is carried out proceeding from the need for its efficient and smooth operations and the economical use of material resources, while keeping the necessary level of resource stocks as low as possible.

In accordance with its plans of economic and social development, the enterprise determines requirements for resources and acquires them by way of wholesale trade or through a centralized procedure.

By way of wholesale trade, the enterprise acquires outside the system of ceilings (central allocations) material resources in accordance with its orders, on the basis of contracts concluded with enterprises and other agencies of material and technical supply or with manufacturers of output.

Certain material resources subject to the system of ceilings (central allocations) are allocated to the enterprise by centralized procedure. The enterprise independently determines, on the basis of contracts with suppliers, the product mix of and the delivery schedules for these resources.

On the basis of direct ties, an enterprise carries out its own material and technical supply independently for output sold on the basis of direct ceiling-free orders, as well as for centrally distributed output.

Wholesale trade is to be expanded and is to become the basic form of material and technical supply to the enterprise.

2. The enterprise bears economic responsibility for the fulfillment of its commitments under delivery contracts. The agencies of material and technical supply must satisfy in good time the valid requirements of enterprises for material resources. Territorial agencies of material and technical supply play a basic role in organizing the reliable supply of material resources to the enterprise and effective monitoring of deliveries. They bear economic responsibility for output deliveries

in instances in which they play the role of supplier. The material and technical supply of construction done by the do-it-yourself method is carried out, regardless of the sources of financing, by territorial agencies of material and technical supply, on the basis of statements of requirement from enterprises.

The enterprise has the right to conclude contracts with agencies of material and technical supply for the organization of comprehensive supply, preliminary preparations for the industrial consumption of delivered materials, the rental of technical devices, the provision of information, and the performance of other services.

3. The consumer-enterprise has a preferential right to the maintenance of existing direct, long-term economic ties with manufacturers and the expansion of such ties, and its selects the form of delivery: directly by the manufacturer or through a supply and marketing enterprise.

Agencies of material and technical supply are forbidden to arbitrarily revise existing direct, long-term ties with enterprises.

4. When the enterprise receives deliveries of output that deviates, in terms of quality, from existing state standards, technical specifications, or concluded contracts, and also when the enterprise is given poor-quality design and technical documentation, it has the right unilaterally to annul a contract with a supplier or developer and to demand reimbursement for losses suffered as a result of the contract's annulment.

At the request of the enterprise, the agency of material and technical supply or the higher-level agency assigns another supplier to it.

5. The shipper-enterprise is responsible for the presentation of freight, demurrage, and the underloading of means of conveyance, and the transport enterprise is responsible for disruptions in making means of transportation available for the delivery or shipment of output stipulated by the plan and contracts and for the on-schedule delivery of freight and its safekeeping, according to a procedure established by legislation. Enterprises that supply water, electricity, heat, and gas and other energy-supply organizations bear economic responsibility to consumer-enterprises for the observance of established ceilings and supply schedules.

### Article 16. The sale of output, work and services

1. The enterprise sells its output, performs work, and provides services in accordance with economic contracts with consumers, trade enterprises, and enterprises of material and technical supply or through its own network for the sale of output, the performance of work, and the provision of services. It is to fulfill completely commitments stemming from contracts in terms of quantity, product mix (assortment), schedules, quality of output (work, services), and other conditions. The fulfillment of orders and contracts serves as a major criterion for evaluating the activity of enterprises and providing material incentives to work collectives. The enterprise must study demand and engage in advertising. Pay-

ment by the consumer for output (work, services) delivered in accordance with the terms of contracts is the final stage of the enterprise's production-and-marketing activity and an inalienable condition for the implementation of full cost accounting and self-financing.

2. On condition that contractual commitments have been fulfilled, the enterprise has the right to use output for its own needs, sell it to other enterprises, organizations, and the population or exchange it with other enterprises, as well as output that consumers and agencies of material and technical supply that have concluded delivery contracts have rejected (with the exception of certain types of output determined by legislation).

3. When contractual commitments are not observed, the enterprise bears economic liability and reimburses losses to the consumer, according to established procedure. The payment of fines and penalties for the violation of contractual terms, as well as reimbursement for losses inflicted, does not free the enterprise from fulfilling its commitments to deliver output, carry out work, or provide services.

4. The purchaser-enterprise must pay on time for output (work, services) supplied to it in accordance with a contract using its own money and, in certain cases, using bank credits. It is responsible for making payments according to established schedules, and it pays a fine for late payments.

When the enterprise does not have its own funds to settle accounts for output (work, services) and lacks the right to obtain credit, the higher-level agency allocates money to it using appropriate centralized funds and reserves, on condition that the money is to be repaid.

*Article 17. Finances and prices*

1. The enterprise's financial activity should be directed toward the creation of financial resources for the production and social development of the enterprise and toward ensuring growth in profits (income) through increasing labor productivity, reducing unit cost, enhancing the quality of output (work, services), and improving the use of production assets.

2. The enterprise carries out financial activity in accordance with five-year and annual financial plans. It is responsible for the on-schedule fulfillment of its commitments to the budget, banks, the higher-level agency, suppliers, contractors, and other organizations. The enterprise must strive for high efficiency in the use of the financial resources remaining at its disposal.

3. The enterprise must take part in the formation of the revenues of the USSR State Budget, the money in which is channeled into the implementation of major economic and social undertakings, the strengthening of the country's defense capability, and other requirements of the state.

The enterprise's financial relations with the state budget are built on the basis of long-term economic normatives. The enterprise pays a charge to the budget for the resources at its disposal, contributes part of its profit (income), and also makes other payments stipulated by legislation, including payments to the local budget, according to established normatives.

Normatives for the distribution of profit (income) between the enterprise and the budget should provide for the state's equally intensive requirements for the use by enterprises of production assets and labor and natural resources.

Charges for production assets are paid, as a rule, on the basis of a norm that is the same for all enterprises. Charges for labor resources reimburse the state's expenditures on training the work force and providing social, cultural, municipal, and consumer services to employees and members of their families. Through charges for natural resources (land, water, commercial minerals), a differential rent that stems from differences in the natural productivity of these resources is withdrawn.

Along with payments to the budget for resources, taxes are levied on the profits (income) of enterprises remaining after payments for resources and the payment of interest on credits.

The withdrawal and redistribution of the profits (income) and other financial resources of the enterprise over and above the established normatives, norms, and rates, as well as in instances not stipulated by legislation, are prohibited.

4. The enterprise must work without showing a loss. In the case of temporary planned-loss operations, the enterprise is financed by the higher-level agency using centralized assets and reserves within the limits of the subsidy established in the five-year plan, with progressive reductions. It must work out measures to strengthen its financial position, to eliminate the unprofitable production of output (work, services) within an established time period, and to ensure operation at a profit.

5. The enterprise makes reimbursement for losses inflicted on other organizations and the state and pays fines, penalties, and other sanctions established by legislation using the collective's cost-accounting income. Sums of money obtained by the enterprise as reimbursement for losses and sanctions are channeled into increasing the collective's cost-accounting income.

6. The enterprise exercises its rights and duties in the field of price formation in accordance with the basic principles of state administration and regulation of prices. Prices should reflect socially necessary outlays on the production and sale of output, its consumer properties, quality, and effective demand. They are used as an active means of influencing growth in production efficiency, improvement in output quality, and reduction in the unit cost of output (work, services). The enterprise must ensure the economic validity of prices and of plans for prices or calculations for them, priority growth for national-economic effect in comparison with outlays, and a relative reduction in output prices for consumers.

7. The enterprise sells its output (work, services) based on prices (rates) that are centrally established, as well as under arrangement with consumers or independently.

8. The enterprise is responsible for the strict observance of price discipline and must prevent the overstating of prices. Profits obtained in an unwarranted manner by the enterprise as a result of violations of state price discipline or nonobservance of standards and technical specifications are subject to withdrawal into the budget (using the collective's cost-accounting income) and are excluded from reporting data on plan fulfillment.

An enterprise that overstates prices and obtains unwarranted profits makes an additional payment into the budget, using the collective's cost-accounting income, in the form of a fine in the amount of the illegally obtained profits. When the producer overstates prices for output (work, services), the consumer has the right to annul the contract that has been concluded for its delivery.

9. Enterprises must be guided by centrally established prices (rates) for output (work, services), as well as by prices (rates) confirmed by ministries and departments.

The enterprise has the right, with the concurrence of the client, to apply markups (discounts) to centrally established wholesale prices for the fulfillment of additional requirements with respect to changes in the consumer properties of output and the making up of complete sets of articles.

10. With a view to expanding independence in economic activity, giving fuller consideration to the individual needs of consumers, and providing incentives for the production of high-quality output, the enterprise has the right to apply prices based on arrangements with consumers (contract prices) for production-and-technical output manufactured to fill one-time and individual orders, new output or output that is in production for the first time and new nonfood consumer goods, as well as certain types of foodstuffs sold under agreement with trade organizations, for a period of up to two years on the basis of an established list, for the final output of research and design organizations, for agricultural output purchased from the population by state farms and other state agricultural enterprises, for output purchased and sold by cooperative organizations, and for other types of output (work, services) stipulated by legislation.

State price-formation agencies determine the procedure for establishing contract prices and monitor their application.

11. The enterprise independently confirms prices (rates) for production-and-technical output, consumer goods and services to which centrally confirmed prices are not applied, as well as for output (services) that is for its own consumption or is sold in its own trade network.

State farms and other state agricultural enterprises have the right to independently establish prices for part of the planned and all of the above-plan agricultural output that is sold through their own trade networks and on collective farm markets.

As full cost accounting, self-financing, wholesale trade, and direct economic ties develop, the application of contract and independently confirmed prices will expand.

## Article 18.  Credit and settlements

1. In conditions of full cost accounting and self-financing, the enterprise uses bank credits for production and social purposes, on condition that the principles of credit operations are strictly observed: the credit is provided, it is directed to a specific purpose, it is granted for a specific time, it is to be repaid, and it is in fact repaid.

Short-term credits are issued by the bank to the enterprise for purposes of current activity on the basis of broad-category objects of credit operations. Long-term credits are granted for purposes of production and social development, with subsequent repayment of the credit using money in the fund for the development of production, science and technology and the fund for social development (or other similar funds).

The enterprise resolves all questions associated with credit operations in the credit institutions at the place where it has its current account or account for financing capital investments.

The enterprise is responsible for the effective use of credits. Sanctions are applied against enterprises that violate the terms of credit operations. When there is a systematic failure to meet schedules for the repayment of loans, the enterprise loses the right to obtain new credits; in certain instances, it may use credits guaranteed by the higher-level agency.

2. The enterprise must settle accounts with respect to its commitments on time. The enterprise pays fines and penalties for late settlements. The enterprise makes all settlements, including payments into the budget and the payment of wages, in the calendar order in which settlement documents are received (when payment dates arrive).

Banks pay the enterprise interest for the use of temporarily free money in its fund for the development of production, science and technology, as well as in the fund for social development.

3. Banks may declare an enterprise that systematically violates payments discipline insolvent, and they report this fact to the basic suppliers of goods and materials and to the higher-level agency. The bank determines the order of priority with regard to payments on such an enterprise's commitments. Creditor-enterprises may stop delivering output to, performing work for, and providing services to an enterprise that has been declared insolvent. The enterprise and its higher-level agency must take steps to eliminate mismanagement and strengthen settlements discipline.

The bank writes off compulsorily exacted fines and penalties and other sanctions to the enterprise's current account. The enterprise is reimbursed by the guilty party for illegally written-off sums in amounts greater than those wrongfully exacted. Disputes over such restitutions are examined by arbitration agencies and courts.

*Article 19. Foreign economic operations*

1. The enterprise's foreign economic operations are an important component of all the enterprise's work. They are carried out, as a rule, on the basis of foreign-currency unsubsidized operations and self-financing; their result is an organic part of the results of the enterprise's economic activity and directly affects the formation of the economic incentive fund and the foreign-currency payments fund.

The enterprise ensures the delivery of output for export as a top priority.

2. Cooperation with enterprises in the socialist countries, the broadening and deepening of socialist economic integration, and the development of effective cooperative arrangements are of priority importance in the enterprise's foreign economic operations.

In relations with enterprises and organizations of the CMEA member-countries, the enterprise:

establishes direct ties, resolves questions of production and scientific-technological cooperation, including the determination of the economic terms of cooperation, including contract prices, and concludes economic contracts;

reaches agreement on the product mix and the volume of export-import deliveries of output based on cooperative arrangements and on the provision of services, and carries out transfers of material resources and the appropriate technical documentation;

conducts research, design, and experimental work, creates joint collectives of scientists and specialists for this purpose, exchanges scientific-technological documentation under mutually agreed-upon conditions, and provides assistance in the training of personnel;

participates in the activity of joint enterprises, international associations, and organizations that are created on the basis of the USSR's international treaties.

3. The enterprise puts into effect economic ties with firms in the capitalist and developing countries according to the principles of mutual advantage and equality. Cooperative production and scientific-technological arrangements on a long-term and balanced basis, as well as the creation of joint enterprises and production facilities, are the basic forms of the development of such ties. The procedures for the creation of joint enterprises and production facilities on USSR territory and for their activity are determined in accordance with Soviet legislation.

4. The right to carry out directly export-import operations (including in markets in capitalist and developing countries) and to create a cost-accounting foreign trade firm for this purpose may be granted to an enterprise that provides substantial deliveries of output (work, services) for export.

Enterprises that do not have the right to independently enter the foreign market participate in determining the best terms for the export of their output (work, services) through the foreign trade associations of their own or other ministries and departments.

5. With a view to strengthening cost accounting, increasing economic interest and responsibility, and expanding independence in carrying out export-import operations, the enterprise:

engages in cooperation with foreign partners on the basis of economic contracts;

creates a foreign-currency payments fund, formed on the basis of stable, long-term normatives from money received through the sale of finished output (work, services) for export, as well as all foreign-currency receipts from operations involving cooperative deliveries and the sale of licenses;

may obtain a bank credit in foreign currency for the creation and development of export production facilities, on condition that the credit is repaid using foreign-currency receipts from the export of output;

bears economic responsibility for the effectiveness of foreign economic ties and the rational use of foreign-currency resources in the interests of developing production and raising its technical level;

pays compensation for losses from the nonfulfillment of assignments for the export of goods or of contractual commitments using its foreign-currency resources;

pays all fines and other sanctions in foreign currency to the foreign purchaser using the foreign-currency payments fund, if the violation of commitments was its fault.

6. With a view to the technical reequipment and reconstruction of production and the performance of research, experimental-design, and other work, the enterprise carries out imports of output using, and within the limits of, the foreign-currency payments fund or borrowed money. It also has the right to acquire in the CMEA member-countries, for the needs of its work collectives, medical equipment and cultural, consumer, sporting, and other goods that are not included in the state allocation plans.

Money in the enterprise's foreign-currency payments fund is not subject to withdrawal and may accumulate for use in subsequent years.

7. The enterprise may acquire in the USSR Bank for Foreign Economic Relations on credit terms, transferable rubles and national currencies of countries of the socialist commonwealth in order to conduct scientific-technological work and to develop efficient production facilities related to cooperative arrangements.

## Article 20. Nature use and environmental protection

1. The enterprise must, in the interests of present and future generations of Soviet people, ensure the efficient use and reproduction of natural resources, make solicitous use of them in accordance with the purposes for which they are

made available to it, protect the environment from pollution and other harmful influences, and carry out the organization of production on the basis of waste-free technologies as the main guideline for preserving the environment.

The enterprise ensures the comprehensive use of commercial minerals and other natural resources; it is to make rational use of agricultural land and conduct the recultivation of land and other measures to protect the environment.

In designs for the expansion, reconstruction, and technical reequipment of production, the enterprise provides for environmental-protection structures and installations; it builds them and sets up their efficient and uninterrupted operation.

2. The enterprise makes established payments for the use of natural resources as part of national property, and it carries out environmental-protection measures using its own money and credits. In certain instances, such measures are financed through centralized sources.

3. In its work with respect to environmental protection and the use of natural resources, the enterprise is under the control of the local soviet and other agencies that exercise state oversight* in the field of environmental protection and the use of natural resources.

The enterprise reimburses damages caused by environmental pollution and the irrational use of natural resources, and it bears material responsibility for the nonobservance of legislation on environmental protection. Enterprise activities that flagrantly violate the established regulations for nature use may be suspended until the violations are eliminated.

## Article 21.  The enterprise's joint production and social activity

1. In order to make more efficient use of production potential, expand the production of goods and services, jointly solve scientific-technological problems, and develop the infrastructure, the enterprise, on its own initiative or at the suggestion of local soviets or other organizations, develops cooperation primarily with enterprises located in the given territory. They may pool their efforts to accomplish interbranch, branch, and regional tasks. With this in view, the enterprise has the right:

to jointly perform work related to the reconstruction and technical reequipment of production, the acceleration of scientific-technological progress, the improvement of output quality, the development of consumer goods production, and the provision of services to the population;

to create, according to established procedure, interbranch production facilities, time-sharing computer centers, and research, design, repair, construction,

---

*Editor's note—In the original CDSP translation this term [gosudarstvennaia kontrol'] was rendered as "state monitoring." It has been changed here and throughout this text in order to maintain consistency with the translation of the manuscript.

trade, and other joint enterprises and associations;

to carry out the construction and operation of facilities of the production infrastructure, auxiliary agricultural operations, environmental-protection structures, residential buildings, and other production, social, cultural, municipal, and consumer-service facilities;

according to established procedure, to amalgamate with other enterprises, up to and including complete merger, if this is dictated by the interests of cooperation and technological ties and the efficient obtaining of final output;

to organize the training of specialists, and to create (in conjunction with educational institutions) production-training enterprises.

In order to carry out the aforementioned and other joint activities, enterprises conclude contracts that provide for the pooling of financial, labor, and material resources on a *pro rata* basis, as well as for the resolution of questions relating to the organization and activities of joint enterprises and associations.

Higher-level agencies and executive committees of local soviets of people's deputies take steps to develop joint activities by enterprises and help them in the fullest possible exercise of the rights they have been granted in this field.

2. The enterprise may participate in the activity of interbranch and interfarm territorial-production associations created by union-republic (in republics not divided into provinces) and autonomous-republic councils of ministers and executive committees of local soviets of people's deputies.

3. Cooperatives may be created under the auspices of the enterprise, according to established procedure. The enterprise provides assistance to these cooperatives, as well as to citizens who engage in individual labor activity under contracts with the enterprise.

## Article 22.  Record-keeping, reporting, and oversight

1. In order to exert an active influence on all economic activity and analyze the ways, forms, and methods of developing production, and with a view to ensuring efficient management and preventing opportunities for the emergence of certain disproportions in the fulfillment of plan assignments, the enterprise keeps records on the results of work, monitors the course of production, and keeps current-operations, bookkeeping, and statistical records.

The enterprise is to:

use advanced forms and methods of record keeping and information processing based on the broad application of up-to-date computing equipment;

compile reporting documents and present them to the appropriate agencies by established deadlines, and ensure the authenticity of reports and balance sheets;

strictly monitor the rational and economical use of material, labor, and financial resources, wage a resolute struggle against mismanagement and wastefulness, take steps to prevent such phenomena, and report embezzlement and flagrant violations of legislation to internal affairs agencies or agencies of the prosecutor's office;

enhance the role and responsibility of the legal, bookkeeping, and other functional services for the observance of legality and contract and financial discipline and for output quality.

Executives of enterprises, structural units, and subdivisions and other guilty parties bear personal responsibility for instances of report padding, eyewash,* and other distortions of state reporting and are subject to disciplinary, material or criminal liability. All instances of report-padding and eyewash are discussed in the work collective.

The forms of the enterprise's reporting documents and the places and times at which they are to be submitted are determined according to established procedure. Requests for and the submission of any other reporting documents are prohibited.

2. Audits and inspections of the enterprise's activity may be conducted by, along with higher-level agencies, financial, banking and other administrative agencies in accordance with the functions of oversight over the enterprise's activity that are assigned to them by legislation. An audit or an inspection may be conducted at the request of law-enforcement agencies or people's control committees.

All types of audits and inspections should promote the increased efficiency of economic management and should not disrupt the normal pace of the enterprise's work. The results of audits and inspections are reported to the labor collective.

3. A People's Control Committee (group, post) is elected at the enterprise; the enterprise's management must provide it with all possible assistance in its work, examine its proposals and recommendations, and take the necessary steps to eliminate shortcomings that are disclosed.

*Article 23. The creation of the enterprise and termination of its activity*

1. Enterprises are created according to the procedure established by the USSR Council of Ministers.

The reorganization (merger, annexation, partition,† detachment, reconstitution†) of enterprises and the termination of their activity are effected, according to established procedure, by decision of the agency that is empowered

---

*Editor's note—We have changed the original *CDSP* rendition of this term [*ochkovtiratel'stvo*] here and below from "hoodwinking" to "eyewash."

†Editor's note—In the original *CDSP* translation the terms *razdelenie* and *preobrazovanie* were rendered as "division" and "transformation," respectively. We have changed them here to "partition" and "reconstitution" in order to maintain consistency with the translation of the manuscript.

to create the enterprise in question.

The enterprise's activity may be terminated:

if there is no need for its further operation and it cannot be reorganized, or for other reasons stipulated by legislation;

when an enterprise has operated at a loss for a longtime and is insolvent, when there is no demand for its output, and in the event that measures taken by the enterprise and the higher-level agency to ensure the profitability of operations have brought no results.

2. When an enterprise is reorganized or liquidated, the higher-level agency guarantees the rights of the dismissed employees as established by the USSR Constitution and legislation. Employees receive personal warnings of the date of dismissal no later than two months before the reorganization or liquidation of the enterprise. They retain their average wages and uninterrupted work records during the job-placement period, but for no more than three months.

The agency that has made the decision to reorganize or liquidate the enterprise and the local soviet of people's deputies provide all possible assistance in the job placement of the dismissed employees. Citizens' claims and suits against the enterprise that is being liquidated may be brought against the higher-level agency.

Employees for whom jobs cannot be found in accordance with their occupations, specialties, or skills are hired for new jobs on condition that they complete retraining within the time period stipulated when the labor contract was concluded.

3. The enterprise has a charter setting the goals of its activity, which is confirmed by the higher-level agency. As of the day that the charter is confirmed, the enterprise becomes a juridical person and enjoys the rights and performs the duties associated with its activity.

The enterprise has a seal bearing its name and a depiction of the USSR Law on the State Enterprise (Association), given the adoption of normative documents pertaining to the practical implementation of this law, and they build their relations with enterprises and associations in strict accordance with the aforementioned law.

### Article 24. On guarantees of the observance of the rights of enterprises (associations)

Agencies of state power and administration are responsible for the observance of the provisions of the USSR Law on the State Enterprise (Association), given the adoption of normative documents pertaining to the practical implementation of this law, and they build their relations with enterprises and associations in strict accordance with the aforementioned law.

*Article 25.  Special features of the application of this law*

Special features of the application of this law in certain branches of the national economy and with respect to certain types of enterprises are determined by the USSR Council of Ministers.

A. GROMYKO
*Chairman of the Presidium
of the USSR Supreme Soviet*

T. MENTESHASHVILI
*Administrative Secretary of the Presidium
of the USSR Supreme Soviet*

# II

# ON CLARIFICATION OF THE PROCEDURES FOR APPLYING ECONOMIC SANCTIONS AGAINST ASSOCIATIONS, ENTERPRISES, AND ORGANIZATIONS UNDER THE CONDITIONS OF RESTRUCTURING OF ECONOMIC MANAGEMENT

Decree No. 1064 of the CPSU Central Committee
and the USSR Council of Ministers, 17 September 1987;
*Sobranie postanovlenii Pravitel'stva SSSR* 1987, No. 45, item 150

In order to strengthen the motivation and the responsibility of associations, enterprises, and organizations for improving the efficiency of production and the final results of their activity, the CPSU Central Committee and the USSR Council of Ministers *decree*:

It is established that from 1987 until the conversion of associations, enterprises, and organizations to operating conditions as provided for in the Law of the USSR on the State Enterprise (Association), funds discharged and received in the form of fines, damages, and other sanctions are treated:

in the case of associations, enterprises, and organizations converted to full cost-accounting and self-financing—as profits (income) remaining at their disposal and deposited in their economic incentive funds in established amounts;

in the case of associations, enterprises, and organizations not converted to full cost-accounting or self-financing—as profits to be deposited in the economic incentive funds and used to cover other expenditures, in accordance with the planned proportions for distribution of this profit (with the exception of funds from fines that, in conformity with the existing legislation, must be remitted to the state budget).

M. GORBACHEV
*Secretary of the CPSU Central Committee*

N. RYZHKOV
*Chairman of the USSR Council of Ministers*

# III

# ON CONFIRMATION OF THE STATUTE OF THE USSR MINISTRY OF FOREIGN TRADE*

Decree No. 1513 of the USSR Council of Ministers, 22 December 1986;
*Sobranie postanovlenii Pravitel'stva SSSR* 1987, No. 5, item 20

The USSR Council of Ministers *decrees*:

1. To confirm the appended Statute of the USSR Ministry of Foreign Trade.

2. To establish that authorization for the importation into and exportation from the USSR of cargo and other property by state, cooperative, and other associations, enterprises, and organizations—including participants in direct ties and joint enterprises, international associations and organizations—as well as for the transit of foreign cargo across the territory of the USSR, is issued by the USSR Ministry of Foreign Trade.

Authorization for the importation into and exportation from the USSR of cargo and other property by organizations belonging to the USSR State Committee for Foreign Economic Relations, the USSR Ministry of the Fish Industry, the USSR Ministry of Geology, and the Main Administration of Geodesy and Cartography of the USSR Council of Ministers, is issued by the USSR State Committee for Foreign Economic Relations.

Associations, enterprises, and organizations maintaining direct production and scientific-technological ties with enterprises and organizations from other socialist countries are granted general authorization, for a year or more—within the limits of the duration of the treaty or protocol on which the direct ties are

---

*Editor's note*—On 15 January 1988 the USSR Ministry of Foreign Trade was abolished by Edict of the Presidium of the USSR Supreme Soviet (see Appendix X, *infra*), along with the USSR State Committee for Foreign Economic Relations. A new Ministry was created by the same Edict: The USSR Ministry of Foreign Economic Relations. Until a Statute is confirmed for the new Ministry, the detailed enumeration of functions and activities contained in the Statutes of the USSR Ministry of Foreign Trade and the USSR State Committee for Foreign Economic Relations can serve as guidelines for foreign commercial firms on the possible scope of activities of the new Ministry, which is now in the process of organization.

based—for the importation into and exportation from the USSR of cargo and other property.

In accordance with the provisions specified in the first and second paragraphs of the present clause, authorization for the re-export of cargo is issued respectively by the USSR Ministry of Foreign Trade or the USSR State Committee for Foreign Economic Relations.

Cargo and other property may be admitted across USSR state borders in the presence of the authorizations specified in the present clause, as well as corresponding authorizations issued by USSR trade missions abroad.

N. RYZHKOV
*Chairman of the USSR Council of Ministers*

M. SMIRTIUKOV
*Administrative Secretary*
*of the USSR Council of Ministers*

# STATUTE OF THE USSR MINISTRY OF FOREIGN TRADE

## Confirmed by Decree No. 1513 of the USSR Council of Ministers, 22 December 1986

1. The USSR Ministry of Foreign Trade is an all-union ministry.

Within the limits of its authority, the USSR Ministry of Foreign Trade is responsible for developing foreign economic relations, for ensuring their effectiveness and the fullest possible utilization of the potentialities offered by the international division of labor in the interest of accelerating the socioeconomic development of the USSR, and for monitoring observance of the USSR's state interests in foreign markets.

The USSR Ministry of Foreign Trade oversees foreign trade in fuels, raw materials, foodstuffs, machinery and equipment (according to the list assigned to the Ministry), and other goods of statewide importance.

2. The primary tasks of the USSR Ministry of Foreign Trade are the following:

the drafting and carrying out of assignments included in the state plans of economic and social development as well as other assignments in the area of the USSR's foreign trade, and the ensuring of strict observance of state discipline;

the implementation of measures aimed at ensuring priority development of the USSR's economic ties with socialist countries based on the principles of socialist internationalism, at improving the system of cooperation with these countries, at making the transition from ties based predominantly on trade to deep specialization and cooperation in production, and at introducing new forms of cooperation;

participation in the drafting of proposals on foreign economic policy and strategy for the development of the USSR's foreign economic relations, including proposals covering individual regions and countries, and primarily of a conception for the development of foreign economic ties with CMEA member countries;

participation in the coordination of state plans between the USSR and the other CMEA member countries;

the all-around development of trade relations and promotion of new forms of cooperation with the developing countries;

the development of stable trade relations with the capitalist countries based on mutual advantage and equality, improvement of the forms of cooperation utilized with them, and the promotion of intensified cooperative activities and joint enterprises;

participation in the drafting of programs for the large-scale expansion of the nation's export potential that are based on the development strategy for the USSR's economic relations;

the protection of the USSR's state interests in multilateral and bilateral trade and economic relations with foreign countries;

enhancement of the effectiveness of the USSR's foreign trade via improvements of the planning of foreign economic operations, improvement of their management and of the structure of exports and imports, enhancement of the competitiveness of export goods, the implementation of measures designed to increase foreign-currency earnings and to make more rational use of foreign-currency funds, promotion of the development of products capable of substituting for imports, and promotion of a balanced development of foreign trade;

within the limits of its authority, ensuring that foreign trade obligations issuing from international treaties entered into by the USSR are honored;

oversight over the observance by ministries, departments, associations, enterprises, and organizations involved in foreign economic ties of the USSR's state interests in foreign markets;

the active introduction of economic methods in interrelations with all-union cost-accounting foreign trade associations subordinate to the Ministry and with associations, enterprises, and organizations belonging to other ministries and departments, by way of developing and strengthening economic cost accounting through the use of contractual relations.

3. The USSR Ministry of Foreign Trade is guided in its activities by the laws of the USSR, other decisions of the USSR Supreme Soviet and its Presidium, decrees and orders of the USSR Council of Ministers, decisions of the State Foreign Economic Commission of the USSR Council of Ministers, the present Statute and other normative acts, and ensures the strengthening of socialist legality and the proper application of existing legislation throughout the Ministry's network, and it organizes and directs legal work in this network.

The USSR Ministry of Foreign Trade publishes consolidated summaries of practice in applying legislation to areas under the Ministry's jurisdiction, drafts proposals designed to improve such application and submits them in the established procedure to the State Foreign Economic Commission of the USSR Council of Ministers.

4. The USSR Ministry of Foreign Trade operates under the direct management of the State Foreign Economic Commission of the USSR Council of Ministers.

5. The unified network of the USSR Ministry of Foreign Trade is comprised of the Ministry itself, its legal representatives at individual regions and sites on the territory of the USSR that hold great importance for Soviet exports, its all-union cost-accounting foreign trade associations (hereinafter "foreign trade associations"), the All-Union Scientific Market Research Institute, the All-Union Foreign Trade Academy, and other subordinate organizations and establishments. The Statute on Legal Representatives of the USSR Ministry of Foreign Trade is confirmed by the USSR Ministry of Foreign Trade.

The USSR Ministry of Foreign Trade bears responsibility for the fulfillment of tasks assigned under the plan on the part of subordinate foreign trade associations, for the effectiveness of their business activity, for their assurance of the safekeeping of socialist property, and for the maintenance of strict oversight in this sphere.

6. Foreign trade associations falling under the jurisdiction of the USSR Ministry of Foreign Trade operate based on the principles of cost accounting, self-recoupment, and self-financing, and based on a system of cost-accounting contract relations.

The USSR Ministry of Foreign Trade does not bear material liability for the obligations of subordinate foreign trade associations, while these foreign trade associations are not liable for the obligations of the Ministry.

7. Beyond the functions enumerated in the General Statute on USSR Ministries, the USSR Ministry of Foreign Trade:

a) prepares and submits to the USSR State Planning Committee and the USSR State Committee for Material and Technical Supply drafts of consolidated plans for exports and imports, and to the USSR State Planning Committee the corresponding summary data on receipts and payments in foreign currency, and prepares drafts of foreign-currency and financial plans of the Ministry, as well as plans for the carriage of export, import, and transit cargo. Drafts of consolidated plans for exports and imports and the corresponding summary data on receipts and payments in foreign currency are based on the plans of ministries, departments, associations, enterprises, and organizations that are granted the right to conduct export-import operations;

b) participates in the drafting of proposals and measures designed to develop socialist economic integration on the basis of the international division of labor, to encourage interstate specialization and broad cooperation in the production of equipment and machinery, and to introduce new and progressive forms of cooperation;

c) drafts proposals on the coordination of the state plans of the USSR with the state plans of the other CMEA member countries;

d) with the participation of the USSR State Planning Committee and the USSR State Committee for Material and Technical Supply as well as the relevant ministries, departments, and organizations that have been granted the right to conduct export-import operations, conducts negotiations on commodity circulation and payments with socialist countries and capitalist countries with whom accounts are settled under clearing agreements, and executes the corresponding documents;

e) grants subordinate foreign trade associations the authority to conduct export-import operations on the basis of contract relations with suppliers of goods for export, customers of import goods, and other organizations;

f) in the established procedure, issues authorizations for the importation into and exportation from the USSR of cargo and other property, for the re-export of cargo, and also for the transit of foreign cargo across USSR territory;

g) carries out measures designed to enhance the effectiveness of operations undertaken by subordinate foreign trade associations, and to promote the more economical expenditure of material resources and foreign-currency and monetary funds; takes part in efforts to develop and strengthen economic cost accounting in the USSR's foreign trade;

h) studies the national economy's export potentialities and import needs, the economies, foreign trade networks, trade policy, and relevant legislation of foreign countries, and also questions related to the development of international trade; undertakes efforts to study competition in international commodity markets;

i) in conformity with existing legislation, submits proposals on the conclusion of international treaties by the USSR concerning issues of foreign trade and on the USSR's adherence to international treaties, and it conducts negotiations and concludes international treaties on behalf of the USSR;

j) organizes and maintains state oversight over the quality of goods exported from the USSR at associations and enterprises where State Acceptance has not been introduced;

k) takes part in the drafting and implementation of measures related to foreign-currency and credit issues in the area of the USSR's foreign trade, and plays a role in the drafting of principles and a methodology underlying the setting of foreign trade prices and rates;

l) together with the relevant ministries and departments, drafts and implements measures designed to organize and improve the carriage of foreign trade cargo;

takes part in the drafting of measures designed to improve the storage and enhance the safekeeping of foreign trade cargo; provides transportation-forward-ing services for export and import cargo, as well as for the transit of foreign cargo across USSR territory;

m) takes part in the organization of international and foreign trade and industrial exhibitions in the USSR, undertakes measures designed to improve coordination of the activities of USSR ministries and departments, foreign trade organizations, associations and enterprises at international fairs and exhibitions, and the conduct of national and trade and industrial exhibitions of the USSR abroad; organizes the participation of subordinate foreign trade associations in fairs and exhibitions;

n) takes part, in the established procedure, in the activities of international organizations and agencies, as well as intergovernmental commissions and committees dealing with the USSR's commercial, economic, and scientific-technological cooperation with foreign countries;

o) takes part in conferences, congresses, symposiums, and meetings devoted to topics of international economic relations; receives foreign delegations arriving in the USSR for the discussion and resolution of questions related to cooperation in foreign trade;

p) conducts informational and promotional work for USSR foreign trade, publishes the journal *Vneshniaia torgovlia SSSR* [Foreign Trade of the USSR], and approves plans for the publication of scientific works, conference materials, and economic literature prepared in the established procedure by subordinate establishments;

q) in the procedures agreed upon with the USSR Central Statistical Administration,* processes data on USSR foreign trade and submits the necessary reports to the former within the specified time limits; prepares and publishes the statistical compendium *Vneshniaia torgovlia SSSR*; prepares proposals aimed at improving the processing of data on USSR foreign trade;

r) provides for the training, retraining, and advanced training of personnel employed in the Ministry's network, as well as of personnel employed in other ministries, departments, associations, enterprises, and organizations that maintain foreign economic ties;

undertakes measures designed to improve working conditions, housing, cultural and communal services, and medical services for employees in the Ministry's network;

s) in the established procedure, gathers and arranges archival documents and materials on USSR foreign trade, and provides for their safekeeping.

8. With the goal of ensuring the observance of the USSR's state interests in foreign markets by ministries, departments, associations, enterprises, and organizations and of conducting unified commercial and economic, foreign-currency, and price policies in foreign markets:

---

*Editor's note*—The USSR Central Statistical Administration was renamed the USSR State Committee for Statistics in August 1987.

with the participation, if required, of the USSR Ministry of Finance, the USSR Foreign Trade Bank,* and other interested agencies and organizations, monitors the conduct of the export-import operations of ministries, departments, associations, enterprises, and organizations;

provides for the coordination and systematic supervision of the operations of ministries, departments, associations, enterprises, and organizations that are related to the conduct of export-import operations;

receives from and provides to ministries, departments, associations, enterprises, and organizations that take part in foreign economic ties, all the necessary documents, proposals, and summaries dealing with issues of foreign trade, including information on the current state of competition in the respective world commodity markets and on exports and imports of individual goods, services, and results of creative activity according to countries or groups of countries and types of currency.

The USSR Ministry of Foreign Trade submits reports to the State Foreign Economic Commission of the USSR Council of Ministers on its work in maintaining such oversight, and these include proposals on eliminating uncovered violations and shortcomings.

9. The USSR Ministry of Foreign Trade is granted the following rights:

a) in the established procedure, to reorganize and liquidate subordinate foreign trade associations;

b) in the established procedure, to authorize subordinate foreign trade associations to create, both within the USSR and abroad, branches, offices, departments, representative offices, and joint-stock companies, and to participate in all forms of organizations whose activities are appropriate to the tasks of the associations;

c) to grant foreign organizations and firms, in the established procedure, authorization to open representative offices in the USSR, and to make decisions on terminating their activities, and also to examine information provided by the heads of representative offices on their activities;

d) upon agreement with the relevant ministries and departments, to award associations, enterprises, and organizations honorary medals and diplomas of the Ministry for achievement of the highest results in the production and delivery of goods for export;

e) within the limits of its jurisdiction, to enter into relations with state agencies, institutions, enterprises, organizations, and official and private persons of foreign countries, both within the USSR and abroad.

Beyond the rights enumerated in the present Statute, the USSR Ministry of Foreign Trade also enjoys rights granted it by the existing legislation.

10. The USSR Ministry of Foreign Trade is headed up by the Minister, who is

---

*Editor's note—The USSR Foreign Trade Bank has since been renamed the USSR Bank for Foreign Economic Relations.

appointed, in conformity with the USSR Constitution, by the USSR Supreme Soviet, and between sessions—by the Presidium of the USSR Supreme Soviet, subject to confirmation by the USSR Supreme Soviet.

The USSR Minister of Foreign Trade is assisted by deputy ministers, who are appointed by the USSR Council of Ministers. The distribution of duties between the deputy ministers is the purview of the Minister.

11. The USSR Minister of Foreign Trade bears personal responsibility for fulfillment of the goals assigned to the Ministry and for the exercise of his own functions, and he establishes the degree of responsibility borne by the deputy ministers and heads of structural subdivisions of the Ministry's central administrative apparatus for the management of the Ministry's various spheres of operations.

12. Within the USSR Ministry of Foreign Trade is formed a Collegium consisting of the Minister (the Chairman of the Collegium), the deputy ministers in accordance with their posts, and other administrative personnel in the Ministry's network.

Members of the Collegium of the Ministry are confirmed by the USSR Council of Ministers.

13. At its regularly scheduled meetings, the Collegium of the USSR Ministry of Foreign Trade examines the following questions:

the Ministry's participation in the drafting of proposals related to foreign economic policy, development strategy for the USSR's foreign economic relations, and the priority development of economic relations with socialist countries;

fulfillment of tasks assigned under the state plans as well as other tasks dealing with foreign trade in fuels, raw materials, foodstuffs, machinery and equipment (according to the list assigned to the Ministry), and other goods of statewide importance, and tasks assigned under the foreign-currency and financial plans of the Ministry;

the introduction of economic methods in the interrelations of foreign trade associations subordinated to the Ministry with associations, enterprises, and organizations of other ministries and departments;

oversight over the observation of the USSR's state interests in foreign markets by ministries, departments, associations, enterprises, and organizations;

supervision over the hiring, selection, distribution, training, and education of personnel by foreign trade associations, organizations, and institutions subordinated to the Ministry;

the preparation of drafts of normative acts and other important documents;

At its sessions, the Collegium hears reports from the heads of the structural subdivisions of the central administrative apparatus, of the foreign trade associations, organizations, and institutions of the Ministry, and of USSR trade representatives and consultants assigned to USSR embassies in foreign countries, and also examines other questions related to the Ministry's activities.

Decisions of the Collegium of the USSR Ministry of Foreign Trade are enacted, as a rule, by orders of the Minister. In the event of disagreements between the Minister and the Collegium, the Minister enacts his decisions while reporting on the disagreements to the USSR Council of Ministers, and the members of the Collegium may in turn make their opinions known to the USSR Council of Ministers.

14. Within the limits of its jurisdiction, and in accordance with and application of the laws of the USSR, other decisions of the USSR Supreme Soviet and its Presidium, decrees and rulings of the USSR Council of Ministers, and decisions of the State Foreign Economic Commission of the USSR Council of Ministers, the USSR Ministry of Foreign Trade issues orders and directives and gives instructions that are binding on the Ministry's legal representatives, foreign trade associations, and other organizations and institutions under its jurisdiction, as well as USSR trade missions and trade advisory bodies in USSR embassies in foreign countries, and sees to and monitors their execution.

Within the limits of its jurisdiction, the USSR Ministry of Foreign Trade issues orders and directives in the area of USSR foreign trade that are binding on ministries and departments, and also associations, enterprises, and organizations regardless of their departmental affiliation.

In the necessary instances, the USSR Ministry of Foreign Trade issues orders and directives jointly or with the agreement of other ministries and departments.

15. The number and composition of employees in the central administrative apparatus of the USSR Ministry of Foreign Trade are confirmed by the USSR Council of Ministers.

The staffing of the central administrative apparatus of the Ministry, as well as provisions for its structural subdivisions, are confirmed by the USSR Minister of Foreign Trade.

The Minister may convert structural subdivisions of the central administrative apparatus of the USSR Ministry of Foreign Trade over to economic cost accounting.

16. The USSR Ministry of Foreign Trade has a seal on which is a depiction of the USSR State Emblem and its appellation.

# IV

# ON CONFIRMATION OF THE STATUTE OF THE USSR STATE COMMITTEE FOR FOREIGN ECONOMIC RELATIONS*

Decree No. 1514 of the USSR Council of Ministers,
22 December 1986;
*Sobranie postanovlenii Pravitel'stva SSSR* 1987, No. 5, item 20

The USSR Council of Ministers *decrees*:

To confirm the appended Statute on the USSR State Committee for Foreign Economic Relations.

To recognize as no longer in force Decree No. 336 of the USSR Council of Ministers of 27 March 1959, "On Confirmation of the Statute of the State Committee of the USSR Council of Ministers for Foreign Economic Relations and of the Structure of the Committee."

N. RYZHKOV
*Chairman of the USSR Council of Ministers*

M. SMIRTIUKOV
*Administrative Secretary*
*of the USSR Council of Ministers*

---

*\*Editor's note*—On 15 January 1988 the USSR State Committee for Foreign Economic Relations was abolished by Edict of the Presidium of the USSR Supreme Soviet (see Appendix X, *infra*), along with the USSR Ministry of Foreign Trade. A new Ministry was created by the same Edict: The USSR Ministry of Foreign Economic Relations. Until a Statute is confirmed for the new Ministry, the detailed enumeration of functions and activities contained in the Statutes of the USSR Ministry of Foreign Trade and the USSR State Committee for Foreign Economic Relations can serve as guidelines for foreign commercial firms on the possible scope of activities of the new Ministry, which is now in the process of organization.

# STATUTE OF THE USSR STATE COMMITTEE FOR FOREIGN ECONOMIC RELATIONS

### Confirmed by Decree No. 1514 of the USSR Council of Ministers, 22 December 1986

1. The USSR State Committee for Foreign Economic Relations (USSR SCFR) is an all-union state agency responsible for the management of the USSR's economic and technological cooperation with foreign countries.

Within the limits of its authority, the USSR SCFR is responsible for developing foreign economic relations, for ensuring their effectiveness and the fullest possible utilization of the potentialities offered by the international division of labor in the interests of accelerating the socioeconomic development of the USSR, and for monitoring observance of the USSR's state interests in foreign markets.

2. The primary tasks of the USSR SCFR are:

assuring fulfillment of the assigned tasks of the state plans for economic development and of other tasks in the area of the USSR's foreign economic relations, securing the increase of foreign-currency receipts to cover the expenditures of Soviet organizations, improving management in the area of the USSR's economic and technological cooperation with foreign countries, increasing commercial activity, and ensuring the strict observance of state discipline;

implementing measures aimed at assuring priority development of the USSR's economic ties with socialist countries based on the principles of socialist internationalism, at improving the system of cooperation with these countries, and at introducing new forms of cooperation;

participating in the drafting of proposals in the area of foreign economic policy and strategy for the development of the USSR's foreign economic relations, including that for individual regions and countries, and primarily in the elaboration of a conception for the development of foreign economic ties with the CMEA member countries;

participating in the coordination of state plans between the USSR and the other CMEA member countries;

implementing measures aimed at expanding and deepening the USSR's economic and technological cooperation with capitalist and developing countries;

protecting the USSR's interests in multilateral and bilateral relations issuing from economic and technological cooperation with foreign countries;

enhancing the effectiveness of the USSR's economic and technological cooperation with foreign countries by improving the planning of foreign economic operations, improving the structure of exports and imports of finished industrial goods and services, by promoting development of the export base on the strength of acceleration of scientific-technological progress, and by developing and reinforcing cost accounting in the operations of all-union export-import associations in the USSR SCFR network;

ensuring fulfillment of the obligations of the USSR tied up in its economic and technological cooperation with foreign countries, in the supply of production and engineering services and the carrying out of other projects involving delivery of equipment and materials, the performance of design and feasibility studies, the dispatching of Soviet specialists abroad, and the training of foreign personnel, in accordance with international treaties entered into by the USSR, and also monitoring observance by foreign partners of their obligations;

monitoring the observance in foreign markets of the state interests of the USSR by ministries, departments, associations, enterprises, and organizations participating in foreign economic relations;

carrying out measures—jointly with the appropriate ministries, departments, suppliers and contractors, and also with design organizations—that have the goal of expanding cooperation in the construction of industrial facilities abroad and promoting allied exports of finished industrial goods and services, of broadening the product mix, and increasing the quality, technical level, and competitiveness of exported equipment;

improving the organization and management of projects calling for the construction and reconstruction of industrial facilities abroad, with the USSR supplying technical assistance, including under contract, as well as projects calling for exploitation of the capacities of constructed enterprises and other facilities and for assuring conditions guaranteeing their effective exploitation;

improving the organization and management of projects calling for the construction in the USSR of industrial facilities involving foreign organizations and firms, including construction-and-installation projects and the performance of allied deliveries of completed equipment;

actively introducing economic methods into interrelations with all-Union export-import associations under the jurisdiction of the USSR SCFR, and with associations, enterprises, and organizations of other ministries and departments, by way of developing and strengthening cost accounting based on contract relations.

3. The USSR SCFR is guided in its activities by the laws of the USSR, other decisions of the USSR Supreme Soviet and its Presidium, decrees and orders of the USSR Council of Ministers, decisions of the State Foreign Economic Commission of the USSR Council of Ministers, the present Statute, and other normative acts, and ensures the strengthening of socialist legality and proper application of the existing legislation in the Committee's network and organizes and directs legal work in this system.

The USSR SCFR publishes consolidated summaries of practice in applying legislation to areas under the Committee's jurisdiction, drafts proposals on improving such application, and submits them in the established procedure to the State Foreign Economic Commission of the USSR Council of Ministers.

4. The USSR SCFR operates under the direct management of the State Foreign Economic Commission of the USSR Council of Ministers.

5. The network of the USSR SCFR is comprised of the USSR SCFR itself, its legal representatives at individual facilities being built in the USSR with the participation of foreign organizations and firms and holding great importance for the USSR's economic and technological cooperation with foreign countries, all-union cost-accounting export-import associations (hereinafter called "all-union associations"), and other subordinate organizations. Legal representatives of the USSR SCFR act in accordance with statutes on them that have been confirmed by the USSR SCFR.

The USSR SCFR bears responsibility for the fulfillment of plan assignments on the part of subordinate all-union associations, the effectiveness of their business activity, their assurance of the safekeeping of socialist property, and for the maintenance of strict oversight in this sphere.

6. All-Union associations under the jurisdiction of the USSR SCFR operate on the principles of cost accounting, self-recoupment, and self-financing, and based on a system of cost-accounting contract relations.

The USSR SCFR does not bear material liability for the obligations of subordinate all-union associations, while these all-union associations are not responsible for the obligations of the USSR SCFR.

7. The USSR SCFR carries out the following functions:

a) together with the appropriate ministries and departments, it elaborates guidelines for the development of the USSR's economic and technological cooperation with foreign countries for the long term, drafts of state plans for economic and technological cooperation, drafts of foreign-currency plans for the USSR SCFR, drafts of plans for project feasibility studies and construction-and-installation projects involved in the construction of industrial facilities both abroad and in the USSR, and also drafts of plans for the selection of Soviet specialists for dispatching abroad as well as plans for the acceptance of foreign specialists and workers in the USSR to provide production and technical training and consulting services;

it drafts proposals designed to enhance the coordination of the state plans of the USSR with those of the other CMEA member countries, and it participates in efforts to bring into agreement the guidelines for development of the USSR's economic and technological cooperation with other socialist countries, including the drafting of proposals on multilateral cooperation with developing countries;

it participates in the drafting of proposals and measures designed to develop socialist economic integration on the basis of the international division of labor, to encourage interstate specialization and broad cooperation in the production of equipment and machinery, and to introduce new and advanced forms of cooperation;

it drafts and submits proposals, in the established procedure, dealing with the development and enhancement of the effectiveness of the USSR's economic and technological cooperation with foreign countries, and participates in the drafting of proposals for the creation of joint enterprises;

b) it examines requests from foreign governments as well as organizations of foreign countries on questions of economic and technological cooperation involving construction and reconstruction of enterprises and other facilities abroad, and in the necessary cases it prepares and submits, in the established procedure, proposals in these areas;

in the necessary cases it issues conclusions regarding proposals of USSR ministries and departments on inviting foreign organizations and firms to construct facilities in the USSR;

c) it issues permits, in the established procedure, authorizing the importation into and exportation from the USSR of goods and other property, and also for the re-export of goods;

d) in conformity with existing legislation, it prepares proposals on the conclusion of international treaties by the USSR concerning issues of economic and technological cooperation and on the USSR's adherence to international treaties, and it conducts negotiations and concludes international treaties on behalf of the USSR;

e) it monitors the fulfillment by ministries, departments, associations, enterprises, and organizations of obligations issuing from international treaties entered into by the USSR and from contracts dealing with economic and technological cooperation;

it exercises the functions of supplier and contractor in those instances where such functions are empowered to the USSR SCFR;

f) for the construction and exploitation of enterprises and other facilities both abroad and in the USSR, in conformity with the USSR's international treaties and contracts, it sees to:

the conduct of feasibility and design studies;

deliveries of finished industrial products, materials, and spare parts, based on the requirement that the delivery of goods for export should take place on a priority basis regardless of whether or not the production plans for the types of products involved and for their supply to other consumers have been fulfilled, and it also secures deliveries of imports;

the dispatching of Soviet specialists abroad and the acceptance of foreign specialists and workers in the USSR for the provision of production and technical training and consultation;

g) in conjunction with the appropriate ministries, departments, associations, enterprises, and organizations, it drafts comprehensive measures and directs efforts designed to better utilize the capacities of constructed enterprises and other facilities and to create conditions for their effective exploitation;

h) it confirms the annual plans of ministries, departments, associations, enterprises, and organizations for project feasibility studies, plans for capital construction and construction-and-installation work on foreign facilities being built under contract, and also quarterly plans for the dispatching of Soviet specialists abroad;

i) it prepares proposals on the establishment of the post of economic adviser at USSR embassies abroad, and on appointment and dismissal of such officials;

in conjunction with the appropriate ministries and departments, it provides guidance and monitoring of the activities of economic adviser-consultants, and it also monitors Soviet specialists dispatched abroad by ministries, departments, associations, enterprises, and organizations in order to provide services related to economic and technological cooperation;

j) it commissions the study, drafting, and introduction of scientific and practical recommendations and recommendations on methods designed to increase the effectiveness of the USSR's economic and technological cooperation with foreign countries, determines the most promising directions of its development, and studies competition on the world market for finished industrial goods;

k) it prepares proposals on improving management in the sphere of the USSR's economic and technological cooperation with foreign countries, and also of the contract relations of all-union associations under the USSR SCFR's jurisdiction with suppliers of products for export, customers for import products, and contractors;

l) it aids in drafting and implementing measures aimed at increasing the production for export of competitive equipment, materials, and spare parts enjoying great demand on world markets, and at securing imports of finished industrial goods and services of world standards for use in facilities under construction in the USSR with the participation of foreign organizations and firms;

m) it takes part, in the established procedure, in the activities of international organizations and agencies, as well as intergovernmental commissions and committees, dealing with the USSR's commercial, economic, and scientific-technological cooperation with foreign countries;

n) it secures the importation of certain types of equipment and services to be used for facilities under construction in the USSR with the participation of foreign organizations and firms, as well as re-export of the same for facilities under construction with the technical assistance of the USSR under contract;

it monitors to see that material resources allocated for facilities under construction abroad with the technical assistance of the USSR (including under contract) are used and expended rationally, economically, and strictly according to their intended purpose, and it also monitors the installation of imported finished industrial goods at facilities under construction in the USSR with the participation of foreign organizations and firms;

it drafts proposals for improving the shipping of freight from producers to construction sites of cooperative facilities in the USSR and abroad, and takes part in the drafting of measures for improving the storage and safekeeping of freight;

o) it oversees the receipt of foreign-currency funds in payment for services rendered by the USSR to foreign customers, and also oversees the repayment of state and commercial credits;

p) it takes part in conferences, congresses, symposiums, and meetings devoted to questions of international economic relations;

it conducts informational and promotional work designed to foster the USSR's economic and technological cooperation with foreign countries;

it receives foreign delegations arriving in the USSR to take part in discussions on issues of economic and technological cooperation;

q) it arranges the collection and transmission to ministries and departments engaged in economic and technological cooperation with foreign countries, of information regarding the demands of the world market for quality and technical levels of complete equipment, and regarding equipment enjoying higher demand, and it makes proposals on measures necessary to increase the competitiveness of equipment, and also supplies information on the status of USSR SCFR's work in implementing foreign economic operations;

r) in the established procedure, it sees to the fulfillment of the USSR's financial obligations to the United Nations, and thereby its obligations issuing from its economic and technological cooperation with foreign countries;

s) it provides for the training, retraining, and advanced training of personnel in higher education institutions of the USSR SCFR network;

it implements measures aimed at improving work conditions, housing, cultural and communal services, and medical services for employees in the USSR SCFR network.

The USSR SCFR also exercises functions provided for in the General Statute on Ministries of the USSR.

8. With the goal of ensuring the observance of the USSR's state interests in foreign markets by ministries, departments, associations, enterprises, and organizations in realizing economic and technological cooperation with foreign countries, and with the goal of ensuring a unified policy in this area, the USSR SCFR:

with the participation, if required, of the USSR Ministry of Finance, the USSR Foreign Trade Bank,* and other interested agencies and organizations, monitors the conduct of export-import operations by ministries, departments, associations, enterprises, and organizations;

exercises coordinating functions and provides systematic guidance for the activities of ministries, departments, associations, enterprises, and organizations in their conduct of export-import operations in this sphere;

receives from and provides to the aforementioned ministries, departments, associations, enterprises, and organizations all the necessary documents, proposals, and summaries dealing with issues of economic and technological cooperation.

The USSR SCFR submits reports to the State Foreign Economic Commission

---

*Editor's note—The USSR Foreign Trade Bank has since been renamed the USSR Bank for Foreign Economic Relations.

of the USSR Council of Ministers on its work in maintaining such oversight, and these include proposals on eliminating uncovered violations and shortcomings.

The USSR SCFR is granted the following rights:

a) to check on the status of commercial work and obtain from managerial personnel of the appropriate ministries, departments, associations, enterprises, and organizations information concerning the fulfillment of tasks assigned under the plan in the area of the USSR's economic and technological cooperation with foreign countries, to make on-sight checks of efforts to fulfill the relevant economic contracts, and to meet assigned goals in the selection and training of specialists for the dispatching abroad and receiving of foreign specialists and workers in the USSR for the provision of production and technical training and consultations;

b) in the established procedure, to create, reorganize, and liquidate all-union associations;

c) to obtain:

from ministries, departments, associations, enterprises, and organizations— memoranda on the requests of foreign countries for the provision of economic and technological assistance as well as the necessary documentation to draft relevant proposals, and also to receive in the established procedure materials necessary for drafting and monitoring the fulfillment of tasks assigned under the plan in the sphere of the USSR's economic and technological cooperation with foreign countries;

from ministries, departments, associations, enterprises, design institutes, and other organizations—information and reports required by the USSR Central Statistical Administration* on the design and construction of facilities abroad, as well as in the USSR with the participation of foreign organizations and firms, and estimates for the construction of facilities and dispatching of specialists thereto;

d) to permit, in the established procedure, subordinate all-union associations to create, both in the USSR and abroad, branches, offices, departments, representative offices and joint-stock companies, repair organizations, bases (warehouses), and technical servicing stations, and to allow these all-union associations to take part in any manner of organization, the operations of which correspond to the goals of the association;

e) to solicit the services of foreign firms, on commercial terms, to serve as intermediaries in concluding and performing foreign economic transactions;

f) to exercise oversight in areas under the jurisdiction of the USSR SCFR over the operations of construction-and-installation organizations engaged in building facilities—both abroad and in the USSR, with the participation of foreign organizations and firms—and export production and assembly centers, with the participation, if necessary, of the USSR Ministry of Finance, the USSR Bank for

*Editor's note—The USSR Central Statistical Administration was renamed the USSR State Committee for Statistics in August 1987.

Financing Capital Investments, and other ministries and departments;

g) to commission scientific research organizations under the jurisdiction of the USSR Academy of Sciences and ministries and departments, with their agreement, to carry out individual studies and projects related to efforts to improve the effectiveness of the USSR's economic and technological cooperation with foreign countries;

h) to conduct checks, jointly with other ministries and departments, of the quality of equipment, machinery, and materials exported from the USSR in compliance with contracts concluded by all-Union associations under the jurisdiction of the USSR SCFR;

i) to provide expert appraisals of feasibility documentation and projects for the construction of facilities, both abroad and in the USSR with the participation of foreign organizations and firms, and to arrive at final decisions on these questions;

j) in the necessary instances, to establish scientific-technological councils, interdepartmental commissions, and groups of experts, and also to call special meetings, inviting representatives from the appropriate ministries and departments as well as design and scientific research organizations, devoted to problems of the USSR's economic and technological cooperation with foreign countries;

k) to authorize, in the established procedure, foreign organizations and firms to open representative offices in the USSR in order to promote economic and technological cooperation between the USSR and foreign countries, and to make decisions on terminating the activities of such representative offices;

l) to conduct on the basis of reciprocity the exchange of technical and economic information with foreign countries, and to obtain toward this end the necessary documentation from ministries, departments, and other Soviet organizations. The amount and nature of documentation to be transmitted is determined by the USSR SCFR with the agreement of the USSR State Planning Committee, the USSR Central Statistical Administration, and the appropriate ministries, departments, and organizations;

m) to enter into contact, within the limits of its authority, with state agencies, institutions, enterprises, organizations, and official and private individuals of foreign countries, both within the USSR and abroad.

In addition to the rights granted it in the present Statute, the USSR SCFR also enjoys other rights accorded it by the existing legislation.

10. The USSR SCFR is headed up by its Chairman, who is appointed, in accordance with the USSR Constitution, by the USSR Supreme Soviet, and between sessions—by the Presidium of the USSR Supreme Soviet subject to subsequent approval by the USSR Supreme Soviet.

The Chairman of the USSR SCFR is assisted by deputies, who are appointed by the USSR Council of Ministers. The distribution of duties between the deputy chairmen of the USSR SCFR is the responsibility of the Chairman of the USSR SCFR.

11. The Chairman of the USSR SCFR bears personal responsibility for fulfillment of the goals assigned to the Committee and for the exercise of his own functions, and he establishes the degree of responsibility of the deputy chairmen and heads of the structural subdivisions of the Committee's central apparatus for management of the Committee's different spheres of operations.

In meeting his assigned obligations, the Chairman of the USSR SCFR enjoys the rights accorded to ministers of the USSR.

12. Within the USSR SCFR is formed a Collegium consisting of the Committee Chairman (or Chairman of the Collegium), the deputy chairmen of the Committee in accordance with their posts, and other management personnel in the USSR SCFR network.

Members of the Collegium of the USSR SCFR are confirmed by the USSR Council of Ministers.

13. At its regularly scheduled meetings, the Collegium of the USSR SCFR examines fundamental questions related to the development of the USSR's economic and technological cooperation with foreign countries, to the fulfillment of tasks assigned under the state plans as well as other tasks in this area, and tasks assigned by foreign-currency and other plans of the Committee, discusses questions related to the management of the Committee's all-union associations and organizations, to verification of the process of selection, distribution, training, and education of personnel, to the preparation of drafts of normative acts and other important documents, hears reports of the heads of the structural subdivisions of the central apparatus of the USSR SCFR's all-union associations and organizations and from economic advisers in the USSR's embassies in foreign countries, and also examines other questions related to the Committee's activities.

Decisions of the Collegium of the USSR SCFR are enacted, as a rule, with the issuance of decrees of the Committee and orders of its Chairman. In the event of disagreements between the Chairman and the Collegium, the Chairman enacts his decision while reporting the disagreements to the USSR Council of Ministers, and the members of the Collegium may in turn make their opinions known to the USSR Council of Ministers.

14. Within the limits of its authority, and in accordance with and in execution of the laws of the USSR, other decisions of the USSR Supreme Soviet and its Presidium, decrees and rulings of the USSR Council of Ministers, and decisions of the State Foreign Economic Commission of the USSR Council of Ministers, the USSR SCFR issues decrees, orders, directives, and recommendations that are binding on the Committee's legal representatives, all-union associations, and other organizations under its jurisdiction as well as the advisory bodies on economic issues in the USSR's embassies in foreign countries,

and it sees to and monitors their execution.

Within the limits of its authority, the USSR SCFR issues decrees and directives generic to the sphere of the USSR's economic and technological cooperation with foreign countries that are binding on ministries and departments as well as associations, enterprises, and organizations, regardless of their departmental affiliation.

In the necessary instances, the USSR SCFR issues decrees, orders, and directives jointly or with the agreement of other ministries and departments.

15. The number and composition of employees in the central administrative apparatus of the USSR SCFR are confirmed by the USSR Council of Ministers.

The staffing of the central apparatus of the USSR SCFR, as well as provisions for its structural subdivisions, are confirmed by the Chairman of the USSR SCFR.

The Committee Chairman may convert structural subdivisions of the central apparatus of the USSR SCFR over to economic cost accounting.

16. The USSR SCFR has a seal on which is a depiction of the USSR State Emblem and its appellation.

# V

# ON PROCEDURES GOVERNING THE CREATION AND OPERATION ON THE TERRITORY OF THE USSR OF JOINT ENTERPRISES INVOLVING SOVIET ORGANIZATIONS AND FIRMS FROM CAPITALIST AND DEVELOPING COUNTRIES*

*Sobranie postanovlenii Pravitel'stva SSSR* 1987, No. 9, item 40

With the goal of further developing trade, economic, and scientific-technological cooperation with capitalist and developing countries on a stable and mutually advantageous basis, the USSR Council of Ministers *decrees*:

## I. General provisions

1. It is established that joint enterprises, with the participation of Soviet organizations and firms of capitalist and developing countries, are created on USSR territory with the authorization of the USSR Council of Ministers on the basis of contracts concluded by the participants in such enterprises.

Joint enterprises are guided in their activities by the 13 January 1987 Edict of the Presidium of USSR Supreme Soviet, "On Questions Involving the Creation and Operation on USSR Territory of Joint Enterprises, International Associations and Organizations, with the Participation of Soviet and Foreign Organizations, Firms, and Administrative Agencies,"[1] the present Decree and other acts of USSR and union-republic legislation, with the exceptions established by the USSR's interstate and intergovernmental treaties.

---

*English translation © 1987 by Current Digest of the Soviet Press. "Rules for Joint Enterprises Published," *Current Digest of the Soviet Press*, Vol. 39 (1987), No. 6. Printed with permission.

1. This Edict was published in *Vedomosti Verkhovnogo Soveta SSSR* 1987, No. 2, item 35 (translated *infra*, in Appendix VI).

*Editor's note*—In the original *CDSP* translation the term *organy upravleniia* was rendered as "management agencies." It has been changed here and throughout this text to "administrative agencies" in order to maintain consistency with the translation of the manuscript.

2. Proposals for the creation of joint enterprises, together with technical and economic substantiating documents and draft articles of incorporation, are submitted by the concerned Soviet organizations to the ministries and departments to which they belong. Republic ministries and departments submit such proposals to the corresponding union-republic Council of Ministers.

The aforementioned USSR ministries and departments and union-republic councils of ministers clear the proposals with the USSR State Planning Committee, the USSR Ministry of Finance, and other concerned ministries and departments.

Once cleared, these proposals for the creation of joint enterprises are submitted to the USSR Council of Ministers.

3. In creating such enterprises, the ministries and departments that have jurisdiction over the Soviet participants in joint enterprises pursue the objective of more fully meeting the country's needs for specific types of industrial output, raw materials, and food products, making advanced foreign equipment and technology, managerial experience, and additional material and financial resources available to the USSR economy, developing the country's export base, and reducing irrational imports.

## II. The participants, assets, and rights of joint enterprises

4. The participants in joint enterprises can be one or several Soviet enterprises (associations and other organizations) that constitute legal entities, and one or several foreign firms (companies, corporations, or other organizations) that constitute legal entities.

5. The Soviet side must have at least a 51-percent share in the charter capital of the joint enterprise.

6. Joint enterprises are legal entities under Soviet legislation. On their own behalf, they can conclude contracts, acquire property and personal nonproperty rights, incur obligations, and be plaintiffs and defendants in a court and in an arbitration court. Joint enterprises are financially independent and operate on the basis of full cost accounting, self-recoupment, and self-financing.

7. A joint enterprise must have a charter which is subject to confirmation by its participants. The charter defines the goal and objectives of the enterprise's operation, its location, the composition of its participants, the amount of the charter capital, the size of the participants' shares, the procedure governing the way charter capital is to be formed (including foreign currency), the structure, composition, and competence of the enterprise's management bodies, the procedure governing the adoption of decisions and the range of questions the resolution of which requires unanimity, and likewise the procedure governing liquidation of the enterprise. The charter can also include other provisions that are not in conflict with Soviet legislation and relate to specific

aspects of the joint enterprise's operation.

8. The term of operation of the joint enterprise is agreed upon by the parties to the agreement to create the enterprise or in its charter (hereinafter: "articles of incorporation").

9. After their articles of incorporation have taken effect, joint enterprises created on USSR territory register with the USSR Ministry of Finance and acquire the rights of legal entities as of that moment. An announcement of the creation of a joint enterprise is published in the press.

10. The charter capital of the joint enterprise is comprised of contributions from its participants. It can be augmented with profits from the enterprise's economic activity and, when necessary, with additional contributions from its participants as well.

11. Contributions to the joint enterprise's charter capital can take the form of buildings, structures, equipment and other material valuables and rights to use land, water, other natural resources, buildings, structures, and equipment, as well as other property rights (including the use of inventions and know-how) and money in the currencies of the countries participating in the joint enterprise and also in freely convertible currencies.

12. The Soviet participant's contribution to the charter capital of the joint enterprise is stated in rubles, on the basis of contractual prices and with due regard for world market prices. The contribution of the foreign participant or participants is valued in the same manner, with the value of the contribution recalculated in terms of rubles, based on the USSR State Bank's official exchange rate on the day that the contract creating the enterprise is signed, or on some other date agreed upon by the participants. In the event that world market prices are lacking, the value of the property being contributed is determined by agreement between the participants.

13. The equipment, materials, and other property imported into the USSR by the foreign participants in a joint enterprise as their contributions to the enterprise's charter capital are exempt from customs duty.

14. The property of a joint enterprise is subject to mandatory insurance through USSR insurance agencies.

15. In accordance with Soviet legislation, the joint enterprise has the right to possess, use, and dispose of its property in accordance with the objectives of its activity and the intended purpose of the property. Its property is not subject to requisition or confiscation by administrative procedure.

The property rights of a joint enterprise enjoy protection in accordance with the provisions of Soviet legislation established for Soviet state organizations. Claims can be assessed against the property of joint enterprises only by decision of the agencies that, in accordance with USSR legislation, can hear disputes involving joint enterprises.

16. The participants in a joint enterprise have the right, by mutual agreement, to transfer all or part of their shares in the joint enterprise to third parties. In each

individual instance, the transfer of such shares is carried out with the permission of the State Foreign Economic Commission of the USSR Council of Ministers. The Soviet participants have priority in acquiring foreign participants' shares.

In the event of reorganization of a joint enterprise, its rights and obligations are transferred to its successors.

17. The rights to industrial property belonging to joint enterprises are protected in accordance with Soviet legislation, including protection in the form of patents. The procedure by which rights to industrial property are transferred to a joint enterprise by participants in that enterprise, and by which a joint enterprise transfers such rights to its participants, as well as the procedure for the commercial use of such rights and their protection abroad, is specified in the articles of incorporation.

18. A joint enterprise answers for its obligations with all the property belonging to it.

The Soviet state and the Soviet participants in a joint enterprise are not liable for the joint enterprise's obligations, and the joint enterprise is not liable for the obligations of the Soviet state and its participants.

Joint enterprises' branches that are set up on USSR territory and that constitute legal entities are not liable for the obligations of the joint enterprises, and the joint enterprises are not liable for the obligations of such branches.

19. Joint enterprises created on USSR territory can open branches and offices, provided that their articles of incorporation grant them that right.

Joint enterprises created with the participation of Soviet organizations on the territory of other countries may open branches on USSR territory by following the procedure established for the creation of joint enterprises.

20. In accordance with USSR legislation, disputes between joint enterprises and Soviet state, cooperative, and other public organizations and disputes among themselves, as well as disputes between the participants in a joint enterprise over questions concerning its operation, are heard by USSR courts or, with the parties' consent, by an arbitration court.

## III. Procedures governing the operation of joint enterprises

21. The highest body of a joint enterprise is the governing board, which consists of persons appointed by its participants. The procedure governing the adoption of decisions by the governing board are specified in the articles of incorporation.

Management of the joint enterprise's day-to-day operation is exercised by management, which consists of Soviet and foreign citizens.

The chairman of the governing board and the general director of the enterprise are USSR citizens.

22. A joint enterprise deals with central bodies of USSR and union-republic

state administration through the agencies with jurisdiction over the Soviet participant in the enterprise, and it deals directly with local administrative bodies.

23. A joint enterprise independently drafts and adopts programs for its business activities. USSR state agencies do not set mandatory plan assignments for the joint enterprise or guarantee the sale of its output.

24. A joint enterprise is granted the right independently to conduct export and import operations necessary to its economic activity, including operations in the markets of CMEA member countries.

The aforementioned export and import operations can also be conducted through Soviet foreign trade organizations or through the foreign participants' marketing networks, on the basis of appropriate contracts.

A joint enterprise's importation into the USSR and exportation from the USSR of goods and other property are conducted on the basis of permits issued in accordance with the procedure established by USSR legislation.

A joint enterprise has the right to carry on correspondence and telegraph, teletype, and telephone communications with organizations from other countries.

25. All foreign-currency outlays of a joint enterprise, including the payment of profits and other sums owed to foreign participants and specialists, must be paid by the joint enterprise with receipts from the sale of its output on the external market.

26. Sales of a joint enterprise's output on the Soviet market and deliveries to the joint enterprise from this market of equipment, raw and other materials, components, fuel, energy and other output are paid for in rubles through the appropriate Soviet foreign trade organizations, at contractual prices, with due regard for prices on the world market.

27. If necessary, a joint enterprise can use credit obtained on commercial terms:

in foreign currency, from the USSR Foreign Trade Bank* or, with the USSR Foreign Trade Bank's consent, from foreign banks and firms;

in rubles, from the USSR State Bank or the USSR Foreign Trade Bank.

28. The USSR State Bank and the USSR Foreign Trade Bank have the right to monitor whether credits issued to a joint enterprise are used for their intended purpose, adequately secured, and promptly repaid.

29. The funds of a joint enterprise are deposited in its ruble or foreign-currency accounts in the USSR State Bank and in the USSR Foreign Trade Bank, respectively, and are expended for purposes related to the enterprise's activity. The joint enterprise is paid interest on the sums credited to its accounts:

in foreign currency, on the basis of interest rates on world money markets;

---

*Editor's note—The USSR Foreign Trade Bank has since been renamed the USSR Bank for Foreign Economic Relations.

in rubles, under the terms and in accordance with the procedure determined by the USSR State Bank.

Differences in exchange rates that affect joint enterprises' foreign-currency accounts or their operations in foreign exchange are reflected in their profit and loss statements.

30. The joint enterprise sets up a reserve fund and other funds essential to its operation and to the social development of its collective.

Deductions from profits are deposited in the reserve fund until the fund reaches 25 percent of the enterprise's charter capital. The amounts of annual deductions are determined in accordance with the procedures established by the articles of incorporation.

A list of other funds and the procedure governing their formation and expenditure are specified in the articles of incorporation.

31. The profits of a joint enterprise, minus amounts deducted to cover dealings with the USSR State Budget and amounts used for creating and building up funds, are distributed among its participants in proportion to their *pro rata* participation in the enterprise's charter capital.

32. Foreign participants in a joint enterprise are guaranteed the transfer abroad, in foreign exchange, of the amounts due them as a result of the distribution of profits from the enterprise's activity.

33. Joint enterprises recognize depreciation in accordance with the directives in effect for Soviet state organizations, unless otherwise specified in the articles of incorporation. The sums recognized as depreciation remain at the enterprises' disposal.

34. The design and capital construction of joint enterprises' facilities, including social facilities, are carried out under contract and paid for with the enterprises' own or with borrowed funds. Prior to final approval, project designs are subject to clearance under the procedure established by the USSR State Construction Committee. Construction-and-installation work by Soviet organizations, and the material resources needed for construction, are allocated to joint enterprises on a priority basis, based on orders placed by them.

35. Joint enterprises' freight is shipped in accordance with the procedures established for Soviet organizations.

## IV. Taxation of joint enterprises

36. Joint enterprises pay a tax in the amount of 30 percent of the portion of profits remaining after payments to the reserve fund, as well as to other funds of the joint enterprise earmarked for the development of production and for research and technology. The tax constitutes revenue for the all-union budget.

Joint enterprises are exempted from payment of the tax on profits for the first two years of their operations.

The USSR Ministry of Finance has the right to reduce the amount of the tax.

37. Computation of the tax on profits is carried out by the joint enterprise.

An advance payment of taxes for the current year is determined by the enterprise with due regard to its financial plan for the current year.

Computation of the final amount of the tax on profits actually realized during the past calendar year is carried out by the joint enterprise not later than 15 March of the year following the accounting year.

38. Financial agencies have the right to verify the correctness of a joint enterprise's computation of its tax.

Overpayment of a tax amount for a past year can be credited to current tax payments or returned to the payer at his request.

39. The amount of the tax on profits for the current year is remitted to the budget in equal payments not later than fifteen days prior to the close of each quarter. The final amount of the tax is paid not later than 1 April of the year following the accounting year.

A penalty of .05 percent per day is exacted for delays in tax payment.

The exaction of overdue taxes is carried out following the procedures established for foreign legal entities by the Statute on the Exaction of Overdue Taxes and Nontax Payments, confirmed by Edict of the Presidium of the USSR Supreme Soviet of 26 January 1981 (*Vedomosti Verkhovnogo Soveta SSSR* 1981, No. 5, item 122).

40. A joint enterprise has the right to protest actions by financial agencies to recover taxes due. An appeal is filed with the financial agency that verified the tax computation. A decision on the appeal is reached within one month of the date on which it was filed.

A decision on an appeal can itself be appealed to a higher financial agency within a month's time.

The filing of an appeal does not stay payment of the tax.

41. Unless otherwise specified by an agreement between the USSR and the foreign state in question, the portion of profits due the foreign participant in a joint enterprise is assessed a tax in the amount of 20 percent upon transfer abroad.

42. The aforementioned procedure governing taxation applies to income received by joint enterprises created on USSR territory and by branches located in the USSR of joint enterprises created with the participation of Soviet organizations in other countries, whether the income is from their activity on USSR territory, on the USSR continental shelf, in the USSR economic zone or on the territory of other countries.

43. Directives on the taxation of joint enterprises are issued by the USSR Ministry of Finance.

## V. Oversight over joint enterprises' operations

44. In accordance with the procedure specified in their articles of incorporation, the participants in a joint enterprise are provided, for purposes of exercising

their rights of oversight, data relating to the operation of the enterprise and the state of its property, profits and losses.

A joint enterprise may have an audit commission, formed in accordance with the procedure specified in the articles of incorporation.

45. Joint enterprises maintain operating, accounting, and statistical records in accordance with the procedure in effect in the USSR for Soviet state enterprises. The forms of this record keeping and reporting are established by the USSR Ministry of Finance, in conjunction with the USSR Central Statistical Administration.*

Joint enterprises bear responsibility, in accordance with Soviet legislation, for observing the procedure governing the compilation of records and reports and their authenticity.

Joint enterprises may not provide any reports of information to state or other agencies of foreign states.

46. The audit of a joint enterprise's financial, economic, and commercial operations is performed for a fee by a Soviet auditing organization operating on a cost-accounting† basis.

## VI. Personnel of joint enterprises

47. Joint enterprises are staffed primarily by Soviet citizens. The management of a joint enterprise is obliged to conclude collective contracts with the trade union organization created at the enterprise. The content of these contracts, including provisions regarding the social development of the collective, is determined by Soviet legislation and the articles of incorporation.

48. The terms of labor remuneration and work and the rest schedules of Soviet citizens employed at joint enterprises and their social security and social insurance are regulated by Soviet legislative norms. These norms extend to foreign citizens employed at joint enterprises, with the exception of questions concerning remuneration, paid vacation, and pension entitlements, which are to be resolved in contracts with each foreign citizen.

The USSR State Committee on Labor and Social Problems and the All-Union Central Council of Trade Unions have the right to determine the specifics as to how Soviet legislation on social insurance applies to foreign citizens employed at joint enterprises.

49. The joint enterprise remits to the USSR State Budget payments for Soviet and foreign employees' state social insurance coverage and contributions to

---

*Editor's note—The USSR Central Statistical Administration was renamed the USSR State Committee for Statistics in August 1987.

†Editor's note—In the original *CDSP* translation the term *khozraschetnyi* was rendered as "profit-and-loss." Here and throughout this text it has been changed to "cost-accounting" in order to maintain consistency with the translation of the manuscript and the other legislation.

Soviet employees' pensions at the rates established for Soviet state organizations. Contributions to the pensions of joint enterprises' foreign employees are transferred to the appropriate funds of the countries of which they are permanent residents (in the currency of those countries).

50. The wages earned by foreign employees of a joint enterprise are assessed an income tax according to the procedure and in the amount specified in the 12 May 1978 Decree of the Presidium of the USSR Supreme Soviet, "On Income Tax from Foreign Legal Entities and Individuals." The unexpended portion of these wages can be transferred abroad in foreign currency.

## VII. Liquidation of joint enterprises

51. A joint enterprise can be liquidated under the circumstances and according to the procedure specified in the articles of incorporation, as well as by decision of the USSR Council of Ministers, if its activities are in conflict with the objectives and tasks set forth in these documents. An announcement of the liquidation of the joint enterprise is published in the press.

52. Upon the liquidation of a joint enterprise or withdrawal from such an enterprise, a foreign participant receives the right to a return of its contribution in the form of cash or goods, on the basis of the residual value of its contribution at the time of the enterprise's liquidation, after repayment of its obligations to Soviet participants and third parties.

53. The liquidation of a joint enterprise is registered with the USSR Ministry of Finance.

N. Ryzhkov
*Chairman of the USSR Council of Ministers*

M. Smirtiukov
*Administrative Secretary*
*of the USSR Council of Ministers*

# VI

# ON QUESTIONS CONCERNING THE CREATION AND OPERATION ON THE TERRITORY OF THE USSR OF JOINT ENTERPRISES, INTERNATIONAL ASSOCIATIONS AND ORGANIZATIONS INVOLVING SOVIET AND FOREIGN ORGANIZATIONS, FIRMS, AND ADMINISTRATIVE AGENCIES

Edict No. 6362-XI of the Presidium of the USSR Supreme Soviet,
13 January 1987;
*Vedomosti Verkhovnogo Soveta SSSR* 1987, No. 2, item 35

The Presidium of the USSR Supreme Soviet *decrees*:

1. It is established that joint enterprises created on the territory of the USSR involving Soviet and foreign organizations, firms, and administrative agencies pay a profit tax in the amount and procedure established by the USSR Council of Ministers. The tax will be entered as income of the state budget.

Joint enterprises are exempt from paying profit tax during the first two years following declaration of a profit.*

The USSR Ministry of Finance has the right to reduce the amount of the tax or to completely exempt individual payers from payment of the tax.

2. Overdue taxes are exacted in the procedure established for foreign legal entities by the Statute on the Exaction of Overdue Taxes and Nontax Payments, confirmed by Edict of the Presidium of the USSR Supreme Soviet of 26 January 1981 (*Vedomosti Verkhovnogo Soveta SSSR*, 1981, No. 5, item 122).

3. Unless otherwise specified in a treaty between the USSR and the foreign state in question, the portion of profits due the foreign participant in a joint enterprise is assessed a tax upon its transfer abroad in an amount determined by the USSR Council of Ministers.

---

*Editor's note—The words in italics are an amendment introduced by Edict of the Presidium of the USSR Supreme Soviet, of 17 March 1988 (*Vedomosti Verkhovonogo Soveta SSSR* 1988, No. 12, item 185. (Prior to the amendment, the sentence ended: "the first two years of their operations.")

4. It is established that land, its depths, waters, and forests may be made available to joint enterprises both for a fee and free of charge.

5. Disputes arising between joint enterprises, international associations and organizations and Soviet state, cooperative, and other public organizations, disputes arising among themselves, as well as disputes between participants in a joint enterprise, international association or organization on questions involving their operations, are examined in the courts of USSR or, under an agreement of the parties, by an arbitration court and, in cases provided for by USSR legislation, by state arbitration agencies.

In connection therewith, in Article 9 of the Law of the USSR of 30 November 1979, "On State Arbitration in the USSR" (*Vedomosti Verkhovnogo Soveta SSSR*, 1979, No. 49, item 844), the following words should be added after the words "and organizations": "joint enterprises and international associations and organizations of the USSR and other CMEA member countries."

A. GROMYKO
*Chairman of the Presidium of the USSR Supreme Soviet*

T. MENTESHASHVILI
*Administrative Secretary of the*
*Presidium of the USSR Supreme Soviet*

# VII

# ON FEES EXACTED FOR THE ISSUANCE OF PERMITS AUTHORIZING THE OPENING OF REPRESENTATIVE OFFICES OF FOREIGN FIRMS, BANKS, AND ORGANIZATIONS IN THE USSR AND FOR THE EXTENSION OF THEIR TERMS OF OPERATION

Edict No. 6338-XI of the Presidium of the USSR Supreme Soviet,
7 January 1987;
*Vedomosti Verkhovnogo Soveta SSSR* 1987, No. 2, item 32

The Presidium of the USSR Supreme Soviet *decrees*:

1. It is established that for the issuance of permits authorizing the opening of representative offices of foreign firms, banks, and organizations in the USSR, a fee is charged in the amount of 500 rubles, and for the issuance of permits authorizing extension of their terms of operation—in the amount of 250 rubles.

2. The foreign firm, bank, or organization pays the fee prior to the issuance of the permit authorizing the opening of its representative office or the extension of its term of operation.

Fees are paid through establishments of the USSR State Bank at the location of the representative office, but if the representative office maintains a current account with the USSR Foreign Trade Bank,* the necessary funds are transferred from this account.

3. In the event a permit authorizing the opening of a representative office of a foreign firm, bank, or organization in the USSR or extension of its term of operation is denied, the paid portion of the fee is returned.

4. It is established that with the goal of promoting mutual exemption from the payment of fees, their exaction may be terminated or limited in accordance with the USSR's international treaties.

The exaction of fees may also be terminated or limited in those cases where the same measures are being applied to the representative offices of Soviet organiza-

---

*Editor's note*—The USSR Foreign Trade Bank has since been renamed the USSR Bank for Foreign Economic Relations.

tions in the relevant foreign state.

5. Fees exacted for the issuance of permits authorizing the opening of representative offices of foreign firms, banks, and organizations in the USSR or the extension of their terms of operation are entered as income of the all-union budget.

6. The USSR Ministry of Finance issues a directive on the procedures for application of the present Edict.

7. The present Edict will enter into force on 1 April 1987.

A. GROMYKO
*Chairman of the Presidium of the USSR Supreme Soviet*

T. MENTESHASHVILI
*Administrative Secretary of the*
*Presidium of the USSR Supreme Soviet*

# VIII

# ON PROCEDURES GOVERNING THE CREATION AND OPERATION ON THE TERRITORY OF THE USSR OF JOINT ENTERPRISES, INTERNATIONAL ASSOCIATIONS AND ORGANIZATIONS OF THE USSR AND OTHER CMEA MEMBER COUNTRIES

### Decree No. 48 of the USSR Council of Ministers, 13 January 1987; *Sobranie postanovlenii Pravitel'stva SSSR* 1987, No. 8, item 38

With the goal of deepening socialist economic integration and binding more closely the scientific-technological and production potential of the countries of the socialist community, the USSR Council of Ministers *decrees*:

1. The standing agencies of the USSR Council of Ministers, USSR ministries and departments, and union-republic councils of ministers are charged with mounting broad efforts aimed at the creation in the Soviet Union of joint enterprises and international associations and organizations of the USSR and other CMEA member countries (hereinafter called "joint enterprises and international associations and organizations").

## I. Primary objectives and procedures governing the creation of joint enterprises and international associations and organizations

2. Joint enterprises are constituted for the purposes of undertaking production, science-production, scientific-technological, and other economic operations in industry, science, agriculture, construction, trade, transportation, and other spheres of the national economy.

Joint enterprises, production enterprises, trade companies, implementation and service organizations, carry out economic operations in their own name on the principal of common socialist property in the interests of the participants of the joint enterprise.

International associations are constituted for the purposes of coordinating

186

production, science-production, and other economic operations undertaken by their participants in industry, science, agriculture, construction, trade, transportation, and other spheres of the national economy.

International associations are created on the basis of the retention of national ownership of the participants' assets, and they carry out their operations guided by the coordinated plans of the participants and the general plans of the international association. If necessary, the participants may combine part of their assets in order to carry out economic operations. Joint organizations (scientific research, design, and others) may be established in order to facilitate scientific research, design, and other activities in the interests of the participants; such organizations constitute common socialist property.

3. It is established that joint enterprises and international associations and organizations are constituted on the territory of the USSR on the basis of interstate or intergovernmental treaties entered into by the USSR.

Provided an interstate or intergovernmental treaty between the USSR and a CMEA member country so stipulates, certain joint enterprises, international associations and organizations of the USSR and the relevant CMEA member country may be constituted on the basis of an international treaty entered into by the USSR that is of an interdepartmental character or on the basis of a management contract.

Joint enterprises and international associations and organizations are guided in their activities by the Edict of the Presidium of the USSR Supreme Soviet of 26 May 1983, "On the Procedures Governing the Operations on the Territory of the USSR of Joint Economic Organizations Involving the USSR and Other CMEA Member Countries" (*Vedomosti Verkhovnogo Soveta SSSR* 1983, No. 22, item 330), the Edict of the Presidium of the USSR Supreme Soviet of 13 January 1987, "On Questions Concerning the Creation and Operation on the Territory of the USSR of Joint Enterprises and International Associations and Organizations Involving Soviet and Foreign Organizations, Firms, and Administrative Agencies,"[1] and by the present Decree as well as other legislative acts of the USSR and the union republics, with exceptions thereto established by interstate and intergovernmental treaties entered into by the USSR.

4. Interested organizations submit proposals for the creation of joint enterprises and international associations and organizations, together with draft agreements and charters (hereinafter called "articles of incorporation")—and in the case of proposals for joint enterprises, also with the technical and economic documentation—to the ministries and departments under whose jurisdiction they operate. Republic ministries and departments forward such proposals to the councils of ministers of the relevant union republics. Such proposals are reviewed by the appropriate USSR ministries and departments and union-republic councils

---

1. *Vedomosti Verkhovnogo Soveta SSSR* 1987, No. 2, item 35 (translated *supra*, Appendix VI).

of ministers together with the USSR State Planning Committee, the USSR Ministry of Finance, and other interested ministries and departments.

Once cleared, proposals for the creation of joint enterprises are submitted to the USSR Council of Ministers, while proposals for the creation of international associations and organizations are submitted to the appropriate standing agency of the USSR Council of Ministers.

5. In creating joint enterprises and international associations and organizations, the ministries and departments having jurisdiction over the Soviet participants to such enterprises, associations, and organizations establish as their goal that of better utilizing the scientific and production potential of the CMEA member countries, more fully satisfying the nation's needs for certain types of industrial products, raw materials, and foods, of introducing advanced foreign machinery and technology, managerial know-how, and additional material and financial resources into the USSR's national economy, of developing the nation's export base, and of reducing irrational imports that must be paid for in freely convertible currency.

## II. Participants, assets, and rights of joint enterprises and international associations and organizations

6. The participants in a joint enterprise or international association and organization may comprise one or more Soviet enterprises (associations and other organizations) that constitute legal entities, and one or more organizations from CMEA member countries that constitute legal entities.

If necessary, administrative agencies of the USSR and other CMEA member countries may also be participants in joint enterprises. Clause 17 of the present Decree also applies to such cases, with due regard to the powers of such agencies as established by legislation.

7. Joint enterprises and international associations and organizations constitute legal entities under Soviet legislation. They may enter into contracts in their own name, acquire property and personal nonproperty rights and carry obligations, and they may be plaintiffs and respondents in courts of law, arbitration, and arbitration courts.

8. Joint enterprises and international associations and organizations must have a charter that is confirmed by the parties to the articles of incorporation.

The charter must define the goal and objectives of the operations of such enterprises, associations, and organizations as well as their location, the composition of their participants, the structure, composition, and authority of their management bodies, decision-making procedures and the range of questions the resolution of which requires unanimous approval, and also procedures governing the liquidation of enterprises, associations, and organizations. The charter may also include other provisions that do not run counter to Soviet legislation and relate to specific aspects of the operations of the joint enterprise or international association and organization.

The term of operation of the joint enterprise or international association and organization is determined by agreement of the participants in the articles of incorporation.

9. After their articles of incorporation have entered into force, joint enterprises and international associations and organizations created on the territory of the USSR register with the USSR Ministry of Finance and acquire the rights of legal entities as of that moment.

An announcement of the creation of a joint enterprise or international association and organization is published in the press.

10. In accordance with Soviet legislation, joint enterprises and international associations and organizations possess, utilize, and dispose of their assets in conformity with the objectives of their activity and the intended purpose of the assets. Their assets are not subject to requisition or confiscation by administrative procedure.

The property rights of joint enterprises and international associations and organizations enjoy protection in accordance with the provisions of Soviet legislation established for Soviet state organizations. Claims may be assessed against the assets of joint enterprises and international associations and organizations only by decision of the agencies that, in accordance with USSR legislation, may hear disputes involving enterprises, associations, and organizations.

The assets of joint enterprises and international associations and organizations are subject to mandatory insurance through USSR insurance agencies.

11. In the event of reorganization of joint enterprises and international associations and organizations, their rights and obligations are transferred to their successors.

12. The rights to industrial property belonging to joint enterprises and international associations and organizations enjoy protection under Soviet legislation, including protection in the form of patents. The procedures by which rights to industrial property are transferred to a joint enterprise or an international association and organization by its participants and by which the joint enterprise or international association and organization transfers such rights to its participants, as well as the procedures for the commercial use of such rights and their protection abroad, are specified in the articles of incorporation.

13. Joint enterprises and international associations and organizations are held liable for their obligations with all the assets belonging to them. The Soviet state and participants in joint enterprises and international associations and organizations are not held liable for the obligations of these enterprises, associations, and organizations; joint enterprises and international associations and organizations are not held liable for the obligations of the Soviet state or their participants.

14. Joint enterprises and international associations and organizations created on the territory of the USSR may open representative offices, and joint enterprises and organizations may also open branches, provided the articles of

incorporation grant them that right.

Joint enterprises and organizations created with the participation of Soviet organizations on the territory of other CMEA member countries may open branches on the territory of the USSR following the procedure established for the creation of joint enterprises and organizations.

The branches of joint enterprises and organizations opened on the territory of the USSR constitute legal entities and are not held liable for the obligations of the joint enterprises and organizations, and these enterprises and organizations are not held liable for the obligations of their branches.

15. Disputes arising between joint enterprises, international associations and organizations and Soviet state, cooperative, and other public organizations, disputes among themselves, and disputes between the participants in a joint enterprise or international association and organization over questions concerning their operations are heard by state arbitration agencies, with the exception of cases in which, in accordance with Soviet legislation, the disputes come under the jurisdiction of other agencies.

## III. Operating procedures of joint enterprises and international associations and organizations

16. The highest organ of the joint enterprise or international association and organization is its council (governing board), which consists of individuals appointed by the participants. The procedures governing the adoption of decisions by the council (governing board) are specified in the articles of incorporation.

Management of the day-to-day operations of the joint enterprise or international association and organization is exercised by the general director (or board of directors), who is appointed by the council (governing board).

The council (governing board) and the board of directors consist of citizens from the participant countries. The general director of the enterprise, association, or organization is a citizen of the USSR.

17. The joint enterprise and international association and organization enter into contact with the central state administrative agencies of the USSR and the union republics through agencies having jurisdiction over the Soviet participant in the enterprise, association, or organization, and they deal directly with local administrative agencies and other Soviet organizations.

18. The joint enterprise and international association and organization independently draft and confirm plans for their business operations. USSR state agencies do not set mandatory plan assignments for them.

19. The importation into and exportation from the USSR of goods and other assets by joint enterprises and international associations and organizations are conducted on the basis of permits issued in accordance with procedures established by USSR legislation.

20. Settlements of accounts and banking transactions in rubles of joint enter-

prises and international associations and organizations, and likewise the holding of cash funds in ruble accounts with USSR banks, take place according to rules applicable to Soviet state organizations.

21. Unless otherwise provided for by interstate or intergovernmental treaties entered into by the USSR, joint enterprises and international associations and organizations deposit their cash holdings in transferable rubles and in foreign currency in accounts with the USSR Foreign Trade Bank,* the International Bank for Economic Cooperation, and the International Investment Bank, and they make payments in transferable rubles or in foreign currency through the USSR Foreign Trade Bank and the International Bank for Economic Cooperation.

22. The USSR Ministry of Finance, with the agreement of the competent bodies of the interested countries, determines the procedure and terms for calculating the exchange rate for foreign currencies in connection with the operations of joint enterprises and international associations and organizations.

23. Joint enterprises and international associations and organizations maintain operating, accounting, and statistical records in accordance with the procedures applicable in the USSR to Soviet state enterprises. The forms of such record keeping and reporting are established by the USSR Ministry of Finance in conjunction with the USSR Central Statistical Administration.†

Joint enterprises and international associations and organizations bear responsibility, in accordance with Soviet legislation, for observing the procedures governing the compilation of records and reports and their authenticity.

24. Joint enterprises and international associations and organizations have the right to carry on correspondence and telegraph, teletype, and telephone communications with organizations of other countries.

## IV. Special features of the operations of joint enterprises

25. The assets of the joint enterprise are regarded as the common socialist property of the USSR and the relevant CMEA member country.

26. Joint enterprises maintain an independent budget and operate on the basis of full cost accounting, self-recoupment, and self-financing.

27. The amount of the charter capital of the joint enterprise, the size of the participants' shares in the charter capital, and the procedures for its formation (including in foreign currency) are defined in the articles of incorporation.

The charter capital of the joint enterprise is formed from contributions of the participants. It may be augmented with profits from the enterprise's business operations, and if necessary, from additional contributions of its participants.

Contributions to the joint enterprise's charter capital may take the form of

---

*Editor's note—The USSR Foreign Trade Bank has since been renamed the USSR Bank for Foreign Economic Relations.

†Editor's note—The USSR Central Statistical Administration was renamed the USSR State Committee for Statistics in August 1987.

buildings, structures, equipment, and other material valuables and rights to the use of land, water, other natural resources, buildings, structures, and equipment, as well as other property rights (including the use of inventions and know-how), and money in the currencies of the participant countries, in transferable rubles and in freely convertible currency.

Contributions to the joint enterprise's charter capital are stated in rubles at foreign trade prices established on the basis of existing provisions within the CMEA. In the event such prices are lacking, the value of the assets contributed are determined by agreement between the participants.

28. Equipment, materials, and other assets imported into the USSR by the foreign participants in a joint enterprise as their contribution to the enterprise's charter capital are exempt from customs duty.

29. The participants in a joint enterprise have the right, by mutual agreement, to transfer all or part of their shares in the joint enterprise to third parties. In each individual instance, the transfer of such shares is carried out with the authorization of the State Foreign Economic Commission of the USSR Council of Ministers. The Soviet participants have the preferential right to acquiring the shares of foreign participants.

30. Joint enterprises are supplied with material and technical resources and their products sold on a priority basis through the wholesale trade network, or through the supply network of the relevant branch of the USSR national economy, or through the appropriate Soviet foreign trade organizations.

Upon inclusion of joint enterprises into the USSR's material-and-technical supply network, they purchase and sell products and services in the USSR at wholesale or contract prices in the procedures established in the USSR.

If joint enterprises obtain supplies through USSR foreign trade organizations, they will purchase and sell products and services at foreign trade prices.

Concrete forms of the material and technical supply of joint enterprises and the procedures for selling their products and services are defined in the articles of incorporation.

31. The design and capital construction of joint enterprises' facilities, including facilities intended for social use, are carried out under contract and paid for with the enterprises' own or with borrowed funds. Project designs and itemized lists for the construction of such facilities are approved by the joint enterprises. Prior to final approval, project designs are subject to clearance under procedures established by the USSR State Construction Committee.

Construction-and-installation projects by Soviet construction-and-installation organizations and the material resources needed for construction are allocated to joint enterprises on a priority basis upon the placement of orders.

32. Joint enterprises' freight is shipped in accordance with the procedures established for Soviet organizations.

33. In carrying out allied export and import operations, joint enterprises have the right to coordinate prices on their manufactured products and to conclude contracts by which their imports will be paid for with their own or

with borrowed foreign-currency funds.

Foreign trade organizations may also conclude such contracts on the basis of agreements between themselves and joint enterprises.

34. If necessary, the USSR State Bank and the USSR Bank for Financing Capital Investments may establish special procedures for joint enterprises by which they may apply for credits and loans, striving to grant them no less favorable terms than are granted to the relevant Soviet state agencies.

If necessary, joint enterprises may utilize credits obtained on commercial terms and in transferable rubles and foreign currency from the USSR Foreign Trade Bank, the International Investment Bank, and the International Bank for Economic Cooperation, or, with the agreement of the USSR Foreign Trade Bank, from foreign banks or companies.

35. USSR banks have the right to monitor whether credits granted to a joint enterprise are used for their intended purpose, adequately secured, and promptly repaid.

36. The products of the joint enterprise are distributed between its participants in proportion to their contributions to the charter capital or by mutual agreement. The procedures for distribution are defined in the articles of incorporation.

37. The joint enterprise makes depreciation deductions in accordance with directives in effect for Soviet state organizations, unless otherwise provided for in the articles of incorporation. The sums calculated as depreciation remain at the disposal of the joint enterprise.

38. The joint enterprise creates a reserve fund and other funds that are essential to its operations and to the social development of the collective.

Deductions from profits are deposited in the reserve fund until such time as the fund reaches 25 percent of the enterprise's charter capital. The amounts of annual deductions are determined by procedures established in the articles of incorporation.

A list of other funds and the procedures governing their formation and expenditure are specified in the articles of incorporation.

39. Unless otherwise specified in the articles of incorporation, the profits of the joint enterprise, minus amounts deducted to cover transactions with the USSR State Budget and sums used for the creation and augmentation of funds, are distributed among its participants in proportion to their *pro rata* participation in the charter capital.

Earnings in freely convertible currency that exceed the needs of the joint enterprise may be distributed in the same proportion (by decision of the management body) with appropriate compensation in transferable rubles.

40. The foreign participants in the joint enterprise are guaranteed the right to transfer abroad sums in convertible rubles and in foreign currency that are due them as a result of the distribution of profits from the enterprise's operations, as well as sums due them from the distribution of earnings in freely convertible currency.

41. In order to exercise their oversight rights, the participants in the joint enterprise are provided, in the procedure specified in the articles of incorporation, with information relating to the operations of the enterprise and the status of its assets, as well as information on profits and losses.

The joint enterprise may have an auditing commission that is formed in the procedure specified in the articles of incorporation.

42. Audits of joint enterprises' financial, economic, and commercial operations are performed for a fee by a Soviet cost-accounting auditing organization.

## V. Taxation of joint enterprises

43. Joint enterprises pay a tax in the amount of 30 percent of the portion of profits remaining after payments are made into the reserve funds, as well as payments to other funds of the joint enterprise earmarked for the development of production, science, and technology. The tax is considered revenue for the all-union budget.

Joint enterprises are exempt from the payment of profit tax during the first two years of their operations.

The USSR Ministry of Finance has the right to reduce the amount of the tax or to exempt altogether individual payers.

44. The joint enterprise is responsible for computing the profit tax.

The enterprise determines an advance payment of taxes for the current year with due regard to its financial plan for the current year.

The joint enterprise must compute the final amount of the tax on profits actually earned during the past calendar year no later than 15 March of the year following the accounting year.

45. Financial agencies have the right to verify the correctness of joint enterprises' computation of the tax.

Overpayments of taxes in the year past may be credited to current tax payments or refunded to the payer at his request.

46. The profit tax for the current year is remitted to the budget in equal payments no later than fifteen days prior to the end of the given quarter. The tax must be paid in full no later than 1 April of the year following the accounting year.

A penalty of .05 percent per day is charged for overdue payments.

The exaction of overdue taxes is carried out in accordance with the procedures established for foreign legal entities by the Statute on the Exaction of Overdue Taxes and Nontax Payments, confirmed by Edict of the Presidium of the USSR Supreme Soviet of 26 January 1981 (*Vedomosti Verkhovnogo Soveta SSSR* 1981, No. 5, item 122).

47. The joint enterprise has the right to protest actions undertaken by financial agencies to exact taxes due. An appeal may be filed with the financial agency that verified the tax computation. A decision on the appeal must be reached within

one month of the date on which it was filed.

A decision on an appeal may itself be appealed to a higher financial agency within one month's time.

The filing of an appeal does not stay payment of the tax.

48. Unless otherwise provided by an agreement between the USSR and the relevant foreign state, the portion of profits due the foreign participant in a joint enterprise is assessed a tax in the amount of 20 percent upon transfer of the profit abroad.

49. The aforementioned procedures governing taxation apply to income received by joint enterprises created on the territory of the USSR and by branches of joint enterprises located in the USSR that have been created with the participation of Soviet organizations and administrative agencies of other countries earned from operations on the territory of the USSR, in the USSR's continental shelf and in its economic zone, and on the territory of other countries.

50. The USSR Ministry of Finance issues directives on the taxation of joint enterprises.

## VI. Special features of the operations of international associations and organizations

51. International associations and organizations have an independent budget (estimate) and finance their operations from the contributions of the participants.

52. In order to finance their operations, including expenditures on the maintenance of their staffs and on business travel by specialists in joint operations, international associations and organizations establish a financial fund, which is valued in both rubles and transferable rubles.

The size of the financial fund of the international association or organization and the procedures governing its formation (including in foreign currency) are specified in the charter of the international association and organization.

Monies may be deposited in the financial fund in the currencies of participant countries in transferable rubles and in freely convertible currency.

Contributions to the assets of the joint organization may also take the form of buildings, structures, equipment, and other material valuables and rights to the use of buildings, structures, equipment, as well as other property rights (including the use of inventions and know-how).

Material valuables submitted by the participants as their contributions are valued at foreign trade prices established on the basis of provisions existing within the CMEA. In the event such prices are lacking, the value of the contributed assets is determined by agreement between the participants.

The Soviet participants in international associations and organizations may also make contributions to the financial fund in the form of credits issued to them by the USSR State Bank and the USSR Foreign Trade Bank.

53. The foreign participants are guaranteed the right to transfer to their

countries monies in transferable rubles and in foreign currency due them as a result of the liquidation of the international association or organization.

54. In carrying out allied export and import operations, international associations and organizations have the right to coordinate prices on cooperatively manufactured products and to conclude contracts by which imports are paid for with their own or with borrowed foreign currency.

Contracts for reciprocal deliveries of cooperatively manufactured products concluded within international associations and organizations are concluded by their participants.

55. International associations and organizations have the right to coordinate prices on and conclude contracts in their own name for imports of licenses, know-how, materials, industrial samples, technology, and other goods and services necessary for the conduct of their operations.

Joint organizations also have the right to coordinate prices on and conclude contracts in their own name for the export of scientific-technological achievements.

The aforementioned contracts may also be concluded by foreign trade organizations on the basis of agreements between themselves and international associations and organizations.

56. International associations that, in addition to coordinating the activities of their participants, also conduct their own business operations using the joint assets of their participants, are guided in these operations by the relevant norms of the present Decree that concern the procedures governing the creation and operation on the territory of the USSR of joint enterprises.

## VII. Personnel of joint enterprises and international associations and organizations

57. The terms of labor remuneration and work and rest schedules of Soviet citizens employed at joint enterprises and international associations and organizations as well as provisions for their social security and social insurance are regulated according to the norms of Soviet legislation. Unless otherwise provided by interstate or intergovernmental treaties entered into by the USSR, these norms apply also to foreign citizens employed at joint enterprises and international associations and organizations.

58. Joint enterprises and international associations and organizations remit to the USSR state budget payments for the coverage of Soviet and foreign employees by state social insurance (security) at the rates established for Soviet state organizations.

59. The management of the joint enterprise is obligated to conclude collective contracts with the trade union organization created at the enterprise. The content of these contracts, including provisions for the social development of the collective, are determined in accordance with Soviet legislation and the articles of incorporation.

60. Wages earned by the foreign employees of the joint enterprise or international association and organization are assessed an income tax in the procedure and amounts stipulated by the Edict of the Presidium of the USSR Supreme Soviet of 12 May 1978, "On Income Tax Exacted from Foreign Juridical and Physical Persons" (*Vedomosti Verkhovnogo Soveta SSSR* 1978, No. 20, item 313). The unexpended portion of these wages may be transferred in the relevant foreign currency.

## VIII. Liquidation of joint enterprises and international associations and organizations

61. The joint enterprise or international association and organization may be liquidated under the circumstances and according to the procedures specified in the articles of incorporation, and also by decision of the USSR Council of Ministers, if their activities do not correspond to the objectives and tasks set forth in these articles. An announcement of the liquidation of the joint enterprise or international association and organization is published in the press.

62. In the event of liquidation of the joint enterprise or withdrawal from it, the foreign participant has the right to the return of its contribution in cash or in kind priced at the residual value of the contribution at the moment the enterprise, association, or organization is liquidated, and after its obligations to the Soviet participants and to third parties have been paid.

63. The liquidation of the joint enterprise or international association and organization is registered with the USSR Ministry of Finance.

\*    \*    \*

64. The present Decree applies also to the creation on the territory of the USSR of joint enterprises and international associations and organizations with socialist countries that are not members of the CMEA. The special features of such application are determined by the State Foreign Economic Commission of the USSR Council of Ministers, and if necessary, the appropriate proposals are submitted to the USSR Council of Ministers.

65. Decree No. 464 of the USSR Council of Ministers of 26 May 1983, "On the Procedures Governing the Submission of Proposals for the Creation on the Territory of the USSR of Joint Economic Organizations of the USSR and Other CMEA Member Countries" (*SP SSSR*, 1983, No. 16, item 80), is hereby considered no longer in effect.

N. RYZHKOV
*Chairman of the USSR Council of Ministers*

M. SMIRTIUKOV
*Administrative Secretary
of the USSR Council of Ministers*

# IX


# ON ADDITIONAL MEASURES FOR IMPROVING FOREIGN ECONOMIC OPERATIONS UNDER THE NEW CONDITIONS OF ECONOMIC MANAGEMENT

Decree of the CPSU Central Committee and the
USSR Council of Ministers;
*Vneshniaia torgovlia* 1987, No. 11, pp. 4–11

It is the conviction of the CPSU Central Committee and the USSR Council of Ministers that transforming into reality the Party's strategic line of accelerating the nation's socioeconomic development, of more fully utilizing the advantages offered by the planned form of management, and of deepening socialist economic integration and the USSR's participation in the international division of labor, requires substantial improvement of the quality of work in the sphere of foreign economic relations and the further strengthening of the role of associations, enterprises, and organizations in the resolution of these questions.

Measures adopted recently on improving the management of the foreign trade complex have shown that their underlying premises are correct. The period just past has seen the almost complete implementation of a series of organizational, legal, and economic measures aimed at securing the broader utilization of the potentialities inherent in the international division of labor capable of accelerating the development of the nation's economy, of involving the actual producers of export products in foreign economic operations, and enhancing their interests in the results of foreign trade. As it was noted at the June 1987 Plenum of the CPSU Central Committee, however, elements of stagnation, of insufficient initiative on the part of enterprises and their work collectives in fostering exports and establishing new forms of cooperation, have yet to be eliminated from the work of the central economic departments, branch ministries, associations, enterprises, and organizations involved in promoting foreign economic relations. Several ministries, associations, enterprises, and organizations are not utilizing to the full the rights granted to them in this area. Cost accounting and economic methods of management are taking root only slowly. Foreign-currency self-recoupment has yet to become a principal form of foreign economic operations in the work of ministries, departments, associations, and enterprises. Nor have there been any substantial changes in import policy. And the decision-making process on questions of foreign trade remains overly cumbersome.

With the goal of further improving foreign economic operations, of increasing the role belonging in this area to associations, enterprises, organizations, USSR ministries and departments, and union-republic councils of ministers, and of simplifying existing procedures governing the conduct of foreign economic operations, the CPSU Central Committee and the USSR Council of Ministers have decreed the following:

To consider as the primary task of the standing agencies of the USSR Council of Ministers, the USSR State Planning Committee, the USSR State Committee for Material and Technical Supply, the USSR State Agro-Industrial Committee, the USSR State Construction Committee, the USSR State Committee for Science and Technology, USSR ministries and departments, union-republic councils of ministers, and associations, enterprises, and organizations engaged in the sphere of foreign economic relations, that of further increasing their effectiveness, of deepening the USSR's economic and scientific-technological integration with the CMEA member countries, of developing the nation's export base, of radically improving the structure of the Soviet Union's foreign trade turnover, of increasing the technical level and competitiveness of goods, and of eliminating irrational imports.

In accordance with the decisions of the June 1987 Plenum of the CPSU Central Committee, to promote with all possible means the development of foreign economic operations on the part of associations, enterprises, and organizations following the provisions of the Law on the State Enterprise (Association). To make a wholesale conversion to the use of economic methods of management, and to more broadly utilize long-term economic indicators as well as foreign-currency self-recoupment. To cultivate direct production and scientific-technological ties with enterprises and organizations from the socialist countries, and to mount an active campaign for the creation of joint enterprises and works with all interested countries as well as other effective forms of economic interaction.

**On improving work toward the creation and operation
of joint enterprises and international associations and
organizations, and toward the development of direct ties
with enterprises and organizations from socialist countries**

To recognize the necessity of simplifying the existing procedures governing the adoption of decisions regarding the creation of joint enterprises and international associations and organizations. To grant to USSR ministries and departments and union-republic councils of ministers the right to make decisions regarding the creation of joint enterprises and international associations and organizations.

With the goals of developing production and fostering cooperation, and notwithstanding the existence of agreements and protocols, to permit associations, enterprises, and organizations to conclude contracts for individual deliveries of manufactured products, industrial samples, instruments, fittings, tools, secondary and recycled raw materials, machinery and equipment, and also the provision of services.

In order to ensure the more complete satisfaction of the population's demand, to expand the assortment of consumer goods reaching domestic trade enterprises and organizations, and consumer and other types of cooperatives, and to make broad utilization of operations involving the exchange of goods with organizations from the socialist countries.

These deliveries and exchange operations are to take place at contract prices and are payable in transferable rubles, the countries' national currencies, or on a clearing basis, and the results of such operations are included in the overall results of the business operation of associations, enterprises, and organizations.

To develop and deepen economic interaction with the socialist countries, making use in such cooperation of a variety of effective forms of joint business activities in production, science and technology, foreign trade, and in financing and credit, including the creation of joint-stock companies, partnerships, as well as other forms of investment and commercial activity.

In entering into intergovernmental agreements with socialist countries in the sphere of economic and scientific-technological cooperation, to recognize the necessity of limiting such agreements only to the most important interbranch problems; in all other areas of this form of cooperation, USSR ministries and departments enter into on an independent basis, and union-republic councils of ministers sponsor, bilateral and multilateral international agreements of an interdepartmental character, while at the same time assuring observance of obligations dictated by intergovernmental treaties entered into by the USSR.

## On the further development of cooperation with firms from capitalist and developing countries, and improving work toward the creation and operation of joint enterprises and industrial projects

To ensure consistent realization of the strategic line of the CPSU of capitalizing on the advantages offered by the world division of labor, of reinforcing Soviet positions in international trade, and of introducing the achievements of world science and technology into the national economy; to recognize the necessity of considerably activating the efforts of ministries, departments, associations, enterprises, and organizations of the USSR aimed at developing cooperation with capitalist and developing countries.

To grant USSR ministries and departments and union-republic councils of ministers the right independently to adopt decisions regarding the creation on the territory of the USSR of joint enterprises involving firms from capitalist and developing countries.

To establish that the joint enterprise determines, in cooperation with Soviet enterprises and organizations, the type of currency to be used in making and accepting payments for products sold and goods purchased, as well as the procedures governing the sale of its products and the procurement of goods on the Soviet market.

Upon agreement between the partners in the joint enterprise, their contributions to the charter capital may be valued both in Soviet and in the foreign currency.

To broaden measurably cooperation with firms from capitalist and developing countries in the spheres of science and technology, trade, finance, services, tourism, and advertising. With these goals in mind, to promote the creation of joint scientific-research and design organizations of engineering, marketing, and advertising firms, to provide for the joint servicing and repair of exported machinery, the training of skilled specialists and workers, and the purchase of stocks, bonds, and other securities as well as their issuance and investment.

To charge the USSR Ministry of Foreign Trade,* the USSR State Committee for Foreign Economic Relations,† the USSR State Committee for Science and Technology, the USSR Ministry of Finance, the USSR Foreign Trade Bank,‡ and the USSR Academy of Sciences with drafting and submitting to the USSR Council of Ministers within three months proposals for measures ensuring the development of these forms of cooperation.

## On the further development of economic methods of management of foreign economic relations

To promote the further improvement of the planning of foreign economic relations as an integral component in the overall system of national economic planning. To enhance the plan's impact on efforts to draw the USSR into active participation in the international division of labor, to deepen socialist economic integration, to make effective changes in the structure of the Soviet Union's exports and imports, to foster the initiative of associations, enterprises, and organizations in increasing the export of competitive products, and to reduce irrational imports. Toward these ends, the USSR State Planning Committee, the USSR State Committee for Material and Technical Supply, USSR ministries and departments, and union-republic councils of ministers, through the system of state orders and quotas, shall ensure unconditional fulfillment of the Soviet Union's

---

*Editor's notes:*
*The USSR Ministry of Foreign Trade was abolished on 15 January 1988. On the same day, the USSR Ministry for Foreign Economic Relations was established.
†Abolished on 15 January 1988.
‡The USSR Foreign Trade Bank has since been renamed the USSR Bank for Foreign Economic Relations.

international obligations, which issue from the following:

the goals of the coordination of the state plans of the USSR and the other socialist countries, and the tasks advanced in the Comprehensive Program for Scientific-Technological Progress of the CMEA Member Countries to the Year 2000;

agreements reached between the USSR and India, Finland, and other countries on commodity turnover and payments;

agreements reached between the USSR and foreign countries on economic and technical cooperation.

To charge the USSR State Planning Committee and the USSR State Committee for Material and Technical Supply with including in plan drafts and physical balances the full volume of gains resulting from agreements reached by USSR ministries and departments on exports to capitalist countries, with the intent of maximizing to the fullest degree possible exports earning freely convertible currency. The union-republic councils of ministers will be guided by this Decree in their relations with republic ministries and departments.

Guided by the Law of the USSR on the State Enterprise (Association), to establish that, with the goal of utilizing positive changes in world market competition, as well as the development of direct ties and other effective forms of business interaction, enterprises (associations) have the right to export machine-building and other finished products, the manufacture of which exceeds the amounts needed to cover state orders and obligations under business contracts.

With the goal of reinforcing the planned foundations of the foreign economic operations of USSR ministries and departments and union-republic councils of ministers, and of associations, enterprises, and organizations, to establish that the sections in their plans covering foreign economic relations should provide, in the form of indicators of the state plan for economic and social development, measures and tasks designed to develop the export base, to increase the production of competitive products in world markets, to foster socialist economic integration—this includes meeting the tasks of the Comprehensive Program for Scientific-Technological Progress of the CMEA Member Countries—to ensure the economical expenditure of foreign-currency funds, to deepen international industrial cooperation, and to promote the operations of joint enterprises and international associations and organizations.

To charge the standing agencies of the USSR Council of Ministers with conducting systematic management and oversight over the compilation and implementation of the aforementioned plan sections.

To cover the products of joint enterprises located abroad that are purchased wholesale by the USSR, as well as products manufactured from recycled raw materials and semifinished goods supplied by the customers, in the production and sales plans of the relevant Soviet associations, enterprises, and organizations, and in export and import plans, in the procedures established by the USSR State Bank.

In order to provide greater incentive to foreign partners for creating joint enterprises on the territory of the USSR, to consider the possibility of exempting these enterprises from the payment of profit tax during the first two years following declaration of a profit.

To recognize the necessity of simplifying the procedures governing the utilization of monies from the foreign-currency funds of associations, enterprises, and organizations, USSR ministries and departments, and union-republic councils of ministers. With this goal, to permit them to purchase products using foreign currency at their disposal, without the need for any form of clearance from the relevant foreign trade associations of the USSR Ministry of Foreign Trade,* from the USSR State Committee for Foreign Economic Relations,* USSR branch ministries and departments, union-republic councils of ministers, or foreign trade companies of associations, enterprises, and organizations. Such purchases are carried out on a priority basis and are included in the fulfillment of the plans of foreign trade organizations.

To ensure strict adherence to the established procedures which dictate that the aforementioned funds must be used to cover imports of machinery, equipment, materials, and other goods to meet the needs of technical retooling and reconstruction, to cover the expansion of production, the implementation of scientific-research, experimental-design, and other types of projects, and that funds in transferable rubles must be used to acquire goods to meet the needs of work collectives.

To invest USSR ministries and departments, union-republic councils of ministers, and associations, enterprises, and organizations with the responsibility for ensuring the effective and economical expenditure of foreign-currency funds at their disposal.

To charge the State Foreign Economic Commission of the USSR Council of Ministers with drafting and confirming procedures to govern the organization and implementation of systematic analyses and monitoring in order to ensure the efficient expenditure of the aforementioned funds.

With the goal of promoting exports, to allow the USSR Foreign Trade Bank to grant to associations, enterprises, and organizations foreign-currency credits:

for the creation and expansion of export production, to be repaid within eight years with foreign-currency earnings from exported products;

for the support of current operations, to be repaid within two years;

against expected future earnings based on current contracts concluded for exports.

In order to promote an enterprising socialist attitude on the part of associations, enterprises, and organizations as well as the expansion of their economic independence, to allow them, as well as USSR ministries and departments, the possibility of pooling monies from their foreign-currency funds, of making these

---

*Editor's note— See note supra.

funds available to other enterprises, ministries and departments, and banks on mutually advantageous terms, including the payment of appropriate interest, and also, with the agreement of USSR ministries and departments, of investing these monies abroad.

To charge the USSR Foreign Trade Bank, in conjunction with the USSR Ministry of Finance, with confirming within two months procedures to govern the aforementioned utilization of foreign-currency funds. In order to provide increased incentive for union-republic councils of ministers, the Moscow City Executive Committee, the Moscow *Oblast'* Executive Committee, the Leningrad City Executive Committee, and the Leningrad *Oblast'* Executive Committee in procuring additional local resources for export and developing border and coastal trade, to increase, beginning in 1988, the quotas for their foreign-currency deductions from exports of goods of services by enterprises belonging to local industries or republic ministries and departments, and by auxiliary enterprises, industries, and other economic organizations under local jurisdiction for all types of foreign currency, and correspondingly, to increase the portion of funds to be left at their disposal.

To institute deductions payable to union-republic councils of ministers from earnings resulting from the export of products processed from the wastes (slag, tailings) of enterprises under all-union jurisdiction situated on the territory of a given republic, in those cases when the recycling is carried out by enterprises under republic and local jurisdiction.

All export earnings from border and coastal trade remain at the disposal of union-republic councils of ministers, *krai* executive committees, and *oblast'* executive committees and are used toward the purchase abroad of consumer goods, machinery and equipment, and raw and other materials.

In order to increase the incentive of associations, enterprises, organizations, USSR ministries and departments, and union-republic councils of ministers for increasing exports to CMEA member countries, to recognize the necessity of instituting, beginning in 1989, wholesale trade in industrial products, medical technology, in cultural, household, sporting, and other types of goods—using transferable rubles at the disposal of associations, enterprises, organizations, USSR ministries and departments, and union-republic councils of ministers—in the interests of developing and expanding production, of introducing new machinery and technology, and also of meeting the needs of work collectives.

To charge the USSR State Planning Committee and the USSR State Committee for Material and Technical Supply, beginning in 1989, with making available for sale through the wholesale trade network and for transferable rubles, a certain portion of products imported from CMEA member countries.

To charge the USSR State Committee for Material and Technical Supply and the USSR Ministry of Finance, in coordination with the appropriate USSR ministries and departments, with confirming procedures governing such trade.

To charge the USSR State Planning Committee and the USSR Ministry of

Foreign Trade,* as well as USSR ministries and departments enjoying the right of direct conduct of export-import operations, and union-republic councils of ministers, in drafting the necessary plans and in clearing annual protocols on commodity turnover with CMEA member countries, providing for utilization of monies from foreign-currency funds in the form of transferable rubles.

To charge the USSR State Committee on Prices, the USSR State Planning Committee, and the USSR Ministry of Finance, in preparing and implementing the radical reform of the system of price formation, with securing an economically sound correspondence of price correlations with world prices based on product groups and types, thus laying the groundwork for progressive changes in the structure of foreign trade, and for the deepening of international specialization and production cooperation, and with the intention of making the conversion in the future to the utilization of foreign-currency exchange rates in the advancement of these goals.

## On measures concerning the supply of personnel for foreign economic operations

The broad application of economic methods of management, the introduction of economic cost accounting into foreign economic relations, and the development of multifarious forms of economic interaction with foreign partners—including the creation of joint enterprises and projects, participation in foreign joint-stock companies, and investment activity abroad—require restructuring of the system of training, retraining, and advanced training of personnel in order that their professional training and business skills are equal to modern demands.

To deem as the task of primary importance today in the procurement of personnel to manage foreign economic operations, the retraining and advanced training of employees engaged in foreign economic relations.

To raise the quality and expand the retraining and advanced training provided to the managerial personnel and specialists of the central economic agencies, ministries and departments, associations, enterprises, and organizations.

With the goal of meeting the needs of associations, enterprises, organizations, ministries, and departments for personnel capable of effective management of foreign economic ties in their modern forms—including joint industrial, scientific-technological, currency and financial, and trade and economic operations with foreign partners—to bring about substantial improvement in the training of specialists in these areas at higher educational institutions.

Toward this end, to review existing and draft new curricula, programs, and assistance programs relevant to issues of foreign economic operations. To establish new criteria for the selection of professors and teachers in the foreign economic disciplines, and to see to their retraining.

---

*Editor's note—See note *supra*.

With the goal of involving as rapidly as possible in foreign economic operations the immediate producers of export products, to recognize the expedience of reassigning highly skilled specialists from foreign trade associations, under temporary labor contracts, to the foreign trade companies of associations, enterprises, and organizations that independently conduct export-import operations in foreign markets.

To recognize the necessity of expanding the training of Soviet specialists in foreign countries, including on-the-job training at enterprises and in companies as well as formal training in higher and specialized educational institutions.

To utilize more fully toward these ends existing understandings and agreements and to conclude new ones, including those calling for specialized training of separately formed groups and individual specialists.

With the goal of assimilating world experience in financial and commercial operations as rapidly as possible, to invite foreign specialists to teach and advise employees directly engaged in the conduct of the USSR's foreign economic relations, and also to set up on the territory of the Soviet Union consulting departments and offices of foreign companies.

To charge the central committees of the union-republic communist parties, and *krai*, *oblast'*, city, and district party committees with improving the quality of party guidance of foreign trade associations of USSR ministries and departments, of the foreign trade companies of associations, enterprises, and organizations, and of other subdivisions engaged in foreign economic operations.

To charge party committees with improving the selection, assignment, and training of personnel involved in foreign economic operations, and with mounting a decisive struggle against shortcomings in this area, including manifestations of indifference and formalism.

\*    \*    \*

The CPSU Central Committee and the USSR Council of Ministers are confident that implementation of these measures will serve considerably to increase initiative on the part of associations, enterprises, and organizations, USSR ministries and departments, and the union-republic councils of ministers, and consequently to enhance by all means available the effectiveness of foreign economic relations in the interest of accelerating the socioeconomic development of the USSR.

# X

# ON THE ESTABLISHMENT OF AN ALL-UNION MINISTRY OF FOREIGN ECONOMIC RELATIONS OF THE USSR

Edict No. 8350–XI of the Presidium of the USSR Supreme Soviet,
15 January 1988;
*Vedomosti Verkhovnogo Soveta SSSR* 1988, No. 3, item 43

The Presidium of the USSR Supreme Soviet *decrees*:
An All-Union Ministry of Foreign Economic Relations of the USSR is established.

The USSR Ministry of Foreign Trade and the USSR State Committee for Foreign Economic Relations are abolished.

A. GROMYKO
*Chairman of the Presidium of the USSR Supreme Soviet*

T. MENTESHASHVILI
*Administrative Secretary of the
Presidium of the USSR Supreme Soviet*

# XI

# THE FOREIGN ECONOMIC ACTIVITY OF COOPERATIVES

### Article 28 of the Law of the Union of Soviet Socialist Republics
### On Cooperation in the USSR;
### *Pravda*, 8 June 1988

1. Cooperatives and their unions (associations) play an active part in foreign economic operations and contribute to the strengthening of the nation's economy, to the enhancing of its international authority, to the accumulation of foreign-currency resources, and to the creation of capacities for accelerating scientific-technological progress and raising the effectiveness of cooperative production.

Cooperatives and their unions (associations) conduct foreign economic operations on the basis of foreign-currency self-recoupment and self-financing.

2. Cooperatives engaged in production activity as well as their unions (associations) may, in the established procedure, be granted the right to conduct export-import operations independently if their products (work, services) are competitive in foreign markets.

Cooperatives and their unions (associations) may also contract with the appropriate foreign trade organizations to provide for the export and import of goods (work, services).

Cooperatives and their unions (associations) have the right, in the established procedure, to conduct foreign trade operations with foreign partners in border trade.

3. In the interest of raising [their] economic stake and responsibility, and expanding [their] autonomy in the conduct of export and import operations, foreign currency earned by cooperatives and their unions (associations) from the export of goods (work, services) and remaining after payments have been made to the state at rates established by the USSR Council of Ministers, is at their full disposal; [foreign-currency earnings] are not subject to withdrawal and may be accumulated for use in subsequent years.

Cooperatives and their unions (associations) may utilize foreign currency earned from the export of [their] goods (work, services) to pay for imports of equipment, raw and other materials, and other goods (work, services) that are required to develop production and increase commodity circulation as well as to acquire a greater base of materials and machinery to serve the sociocultural sphere.

If the right independently to conduct export-import operations is granted to a union (association) of cooperatives, then [its] foreign-currency earnings from foreign economic operations, after payments have been made to the state, are distributed to each cooperative in a proportion commensurate with its contribution to the foreign-currency receipts. With the general agreement of the member cooperatives of the union (association), part of their foreign-currency earnings may be deposited in the central fund of the given union (association).

4. In the interests of accelerating scientific-technological progress and enhancing the competitiveness of manufactured goods and of services, cooperatives engaged in production activity may create joint enterprises, international associations and organizations with the appropriate organizations from CMEA member countries, from other socialist countries, and they may create joint enterprises with firms from capitalist and developing countries.

Together with their foreign partners, cooperatives determine the specialization of joint enterprises (organizations) and the volumes and structure of production with reference to the effective demand for [their] products (work, services) and the conditions for their sale, including prices (rates). Joint enterprises (organizations) may be constituted both on the territory of the USSR and on the territory of foreign countries.

Cooperatives and their unions (associations) enter into and develop scientific-technological and production cooperation with the corresponding enterprises (organizations) of foreign countries, organize joint scientific research, design, and experimental projects, create multinational collectives of specialists, exchange scientific-technological data—in the established procedure—on mutually agreeable terms, and provide assistance in the training of personnel.

5. In the interest of developing effective cooperation with cooperative organizations from other countries, cooperatives and their unions (associations) may take part in the activities of international cooperative organizations, provided such involvement does not conflict with their charters, and they may take part in international exhibitions and fairs.

6. USSR banks may grant credits in Soviet and foreign currency, and also in convertible rubles, to cooperatives and their unions (associations) engaged in foreign economic activity; these credits must be repaid in foreign currency earned from the sale of [exported] products or from other funds of the cooperatives and their unions (associations).

7. Cooperatives and their unions (associations) bear economic responsibility for the effectiveness of their foreign economic operations and for the economical use of foreign-currency funds applied toward the development of production. If they fail to fulfill export or other contractual obligations, they compensate damages with all their assets, including foreign-currency funds, and they use foreign currency from their foreign-currency savings to pay fines and other sanctions to a foreign customer if the violation occurred due to their own fault.

# ABOUT THE AUTHORS AND THE EDITOR

Professor M. M. Boguslavsky is a prominent Soviet jurist and an internationally recognized specialist in the fields of private international law, copyright and patent law, and legal-economic relations with other countries. He is the author of over 150 publications in these areas, and numerous of his books have been published outside the Soviet Union in English, German, Japanese, Spanish, and other languages. A holder of the degree of Doctor of Juridical Sciences, he currently occupies the position of Section Chief at the Institute of State and Law of the USSR Academy of Sciences.

P. S. Smirnov is a high-ranking Soviet foreign trade official who has published extensively in the major Soviet scholarly and business journals. He is currently Deputy Chief of the Department of International Economic Organizations of the USSR Ministry of Foreign Trade, and he holds the degree of Candidate of Juridical Sciences.

Serge L. Levitsky is one of the world's foremost specialists in the fields of international copyright law and legal issues of East-West trade. His publications in these areas number in the hundreds, among which are *Introduction to Soviet Copyright Law* (1964) and *Copyright, Defamation, and Privacy in Soviet Civil Law* (1979). Formerly Vice-President of Chase Manhattan Bank and Professor of Law at the New York Law School, Professor Levitsky currently serves as acting editor of the *Review of Socialist Law*, a quarterly published by the Documentation Office for East European Law of the University of Leyden, and editor of the quarterly *Soviet Statutes and Decisions*.